Neuro-Hypnosis

Neuro-Hypnosis

USING SELF-HYPNOSIS TO ACTIVATE

THE BRAIN FOR CHANGE

C. Alexander Simpkins

Annellen M. Simpkins

W. W. NORTON & COMPANY

NEW YORK • LONDON

For information about permission to reproduce selections from this book, write to
Permissions, W. W. Norton & Company, Inc., 500 Fifth Avenue, New York, NY 10110

For information about special discounts for bulk purchases, please contact
W. W. Norton Special Sales at specialsales@wwnorton.com or 800-233-4830

Manufacturing by Malloy Printing
Book design by Jonathan Lippincott
Production manager: Leeann Graham

Library of Congress Cataloging-in-Publication Data

Simpkins, C. Alexander.
Neuro-hypnosis : using self-hypnosis to activate the brain for change /
C. Alexander Simpkins, Annellen M. Simpkins. — 1st ed.
p. cm. — (A Norton professional book)
Includes bibliographical references and index.
ISBN 978-0-393-70625-3 (pbk.)
1. Autogenic training. I. Simpkins, Annellen M. II. Title.
RC499.A8.S566 2010
615.8'5122—dc22
2010013105

ISBN: 978-0-393-70625-3 (pbk.)

W. W. Norton & Company, Inc.,
500 Fifth Avenue, New York, N.Y. 10110
www.wwnorton.com

W. W. Norton & Company Ltd.,
Castle House, 75/76 Wells Street, London W1T 3QT

1 2 3 4 5 6 7 8 9 0

We dedicate this book to:

Our parents, Nathaniel and Carmen Simpkins and Herbert and Naomi Minkin, who saw us through our training.

Our hypnosis teachers, Ernest L. Rossi, Milton H Erickson, G. Wilson Shaffer, and Harold Greenwald, who steered us on the course to deep understanding and respect for hypnosis, and to Jerome D. Frank, who set us on the path of rigorous thinking about the effectiveness of psychotherapy.

Our children, Alura L. Aguilera and C. Alexander Simpkins Jr., who not only came to be through the use of hypnosis in childbirth, but who have continued to turn to hypnosis creatively as a useful tool to foster excellence in their own lives.

Our many clients through the years who have openly and willingly embraced hypnosis, experimented with many of the techniques included in this book, and allowed hypnosis to help them reach their full potential.

And

To our readers and clients of the future, who will develop inner resources through their creative use of hypnosis.

Contents

Part III: Experiencing Self-Hypnosis

Part IV: Applying Self-Hypnosis

Neuro-Hypnosis

Introduction

The most recent effort attempts to bridge the sciences, which are traditionally concerned with nature and the physical world and the humanities, which are traditionally concerned with the nature of human experience, and to use the bridge for the improvement of mentally and neurologically ill patients, and for the general betterment of mankind.

—Larry R. Squire & Eric R. Kandel, *Memory: From Mind to Molecules,* p. 215

The Mind Can Change the Brain

Hypnosis has long been known to be an effective and expedient way to bring about real and measurable change. With the new neuroimaging technologies, we now know that hypnosis has a therapeutic influence on the brain. Drawing on innovative studies of neurological effects, *Neuro-Hypnosis* offers a new look at hypnosis as an exciting way to effortlessly bridge human physiology and human experience.

People have understood for several decades that the brain can influence how people feel and think, and drug therapies have been used to help people feel better, altering their brain chemistry. But the most recent research has revealed that the changes work both ways: The experiences we have, including thoughts and feelings about those experiences, bring about measurable changes in brain functions and structures. These changes result in new neuronal connections (known as *neuroplasticity*) and the birth of new neurons (known as *neurogenesis*). So, if you give yourself the right experiences, you can bring about real and lasting mind–brain change, for a better and happier life. *The mind can change the brain!* Hypnosis can be your source for the kinds of new experiences that will foster mind–brain change.

Hypnotizing Yourself

This book is about self-hypnosis. In a sense, all hypnosis is self-hypnosis, since the effects ultimately take place within the person undergoing the experience. With self-hypnosis, you act as hypnotist and subject simultaneously. You may not know it, but you have the ability to do many things automatically and spontaneously, flowing seamlessly between tasks without having to think about it. These moments are often your finest ones, when action flows naturally as you perform perfectly and effortlessly. The dilemma in self-hypnosis is how to deliberately be spontaneous, to voluntarily do the involuntary, and to form a rapport with your own inner processes. This book will show you how to utilize your natural capacity to set yourself to spontaneously overcome your problems. This approach to self-hypnosis harnesses the potential in your brain, to allow natural healing and growth to take place automatically.

Returning to Natural Balance

Doing self-hypnosis returns you to balance. Both the conscious and unconscious processes can work together for orienting and problem-solving in hypnotic work. You will learn to return to natural functioning with your unconscious and to cooperate with your inner needs in a healthy and positive way.

In performing self-hypnosis, a balance is found between specific and nonspecific methods. Some techniques target specific brain areas and mental processes. Others target nonspecific influences such as your hopes, expectations, and general sense that you are OK and you can succeed.

You Are Unique

Brains share many commonalities, but every brain is also unique, and so your own individuality will be expressed when you work with your brain to use your inner sensitivities, talents, and needs. As your specific abilities unfold, you can develop openness to creative therapeutic processes in general, and thereby tap a positive reservoir of potential from within. Acknowledging that you might have capacities beyond those you are consciously aware of makes it possible for better solutions to problems and difficulties to emerge. The unexplored regions of your unconscious mind have vast reservoirs of potential, waiting to be tapped.

People vary in how they respond to hypnosis. Some people will feel things develop in their bodies from merely an imagined thought. They may watch in amazement as their hand lifts up, seemingly of its own volition. Others, who are naturally comfortable with trance, may feel as if they fell deeply asleep, and remember nothing afterwards. Once you become familiar with your own personal response to hypnosis, you can broaden and evolve to learn other responses.

Inviting Novel Responses

Self-hypnosis facilitates novel responses and better use of potential abilities. Normally, we have routine patterns of thoughts, attitudes, concerns, and feelings. For example, if you use an outdated computer with limited RAM and hard-drive space, you adapt by using only older, limited programs that will run on that machine. Then, one day you become curious about new possibilities and decide to add more RAM and get a hard drive with greater storage capacity. Suddenly you can update your system and get the latest programs with many new options. Similarly, your assumptions about your own abilities may limit you to a certain range of possible experiences. Other mental and physical events are either disregarded or experienced as meaningless or too difficult. Exercising more of your capacities through hypnosis draws in new data and additional perspectives. Added potentials may be integrated to expand the horizons of brain processing and experiencing.

You can build on your natural responsiveness. Spontaneous reactions will occur, rather than redundant conditioning. We invite you to interact with your inner resources and use them creatively.

About This Book

Self-hypnosis develops an art of inner communication that can be used for many positive purposes. *Neuro-Hypnosis* is written for the person who is interested in developing skills in self-hypnosis to bring about change. It is also intended for professionals in the therapeutic field who want to help themselves or their clients use some hypnotic facilitation. We recognize that professionals are accustomed to a complex lexicon, but wherever possible, we have used simpler terminology for the convenience of the intelligent layperson.

This book is divided into four parts. Part I, Understanding Self-Hypnosis, provides a new perspective on the history of hypnosis, showing how changes in the brain have always been a part of how hypnosis works. Included are early developments and clinical applications, along with recent research findings. We offer a new theoretical synthesis, centered on the close interaction between mind and brain, which integrates the major theories of hypnosis. You can use these historical and theoretical understandings to help guide your experience of self-hypnosis.

Part II, Tools of Self-Hypnosis, provides an overview of the fundamental tools used in self-hypnosis: attention, unconscious processing, and suggestion. We begin with a brief description of the brain and how it functions, to help you understand the many ways that these methods alter brain structures and functions for your benefit. Then we show how the mind changes the brain, through many powerful psychological effects. Exercises are also offered, so you can develop the tools you will need for self-hypnosis.

Part III, Experiencing Self-Hypnosis, gives systematic instructions for inducing hypnosis in yourself. Find your way into a deeper trance by trying various self-hypnotic techniques. We encourage you to experiment with the many kinds of exercises that are offered. Each presents opportunities to try out new skills. Special work with resistances can help if you find it difficult to develop a trance or respond to self-suggestion.

Part IV, Applying Self-Hypnosis, offers approaches to specific problems, using and developing the self-hypnotic skills taught earlier in the book. Self-hypnosis can be a practical tool for specific target areas, but it also facilitates a general, nonspecific constructive process within the self. We cover problems that hypnosis has been especially effective for treating, including: stress, depression, substance abuse, weight management, pain, anxiety, fears, and sports performance. These applications can also be viewed as paradigms for more general personal development.

How to Use This Book

Some readers of this book will want to understand the theory and history of self-hypnosis first, to gain a map for the journey that will better guide their experience from a firm theoretical orientation. But others may not want to start at the beginning with history and theoretical sections. Hypnosis is an experience, so you might prefer to try it first, going directly to the exercises, and then learn about the theory and history of hypnosis later. Both ways can work, and probably, you will try both approaches eventually.

We encourage you to experiment with the exercises throughout the book. Many of the exercises have instructions that might seem complex or difficult to remember. You will probably achieve the greatest success by reading through each exercise you want to try at least twice. Then set the book aside, find a comfortable, quiet place to sit or lie down, and try to do the exercise. Since these exercises are mostly directed toward unconscious response, you do not need to remember every instruction. The unconscious tends to find its own way when given the opportunity. Repeat an exercise over a span of time scattered through the week for maximum results. Trance instructions offered in the earlier chapters should be practiced thoroughly, so you can develop your self-hypnotic skills before attempting the applications in Part IV.

The exercises are intended to have wider applications than their specific provided contexts. Please individualize them in ways that are most useful, positive, and meaningful for you. Be creative and adapt them to your own resources, interests, and talents. With these experiments you can discover techniques and ways of helping yourself.

We believe that you will learn the hypnotic perspective best from experiencing it personally. Thus, anyone who wants to make a change or any professional helper who intends to use hypnosis with clients should do the exercises to gain a felt sense of the process. Reactions to the exercises should be felt and thought about. We hope you will be able to find your own positive potential for growth and development through the use of this book.

Note to Professional Therapists

The Stanford University researcher Ernest Hilgard believed that hypnosis had a great deal to offer to the field of psychology in general. The history of hypnosis is intimately intertwined with the early formulations of psychotherapy itself. Many of the theories of attention and absorption, suggestion, the unconscious, and the mind-brain relationship grew out of early hypnosis research and continue to evolve today in modern research.

Clinicians who are looking for helpful techniques that facilitate the therapeutic process will find useful methods here. Theory and applications provide the background that will allow therapists to make these methods their own. In addition, the early chapters provide the research evidence and practical considerations that therapists need in order to incorporate these proven methods into treatments.

The best way to begin to add hypnosis into practice is to experience it personally. Perform the inductions and trance phenomena found in Chapters 8 and 9. Once you have a personal "feel" for trance, you will be better equipped to help others. If you find that you like hypnosis, you can seek further training through professional organizations that teach hypnotherapy. The Milton H. Erickson Foundation and the American Society of Clinical Hypnosis offer excellent opportunities for learning.

Although the book is primarily directed to the consumer, the case examples are therapeutic ones. The application chapters in Part IV include useful approaches to working with specific problems that you may face with clients. For example, if you are working with a blocked or resistant client, refer to Chapter 10 for ways to facilitate progress that can be incorporated into most forms of psychotherapy.

Hypnosis can be integrated into treatment by providing time for trance induction during the session. Clients can also bring therapy home by practicing self-hypnosis between sessions, which reinforces therapeutic discoveries made during the session and improves their sensitivity to unconscious functioning. The exercises are directed to the reader performing them, and can be read verbatim or creatively adapted for the specific needs of each client.

We have found that hypnosis provides clients with comfort, the experience of mastery, and opportunities for novel experiences to facilitate brain plasticity, to name just a few benefits. We hope that these methods will become a useful part of your therapeutic toolbox.

About the Authors

We have been teaching, researching, and practicing hypnotherapy since the 1970s. Our first hypnosis teacher, G. Wilson Shaffer, dean of Johns Hopkins University and director of the University Counseling Center, taught us how to develop hypnotic capacities and then integrate them, with suggestion, into therapeutic methods. Harold Greenwald, founder of direct decision therapy, taught us how to use the fundamental decisions clients make to help them change. Milton H. Erickson showed us the vast positive potential of the unconscious and taught us how to facilitate change through these natural automatic abilities. Ernest Rossi guided us throughout in theory, research, and practice of hypnosis and the facilitation of the brain. He always encouraged us to recognize the close interaction between the body, mind, and brain, expressed at the deep and fundamental level of the genes.

We have taught self-hypnosis and have treated many problems using these methods for several decades. We have also applied them to ourselves and family for many purposes. Perhaps the most important lesson we have drawn from our years of work with hypnosis is to have a deep respect for the potential of the natural capacities within, already there, just waiting to be released and used. And so, we encourage you to open yourself to these methods so that you too can experience for yourself the vast potential of your mind to activate your brain for change.

PART I

Understanding Self-Hypnosis

1

Early History of Neuro-Hypnosis

The point we emphasize is strong confidence in our original nature.
—Shunryu Suzuki, *Zen Mind, Beginner Mind,* p. 3

YOUR brain–mind system has amazing capabilities. When functioning as it should, your brain helps you to know when you are hungry or tired, and your mind responds by thinking about food and preparing to go to sleep. You instinctively seek loving relationships and know how to enjoy them when you find them. Soto Zen master Shunryu Suzuki's advice given above implies that you can have strong confidence in your inherent brain–mind abilities.

People have known for centuries that hypnosis can have a powerful influence on the mind and brain, but they did not understand why. Recent neuroscientific findings have shed new light on how hypnosis influences the brain and mind. Now we can look back upon the history of hypnosis with a fresh perspective, and apply our newer understandings about the brain–mind system, which have emerged from recent discoveries.

In looking back, we find a common thread that synthesizes the different historical views. All of the key figures in the history of hypnosis believed that the phenomenon of hypnosis brings about an alteration of the nervous system. Whether the theory was that hypnosis originates in the mind through suggestion and imagination, or in something found in the environment, such as a magnetic force or a social role, or whether hypnosis was seen as a normal physiological process or an abnormal condition, what we find at the heart of all these approaches is that *hypnosis can change the nervous system for the better.*

This common thread leads to a fascinating story of how hypnosis, with its many different conceptions and approaches, always comes back to the alterations that occur in the mind–brain system. We will touch on the key theories offered by important figures and ideas that show how conceptions of hypnosis evolved over time. Directing a spotlight on the neurological influences will shed new light upon this fascinating and often enigmatic phenomenon, emphasizing a perspective that will be helpful in understanding how you can most effectively use hypnosis to help yourself.

From Ancient Roots to Modern European Innovation

Hypnotic phenomena have been observed for thousands of years. In fact, many of the basic concepts of hypnosis were understood and described even before hypnosis was isolated as a discipline of its own. The ancient Egyptians and early Greeks made reference to its practice. For example, the famous Ebers papyrus of Egypt, dated about 1550 BC, described procedures identical to modern hypnosis. Beginning around 300 BC, the ancient Greek medical sect of Asclepius (the Greek god of medicine and healing) practiced a healing treatment that utilized a combination of sleep with suggestion—two fundamental components of many modern theories of hypnosis (Klein, 1905; Janet, 1925).

Although hypnotic phenomena were used at times throughout history, it was not until the eighteenth century, in the United Kingdom and Europe, that hypnosis was both studied scientifically and practiced extensively. Two main branches of hypnosis developed during this period: Animal magnetism and somnambulism. The two methods differed in many respects, but they shared the idea that hypnosis had a profound effect on the nervous system, and that this effect on the nervous system could help cure diseases.

The Powers of Magnetism to Alter the Nervous System

Franz Anton Mesmer (1734–1815) is credited with having founded the field of hypnosis through his method, which was eventually named *mesmerism* in his honor (Figure 1.1). Mesmerism evolved from mid-sixteenth-century ideas about harnessing physical forces of nature to promote healing.

Mesmer's approach to hypnosis was drawn from the earlier view that magnets had a curative power. In medieval times, people wore magnetized necklaces and bracelets in order to cure their physical and psychological problems. It may not be immediately clear how magnets could possibly help with healing, and in fact, many theories were created to explain the healing effects of magnets that people believed in. Eventually, ideas about magnets and healing expanded, and it became commonly believed that magnetic properties resided within the human body as well (Binet and Féré, 1888). One of the first to explore human magnetism was Paracelsus (1493–1541), a physician and mystic who believed that each person is a small microcosm of the larger universal macrocosm. He theorized that the human body was under a magnetic-like force from the stars, part of the larger harmony. As an interesting side note, Paracelsus was also one of the first individuals to mention the unconscious in connection with psychosomatic disorders. He wrote that sometimes an unconsciously held opinion or belief is so strong that it literally alters what the individual sees or hears (Waite, 2002). The unconscious processes play an important role in hypnosis, as will be seen.

Jan Baptist van Helmont (1579–1644) coined the name for the magnetic effect on humans: *animal magnetism*, with *animal* referring to the fact that the effects were biological. He believed that a magnetic fluid emanated from human beings, and this fluid could be influenced by the will. Maximilian Hell (1720–1792), a Jesuit priest and astronomer, experi-

Figure 1.1. Anton Mesmer.

mented with the medical use of magnets. Many of those who accepted the theory of animal magnetism wrote prolifically about it, and Mesmer was likely to have read a number of these books.

Mesmer's Version of Animal Magnetism

Mesmer developed his own method of animal magnetism for healing, based on a series of 27 propositions he formulated. He believed that there is a responsive influence or force between the stars, the earth, and the body. The body receives the influence of this force through a universally diffused fluid. This connecting fluid transmits a magnetic force between objects and people, but it also accounts for how many types of forces are transmitted, such as electricity, light, and heat. He also posited that this force is subject to mechanical laws. The influence of the magnetic force carried by the fluid is felt directly in the nervous system of human beings, and therefore, it can bring about cures for nervous disorders. In short, Mesmer believed the phenomena was caused by an external force and carried by a fluid, but its effects were felt in the nervous system. Here we see the beginnings of a theory that hypnotic phenomena bring neurological change.

Figure 1.2. The baquet.

Mesmer seemed to hold the key to tremendous power because he was able to create visible results, known as the crisis, that caused his patients to faint, to go into convulsions, to shout out, cry, laugh, etc., followed by a deep dream state. After this intense experience, his patients were apparently restored to health, losing chronic, troublesome symptoms. By 1780, Mesmer's cures were legendary. He had so many patients that he created a group-treatment method known as the *baquet* where many patients with different ailments could be treated together at one time (Figure 1.2).

Early Roots of Self-Hypnosis

Mesmer's approach underscored the power that the magnetizer had over the subject, which led to a sense that changes in the nervous system were brought about by the dominance of one person over another. But what is less well known is that Mesmer performed animal magnetism on himself—a form of self-hypnosis—and also encouraged it in his followers. Charles Nicholas D'Elson (1750–1786) was one of Mesmer's supporters and a practitioner of animal magnetism who wrote about his experiences with Mesmer. According to D'Elson, when Mesmer began to feel ill from a blockage in his bowels, "he decided that this was a good opportunity to apply the proverb *Physician heal thyself*" (D'Elson in Gravitz, 1994, p. 51). Mesmer reported that he was successful in curing himself and encouraged his other magnetizers to use self-treatment to cure their own ills. Mesmer believed that just as magnetizers transmitted a healing magnetic fluid to their patients, so could they transmit it to themselves. A number of nineteenth-century practitioners used self-magnetization, which provided a precedent for the founding fathers of self-hypnosis, Braid and Coué, who would later develop self-hypnosis into a viable treatment method (Gravitz, 1994).

Mesmer's Failure to Secure Scientific Acceptance for Animal Magnetism

Mesmer sought approval for his method from the medical community. In 1787 the Royal Society of Medicine, the most influential scientific organization of the time, formed a commission to hear Mesmer's request. The panel included the American expert on electricity Benjamin Franklin, the famous chemist Antoine Lavoisier, and the inventor of the guillotine, who was also a well-known physician, Joseph-Ignace Guillotin. The group decided that animal magnetism did not exist and that the Mesmer's cures were due to suggestion and imagination, and therefore invalid. Today, with our understanding of the measurable effects of suggestion and imagination on the nervous system, we might not be as likely to downplay the importance of Mesmer's cures, but such ideas were unknown in Mesmer's time. This rejection was the greatest disappointment of his life. He left France and settled in Switzerland. In France, the outbreak of the French Revolution dominated public attention, and thus few investigations of animal magnetism took place. However, though temporarily restrained, mesmeric currents seethed beneath the surface of the times, to flow again later.

The Power Is in the Mind: The Rise of Somnambulism

Despite Mesmer's failure to gain approval from the scientific community, interest in the phenomenon of hypnosis did not disappear. In the early 1800s several French, Scottish, and English scientists continued to investigate the phenomena. These pioneers quietly experimented in their own homes and offices, and through their discoveries they gave us some of the theories that helped to lay the foundation for modern hypnosis.

One of Mesmer's followers, a military officer from a prominent family known as the Marquis de Puységur (1751–1825), researched electricity and animal magnetism. He learned that animal magnetism might not be based in the bizarre reactions that Mesmer's patients showed, such as convulsive movements. When one of Puységur's employees underwent the procedure of being commanded to sleep, he became more alert, perceptive, and self-confident. As a result, Puységur considered animal magnetism to be a form of active sleep, leading him to call it artificial somnambulism. It was considered artificial because it was induced rather than naturally occurring, and referred to as sommanbulism because it had many of the same behaviors as sleepwalking, but with some important differences (Gravitz, 1991). For example, in this state, people could converse, which they could not do while asleep, but people in this state often would speak more openly than they usually would when fully awake. This ability to speak freely suggested the possibility of using artificial somnambulism as a method to facilitate psychotherapy.

The Abbé Faria (1746–1819), a notable cleric, believed that a magnetic fluid was not the primary cause of magnetism. He found that he could induce sleep-like states, which he called lucid sleep, by giving a dynamic command, such as confidently saying to patients, "I wish you to go to sleep." He used this method with dramatic success to the benefit of many people. He is credited as the founder of the technique of rapid induction, commonly used by skilled practitioners today.

Alexandre Bertrand (1795–1831) was one of the first to state that artificial somnambulism was due solely to the workings of the subject's imagination. He believed that suggestion was the determiner of the state, not fluids or magnets. In his book *Traité du Somnambulisme* (1823), Bertrand described the movements, actions, and hallucinations that could be aroused in the mind of the subject. Francois Joseph Noizêt (1792–1885), a friend of Bertrand, wrote a book that linked him with the doctrine that later became integral to an important formative influence on hypnosis known as the Nancy School. He stated:

> The fundamental psychological law, which is at work, is the law in accordance with which every idea tends to become an action; the suggested action is performed because the idea of the action has made its way into the subject's consciousness. (Janet, 1925, p. 157)

This definition is central in our modern conception of how suggestion works. Thanks to the pioneering work of Bertrand and Noizêt, the foundation of modern artificial somnambulism could now be viewed as a normal state, working in accordance with the general laws of imagination, expectant attention, and desire to alter the nervous system.

James Braid and Neuro-Hypnosis

James Braid (1795–1860) has been called the father of modern hypnosis (Figure 1.3). He shifted the scientific focus from external power to inner influence, and paved the way for hypnosis to become a subject for scientific exploration.

The Naming of Hypnosis

For many years, James Braid was credited with coining the term *hypnosis*. But modern historians have found that the term was used earlier in France (Gravitz, 1993). Etienne Félix d'Hénin de Cuvillers (1755–1841) was a military man who was honored for his service. After he retired, he developed his longtime inter-

Figure 1.3. James Baird.

est in animal magnetism, authoring books and founding a journal on the topic. He was a proponent of the idea that animal magnetism involved mental factors. He called it *hypnosis*, to distinguish it from the work of the magnetizers, drawing on the name of the ancient Greek god of sleep, Hypnos. A prominent expert in the history of hypnosis, Mel Gravitz, points out that the word "hypnosis" can be found even earlier, in 1809, and that although Cuvillers may not have created the term, he certainly popularized it (Gravitz, 1993).

Braid may have read some of these earlier French books and journals to come up with the term *hypnosis* in naming the phenomenon he was exploring. His first choice for the name was *neuro-hypnosis*, based on his primary belief about the nature of the phenomena, namely, that it always involved a change in the nervous system. In Braid's own words: "By the term neuro-hypnotism, then is to be understood nervous sleep, and for the sake of brevity, suppressing the prefix 'neuro' by the term *hypnotism* will be understood as the state or condition of nervous sleep and *hypnotize*, to induce nervous sleep" (Braid, 1960, p. 94).

Since hypnosis had an influence on the nervous system, it could cure many nervous disorders, including psychological problems and brain syndromes. Today we know that the mind, body, and brain function in a closely interactive system, and that psychological change can elicit real structural brain changes (Simpkins & Simpkins, 2010; Rossi, 2002; Rossi & Lloyd, 2009; see Chapter 4). This close interaction may help to explain how hypnosis can have a positive influence on some physical problems as well as psychological ones.

Braid's approach consisted primarily of intensely focusing the attention, particularly paralyzing the nervous centers of the eye by staring, which altered the equilibrium of the nervous system to produce hypnotic phenomena. Braid wrote,

The phenomena of mesmerism were to be accounted for on the principle of a derangement of the state of the cerebro-spinal centers, and of the circulatory and respiratory and muscular systems, induced, as I have explained, by a fixed attention and suppressed respiration concomitant with that fixity of attention that the whole depended on the physical and psychical conditions of the patient, arising from the causes referred to, and not at all on the volition or passes of the operator, throwing out a magnetic field, or exciting into activity some mystical universal fluid or medium. (Braid, 1960, p. 102)

Fixation of attention was understood to be key to hypnosis, and as will be seen, this quality of mental absorption alters brain activity in important ways. Braid's method required subjects to keep their eyes fixed on an object approximately 15 inches from the eyes, placed slightly above the forehead. At the same time, the mind was held on one idea. Eventually, the eyes became strained and the subject felt compelled to close them.

Braid distinguished his method from mesmerism in certain respects. Braid felt his method was far more generally applicable and practical than magnetizing. Magnetizers, especially those of Mesmer's tradition, claimed to have power over their subjects, but Braid found that hypnosis was most effective when the subject consented to do it. Since hypnosis takes place when the subject consents to focus his or her attention, then it followed that self-hypnosis would be possible. In a sense one could say that all hypnosis is ultimately self-hypnosis, since the phenomenon takes place by the deliberate actions of the individual, within the individual. This idea paved the way for the scientific development of self-hypnosis, which Braid explored with his experimental subjects.

Charcot's Neurological Approach to Hypnosis

Jean-Martin Charcot (1825–1893) has been called the founder of the field of neurology in France, and he is also considered one of the pivotal founding fathers of modern hypnosis (Figure 1.4). He developed what became one of the two main

Figure 1.4. Jean-Martin Charcot.

forms of hypnosis in France: the Salpêtrière school of hypnosis, sometimes called the Paris school. (The other form of hypnosis, known as the Nancy school, is described in the next section.)

Charcot's Contributions to Neuroscience

Charcot was one of the most influential neurologists of the nineteenth century (Goetz, 2000) and worked for 33 years as a physician at the Salpêtrière Hospital, located in Paris, treating nervous disorders. He gave Parkinson's disease its name and helped to clarify the symptoms. He offered dynamic, "multimedia" lectures, with posters hung around the room and patients brought in for dramatic demonstrations of symptoms. These teaching seminars covered topics in neurology and hypnosis.

During the nineteenth century, doctors based their diagnoses upon abstract constructs, influenced by the ancient Greek methods of categorization, such as Plato's forms and Aristotle's first principles. Charcot believed that the diagnosis should instead be derived from close observation of the patient's actual symptoms. Charcot formulated a special method for studying neurological problems, with clinical observation as the essential starting point. He drew from the positivist philosophy of Auguste Comte and the empirical method of David Hume. As he said, "I do not have to concern myself with functions and properties. I am and remain empirical" (Goetz, 2000, p. 1843). Many of the students who attended Charcot's teaching seminars—including Sigmund Freud, Alfred Binet, Pierre Janet, and William James—would later became pivotal figures in psychology.

Charcot's ideas on the relationship between mind and body can be found in contemporary neuroscientific theories of the relationship between mind and brain. He believed that psychological disorders share their roots with the nervous system, like two trees. He expressed this idea poetically:

The two trees live side by side. They communicate through their roots and they interrelate so closely that one may wonder if the two are not the same tree. If you understand this concept, you will appreciate what occurs in most neurological conditions; without this understanding you will be lost. (Goetz, 1987, p. 74)

An Empirical and Neurological Approach to Hypnosis

Charcot applied empiricism and neurology in his work with hypnosis, and as a result he singlehandedly established it as worthy of scientific exploration. He researched hypnosis scientifically by narrowing his study to observable physiological manifestations: the movements and reflexes of his subjects. He considered describing the psychological dimensions without the neurological component to be unscientific, calling this approach "minor hypnosis."

The dimension that Charcot approved and classified was called "major hypnosis." He developed classifications of phenomena according to three reactions: lethargy, catalepsy, and somnambulism. With lethargy the subject's eyes closed as they went into profound unresponsive slumber. In catalepsy the eyes opened suddenly and the limbs retained any position imposed by the experimenter. During somnambulism subjects could hear, speak, and manifest readiness to accept suggestions.

Charcot's research was based upon his work with his patients at the hospital. The best subjects proved to be females who suffered from the psychological disorder known at that time as hysteria (today we would call such a condition a psychosomatic one, conversion disorder, or somatization disorder, in which the physical complaint is psychologically caused). The intense responsiveness he observed in these patients led him to believe that hypnosis was a pathological state. This was a shortcoming of his understanding; we know today that hypnosis is a healthy phenomenon. Despite or perhaps because of his narrow conception of hypnosis, Charcot was able to gain acceptance for his hypnotic research in 1881 from the same academy that had rejected Mesmer nearly a century before. Paradoxically, this gradually ended the condemnation of hypnosis and ultimately allowed its practice to flourish. Although he was mistaken about some aspects of the process, Charcot's work firmly established that hypnosis affects the nervous system.

The Nancy School: How the Mind Can Change the Brain

Another approach to hypnosis that developed in eighteenth-century France proposed that the power of hypnosis came from the mind through the use of attention, suggestion, and imagination. The developer of this approach, Ambroise-Auguste Liébeault (1823–1904), practiced hypnosis near the French city of Nancy (Figure 1.5). Liébeault was a humanitarian who provided free medical hypnosis to thousands of patients suffering from diverse physical symptoms. He was reputed to have successfully hypnotized over 8,000 hospital patients (Bramwell, 1903) and was considered by some to be the true father of modern hypnosis (Kroger, 1977).

The Nancy school was in conflict with Charcot's school, partly because of the differences in their theories, as one seemed to be psychologically based (Nancy school) and the other seemingly physiologically based (Salpêtrière school). And although the Nancy followers did believe that hypnosis arose from the use of the mind, particularly suggestion, Liébeault's understanding of how the mind influenced the body was intimately linked to how the mind is related to the nervous system. Liébeault based the effects of hypnosis in three mental elements that could influence the body: thoughts, memory, and attention. "Attention is the propeller, the thought is the propelled element, and memory is the element's receptor. To express this in the most precise way, the mind must be defined as the result of attention bearing on thoughts in the field of memory" (Carrer, 2002, p. 42). Through the action of these elements, Liébeault argued, the mind influences the body. Liébeault described how the mind and brain work together in his own preliminary definitions of what makes somnambulism possible:

Figure 1.5. Ambroise-Auguste Liébeault.

But if we cannot conceive of the mind without its three building blocks, [attention, thinking, and memory] it is equally impossible to fathom its formation without the existence of the senses, their nerves and the external objects of focus which are the starting points of thought-images; it is even more impossible to understand this formation without the unity of our organism. It is through the latter, under the influence of attention and the mind, that with the help of sensory organs and their nerves, our being engages with its immediate surroundings and with itself. But the organism is not a mere intermediary between thinking beings and their exterior world; it is also the double, or more exactly, the written expression of the mind, absolute master reigning over the brain, with the power to mold unconsciously the body to its image and, consciously in some circumstances, the power to modify it at will. " (Carrer, 2002, p. 35–36)

Attention was seen as a force that transported itself throughout the entire nervous system, often traveling through a specific sense organ, which allowed impressions, perceptions, and sensations to take place often automatically, without our being aware. In this sense, attention could be "a true creator" (Liébeault in Carrer, 2002, p. 35). In some ways, the Nancy school's approach anticipated what we now understand as experience-based neuroplasticity (which you will learn how to activate later in this book).

Attention could be conscious or unconscious, and while in a state of hypnosis-induced artificial sleep (a state similar to normal sleep), a subject would be more responsive to suggestions that could lead the mental processes toward cure. The Nancy school compared hypnosis to sleep. Whether artificial or spontaneous, the sleep state is a cerebral condition that focuses reasoning faculties. The nervous system fixates upon images or suggested ideas. Sleep favors the production of suggestions by suppressing or lessening distracting influences.

Hippolyte Bernheim (1840–1919) developed Liébeault's theory further (Figure 1.6). He had heard that Liébeault had used hypnosis to cure a stubborn case of sciatica, which Bernheim had tried unsuccessfully to cure. He traveled to Liébeault's clinic planning to expose Liébeault as a fraud, but instead was amazed by Liébeault's abilities. He undertook a study with the master, and eventually became the spokesman for the Nancy school. Later, Sigmund Freud would translate Bern-

Figure 1.6. Hippolyte Bern-heim

heim's book on hypnosis and suggestion (Bernheim, 1973) helping to further spread the influence of this approach.

The whole explanation of hypnotic phenomena, according to Bernheim, can be found by understanding suggestion. Bernheim defined suggestion as the influence exerted by an offered idea and received by the mind. An idea initiated in the mind gives rise to a corresponding sensation in the body. This occurs automatically, with no conscious thought involved. As Bernheim wrote, "It is impossible to be seized by a vivid idea without the whole body being placed in harmony with this idea" (Bernheim, 1973, p. 129). Everyone experiences this on a daily basis, when characteristic facial expressions and body gestures accompany emotions. For example, when someone mentions a tart lemon, apple pie, or chocolate cake, we automatically salivate. If we are happy, we smile. Bernheim called these *instinctual acts*. This central concept marks the origins of the Ideomotor theory, central to hypnosis and self-hypnosis today. You will learn how to use the ideomotor effect in Chapter 7.

During hypnosis, attention is focused and consciousness is reduced, permitting automatic responses to occur. In trance, the subject's transformation of thought into action, sensation, movement, or vision is quickly and actively accomplished. Rational inhibition has no time to intervene. Unlike some hypnotists, who thought that conscious activity is completely paralyzed by hypnosis, Bernheim saw the ego involved as an observer. For example, a patient in hypnosis could not open his eyes. Upon awakening he said he heard everything but could not prevent his hands from rising and his eyes from closing. Bernheim argued that suggestion, not weakening of the will, is the central force of hypnosis:

> There is an increase of this reflex ideomotor, ideosensitive, and ideosenso-rial excitability. With hypnotism the ideo-reflex excitability is increased in the brain so that any idea received is immediately transformed into an

act, without the controlling portion of the brain, the higher centers, being able to prevent the transformation. (Bernheim, 1973, p. 138)

The Nancy School inspired many to work with hypnosis, firmly establishing it as a viable therapeutic method.

The Neo-Nancy School of Self-Suggestion and Self-Hypnosis

By the early 1900s, self-hypnosis had not been explored very much, with the exception of Braid's work in the 1800s. In Braid's view, hypnotic phenomena occur in the mind of the subject, rather than coming from the external source of the hypnotist. These concepts, though not inconsistent with Liébeault's and Bernheim's theories, remained undeveloped by the Nancy School.

Émile Coué (1857–1926) was a pharmacist for 25 years. He studied with Liébeault and assisted him in some of his experiments (Figure 1.7). Coué eventually began to apply what he learned from Liébeault to his customers at the pharmacy, offering suggestions when he gave his customers their drug orders. He consistently observed more positive response to the drug when it was accompanied by a suggestion. He theorized that ultimately the suggestions he gave became autosuggestions patients gave to themselves, now known as self-suggestion. Coué founded the Neo-Nancy School in 1910, introducing an original approach that abandoned trance entirely and taught people how to work with waking suggestion. In this way, he taught people how to facilitate their own healing process through deliberate self-suggestion.

Figure 1.7. Émile Coué.

Coué's method was based on consciously harnessing the effects of autosuggestion that he believed stemmed from the imagination. He distinguished between willpower and imagination. Any effort to bring about a change always begins in the imagination, not from willpower, as might be expected.

Coué developed an uncomplicated system that taught people how to harness their imagination, stemming from the unconscious. An unconscious self-suggestion could activate the imagination. These unconscious self-suggestions would link directly to the nervous system to bring about changes. He gave patients some simple ideas to vividly imagine each morning, such as: "Day by day, in every way, I am getting better and better" (Coué, 1923, p. 101). He encouraged people to imagine the positive results they wanted to achieve and stop trying to will themselves to accomplish them. Many modern self-hypnosis practitioners apply variations of these same principles today.

Charles Baudouin (1893–1963) developed a theory of autosuggestion and self-hypnosis drawn from Coué's theory of autosuggestion, but unlike Coué, he included trance. Baudouin (1921) defined suggestion as the subconscious realization of an idea, or as he wrote, "The idea of an idea gives birth to this idea" (p. 47). Thus, the mental representation that we hold in mind is what can bring about changes in the nervous system, through the sensory, affective, and motor systems. These nervous system changes alter how we think, feel, and act. The mind, body, and brain are all linked together by autosuggestions. We give ourselves autosuggestions constantly throughout the day without realizing it. These autosuggestions influence what we can or cannot accomplish. Autosuggestions follow three general laws. First, ideas that are concentrated on tend to be realized. Second, ideas accompanied by emotion tend to be more easily realized. Finally, and perhaps most important to consider for fostering therapeutic change, any idea tends to evoke the counter-idea. This third law helps to explain why many of our new year's resolutions lose momentum after a few weeks.

Baudouin found that the best way to implement autosuggestions was during self-hypnosis. During hypnosis people are relaxed and yet focused. Under these circumstances, ideas can be accepted as suggestions without any resistance occurring. When consciousness is riveted on a single idea in trance, reverse suggestions cannot dominate, and the nervous system can be altered in the therapeutically intended direction.

Dissociation Theorists: Janet, Sidis, & James

Pierre Janet (1859–1947), a student of Charcot's, is a central figure in the history of hypnosis, influencing many with his books and ideas (Figure 1.8). He wrote extensively about what he called *automatism*, which in many ways predates Freud's idea of the unconscious. He theorized that complexes of ideas exist in a state that is split off or dissociated from personality. "The power of such ideas depends upon their isolation. They grow, they install themselves in the field of thought like a parasite, and the subject cannot check their development by any effort on his part, because they are ignored, because they exist by themselves in a second field of thought detached from the first" (Janet, 1925, p. 600).

Janet believed that hypnosis was not a state of sleep, and should not be characterized as suggestibility; rather, it profoundly altered the normal brain–mind state. The modification was considered a temporary state, in which the individual's personal memory is dissociated. In fact, the modification of personal memory is one way we can discern the difference between a state of hypnosis and a normal state. He cited an example: Though he might be tired and depressed, he still remembered how he felt earlier when he was not feeling tired and depressed. But in trance these conscious balances and tendencies are replaced by repressed tendencies. Another life, another character, another memory can be evoked in place of the usual one. For this reason, hypnosis can be useful in working with neurosis, since it gives people relief from their everyday tensions and problems.

Hypnosis can activate dissociated parts of the personality Janet called "tendencies." Ordinarily, unused tendencies atrophy, but during trance these tendencies can be reintegrated into the waking personality. Thus, through hypnosis, dissociated thoughts and experiences could become part of consciousness once again. Janet anticipated many of the ideas prevalent in modern hypnosis when he stated that "the unconscious mind is a reservoir of untapped potential beyond the limits of conscious awareness" (Janet, 1925, p. 147).

Figure 1.8. Pierre Janet.

Boris Sidis (1898), a Harvard University researcher, attempted to unify the views from the Salpêtrière and Nancy Schools:

> With the Nancy School, we agree that suggestion is all-powerful in hypnotic trance; the hypnotic trance is in fact, a state of heightened suggestibility, or, rather of pure reflex consciousness; but with the Paris School, we agree that a changed physiological state is a prerequisite to hypnosis, and this modification consists in the disaggregation of the superior from the inferior centres, in the segregation of the controlling consciousness from the reflex consciousness. (p. 70)

Thus, we see in Sidis's synthesis the basis for our modern neurological perspective, which views different hypnotic phenomena as activating the brain and bringing about new thoughts, feelings, and behaviors.

Sidis applied a neurological interpretation to Janet's ideas on dissociation as well. The higher, conscious levels of controls were dissociated from the reflexes and automatic, lower levels. During hypnosis a suggested movement or idea is carried through without interruption from the conscious mind. Neuroscience calls this bottom-up processing, and later in this book we will show you how to foster this capacity in self-hypnosis, to carry out tasks you normally find difficult.

Figure 1.9. William James.

William James (1842–910), who is considered the American father of modern psychology, was also influenced by Janet's hypnotic theory (Figure 1.9). In the normal waking state, James believed people retain both a "normal" consciousness and a subliminal consciousness. "In hypnosis, waking consciousness is split off from the rest of the nervous system while subliminal consciousness is laid bare and comes into direct contact with the external world" (James, in Taylor, 1982, p. 42).

This secondary consciousness is intelligent as well, attending t... 's own concerns without interfering with ... ...ould be but an extract of a vast ... Taylor, 1982, p. 42). James point... ...uroscience distinguishes betwe... ...awareness and language usage, ...ons and habits.

Unlike Janet... ...tor of hypnosis. In trance, th... ...can easily be translated to ide... ...ion. Suggestibility also causes... ...one idea that produces an inten... ...d, creating a state of focused co...

James explain... ...mmediately from a correspond... ...on flows so automatically that ...

> We may then l... ...movement awakens i... ...object; and awakens in... ...doing by an antagonis... ...to the mind. (James, 1896, p. ...)

This ideomotor effect occurs naturally when a thought, image, or experience is automatically translated into bodily experience, movement, or sensation. There is no actual separation: thought becomes action, image becomes motor response, imaginary sensory experience becomes actual sensory phenomena.

Using Hypnosis to Unblock Unconscious Conflicts:
Freud and Psychoanalysis

Josef Breuer (1842–1925) introduced psychoanalytic applications of hypnotic therapy. Previously, the therapeutic use of hypnosis had been direct symptom removal.

Figure 1.10. Sigmund Freud.

Working with his patient Anna O., Breuer discovered that the original trauma related to her hysterical symptoms could be brought to the surface of her consciousness by hypnosis, resulting in a cure of her symptoms. Pierre Janet simultaneously arrived at the technique of liberating repressed emotions associated with traumatic memories, but Breuer is given historic credit for the discovery.

Sigmund Freud (1856–1939) became fascinated with hypnosis and studied it ardently (Figure 1.10). He translated both Charcot and Bernheim's books into German. His interest was so intense that he traveled to Nancy to visit Bernheim and Liébeault and brought one of his patients with him for Bernheim to hypnotize. He published a book on hypnosis with Breuer entitled *Studien Uber Hysterie* (Studies on Hysteria) in 1895. They stated:

> The individual hysterical symptoms immediately disappeared without returning if we succeed in thoroughly awakening the memories of the causal process with its accompanying affects, and if the patient circumstantially discussed the process in the most detailed manner and gave verbal expression to the affect. (Breuer & Freud, 1957, pp. 3–4)

They concluded that symptoms developed as a result of experiences so damaging to the individual that the memory of the experience was repressed. Energy became blocked due to the unconscious conflict between the mind and the repressed memory. Freud used hypnosis and suggestion as a method to release blocked energy and thereby cure patients.

At first Freud used suggestion and hypnosis as his primary techniques until he encountered a patient, known as Lucy R., who was unable to go into trance. Freud remembered that Bernheim's patients often recalled their trance experiences when awake. Freud recognized the potential. He decided to try encouraging Lucy to say every thought that came into her mind, hoping she would express her unconscious conflict. His difficulty with inducing trance led him to develop an alternative technique, *free association*, to accomplish the therapeutic catharsis that hypnosis had usually brought about. Although Freud stopped using hypnosis, many of his concepts of psychoanalysis were influenced by hypnosis. Later, psychoanalysts reincorporated hypnosis to facilitate the analytic process.

Hypnosis as a Forerunner to Psychotherapy

The early 1900s were a period when the medical model predominated, and thus psychotherapy was struggling to become an accepted treatment method. Some doctors recognized the importance of the mind–body interaction and attempted to persuade other medical professionals to include mental processes in their work. Henry S. Munro was one of those medical doctors. He lectured around the country to other doctors about the value of psychotherapy, which he termed *suggestive therapeutics* (Munro, 1911). He tried to show that psychotherapy could be an important adjunct to clinical work because of the close affinity between mind and body:

> In the study of the nervous system we find for every difference of experience—whether of quality, intensity, or structure, a corresponding physical change. The end sought in psychotherapeutic treatment is to bring the patient under the influence of such experiences as will produce such brain changes that will promote the normal functioning of the organism on the one hand, and that will serve to adapt the individual to his environment on the other. (Munro, 1911, p. 44)

For Munro, psychotherapy was synonymous with hypnosis and suggestion, occurring through three basic methods: hypnotic suggestion, waking suggestion, and persuasion, reasoning, or re-education. Thus we see the important role that hypnosis played in the early development of psychotherapy.

Suggestion was central to Munro's view. In order for a suggestion to be assimilated as a self-suggestion, he argued, people need a mental attitude of conviction. The right mental attitude could make a difference:

This mental attitude evokes or calls forth latent powers or inherent psychic activities, and renders the reserve energy available or useless as he has confidence or lack of confidence. (Munro, 1911, p. 145)

Suggestion, along with a positive mental attitude, could promote healing and health. Munro encouraged the family and friends of his patients to create a positive, suggestive environment. He emphasized that it is of vital importance for all good psychological treatment to be accompanied by the teaching of healthy habits to unify the mind and body in patients. Due to his beliefs and work, he can be seen as a forerunner of cognitive therapy and preventive medicine.

Despite the efforts of these fine hypnotic researchers, many doctors of the early 1900s continued to consider hypnosis unscientific. The benefits of hypnosis were disregarded until World War I, when many soldiers suffered from injuries and the trauma of war. Hypnotherapy was revived to facilitate therapy for shell shock (now known as post-traumatic stress disorder) and other conditions. Numerous accounts of rapid and effective treatment were given during this period, which led to renewed interest in hypnosis, laying the foundation for a new era of hypnosis.

Conclusion

Some hypnotists thought that the mind instigates physiological changes and is thus preeminent, such as the Nancy school, while Charcot and others thought that physiology alters the mental experience. Some answers are found in the relationship between the mind and brain. Historical and contemporary theories of hypnosis can be better understood through the lens of neuroscience, as the next chapters will show.

2

Recent History: Research, Neuroscience, and Practitioners

My own preference is to see hypnosis "domesticated" as a part of normal psychology, on the assumption that understanding of the normal human mind will be enhanced if hypnosis is taken seriously along with perception, learning, motivation, and the other accepted topics of general psychology.

—Ernest R. Hilgard, *Divided Consciousness: Multiple Controls in Human Thought and Action,* p. x

MANY innovative investigators of hypnosis in the eighteenth and nineteenth centuries helped make hypnosis a recognized phenomenon worthy of study. From the late nineteenth century to the present, hypnosis has been brought into the laboratory to help answer some of the age-old questions, such as: How does hypnosis work, and what does it do to consciousness? New technologies have made it possible to see the brain during hypnosis. Furthermore, clinical studies have shown that hypnosis is an effective form of treatment, and that it is especially helpful for certain kinds of problems. This chapter offers highlights from pivotal studies that have helped to shape our understanding about the nature of hypnosis and its therapeutic effectiveness. Reading this chapter, you may learn more in general about how you think, feel, and behave.

The Largest Historical Hypnosis Study

Today we often think we know more and can do better than our predecessors. Scientists are always trying to improve their methods. But one of the largest hypnosis studies took place more than 100 years ago. Many prominent hypnosis practitioners from around the world collaborated together to investigate hypnotic susceptibility. Their data was based on 8,705 hypnotized subjects from 15 different countries. The results were published as the First International Statistics of Susceptibility to Hypnosis in 1892 (Bramwell, 1903). All participating hypnotists kept track of their own results with trance phenomena and induction, and then these statistics were correlated together. Later, the statistical results were combined with two other large studies done around the same period of time to give a grand total of 19,534 subjects in all (Hilgard, 1965, p. 75)—quite an impressive subject sample! Rarely do we find such large studies performed today.

The compiled findings indicated that most of the population is responsive to hypnosis. Only 9% were unresponsive, while 29% produced light trances, 36% showed moderate trances, and 26% went into a deep, somnambulistic trance. The study noted no significant differences among the many different countries. For example, some of the researchers had expected that the French would be more susceptible to hypnosis than other nationalities, since many of hypnosis's founders were French, but all participating nations had comparable results. Subjects in Sweden, Germany, England, Scotland, India, and Australia were no different from the French in their trance abilities.

The researchers did find some distinctions. For example, the age of subjects made a difference in susceptibility. Children were more readily able to respond than adults, and most children aged 3 to 15 could readily experience trance phenomena. For adults, responsiveness remained fairly steady up to 63 years of age, when susceptibility dropped slightly.

Most people expect that subjects who firmly believe that they will be hypnotized will respond more strongly than those who are skeptical, but the study found that people responded equally no matter what they expected. These results helped to dispel the assumption that faith or belief in hypnosis was a necessary component of effective hypnosis. For example, some subjects laughed at the process and believed hypnotized people were imposters—and yet, these subjects were often quickly hypnotized without realizing what was happening.

The misconception regarding differences between men and women was also corrected. At the time of the study, many people believed in the stereotype that women were the "weaker sex," and therefore researchers expected them to be more susceptible to hypnosis. However, they found no such result: Men and women were found to be equally hypnotizable. Another myth is that hypnosis is for the weak-minded. The study actually found that intelligent, imaginative subjects were more hynotizable than duller, unimaginative ones. People who were intellectually passive, with poor concentration abilities, were not as easily hypnotized as subjects who could direct their attention at will.

The sheer magnitude of these early hypnosis studies lends credibility to their findings. However, there were some problems in the research methods. Even though the nineteenth-century researchers collected large numbers of observations of hypnotic phenomena, they did not carefully standardize their induction methods. The same hypnotic technique meant different things to different hypnotists. For example, one researcher gave suggestions forcefully as a command, while another offered suggestions gently, as a subtle inference. Some made suggestions verbally, while other used nonverbal means of suggestion, such as touching the subject. We now know that keeping all the independent variables constant produces more reliable results. But despite these shortcomings, this study offers an early meta-analysis that points to the idea that hypnosis reaches beyond any one theory or approach, given that it occurred in a majority of subjects no matter what method was used. Clearly the techniques of hypnosis are robust. From these foundations, modern hypnosis research has confidently moved forward to explore what characterizes hypnosis and how best to use it for healing.

Pavlov's Work with Hypnosis

Ivan Pavlov (1849–1936), the Russian researcher most famous for his formulations of stimulus-response conditioning with dogs, also did extensive studies of hypnosis (Figure 2.1). He devised a neuro-physical theory of suggestion and hypnosis,

Figure 2.1. Ivan Pavlov.

defining suggestion as a form of signal processing and hypnosis as a form of sleep.

Pavlov believed that the cerebral cortex influences the entire organism in a complex manner he called the *primary signaling system*. All animals have this signaling system to maintain balance between organism and environment. Human beings distinguish themselves from animals by having a secondary signaling system of higher thinking and speech. Language is a conditioned stimulus that affects the higher nervous activity. In this sense, words are like signals. Through this process, one person's words can powerfully affect another. As one of Pavlov's students explained, "A word is as real a conditioned stimulus for man as all the other stimuli in common with animals, but at the same time more all-inclusive than any other stimuli (Platonov, 1959, p. 15).

Once words have been paired with unconditioned responses, language influences action. For example, the phrase "ice cream" acquires definite meaning once you have tasted ice cream at least once. Then the verbal stimulus can evoke a hunger response simply upon hearing the phrase. Pavlov believed that suggestion was the simplest form of conditioned reflex, signaled by a word's associated meanings. The hypnotic command concentrates excitation in a narrow area of the subject's cortex, while at the same time intensifying the inhibition in other areas (Pavlov, 1927).

Pavlov defined hypnosis as a neurological state of partial sleep that is similar to natural sleep. Hypnosis, he posited, is induced by signaling through words or symbolic gestures associated with sleeping. "In this manner any stimulus which has coincided several times with the development of sleep can now by itself initiate sleep or a hypnotic state. The mechanism is analogous to the inhibitory chain reflexes" (Pavlov, 1927, p. 406). Sleep involves the internal inhibition of the cortex. After exhaustion of the cortex from being awake, inhibition replaces excitation, giving the cells a chance to be restored. During hypnosis, as in natural sleep, internal inhibition spreads over the cerebral cortex. But being a form of partial sleep, some parts of the cerebral cortex undergo inhibitory response while others do not. Scattered areas of sleep take place in a complex pattern throughout the cortex. Pavlov believed that this accounts for the individualized, different levels of hypnosis that occur. Suggestion and autosuggestion are based upon the transition of certain cortical cells to an inhibitory state, while others are selectively stimulated, resulting in a reflex in the brain that brings about an intensified response.

Clark Hull: Incorporating Technology for Hypnosis Research

Clark Hull (1884–1952) attempted to give a scientific account of hypnosis using the most up-to-date experimental methods of his time (Figure 2.2). Hull set up a laboratory at Yale University, where he tested many aspects of hypnosis. He thought that through careful scientific study, some of the many questions about the nature of hypnosis could be resolved. He used and created devices including an apparatus to measure and record eyelid movements, a mechanical set of strings and pulleys that recorded postural swaying, and a galvanic skin response (GSR) machine measuring the electrical resistance of the skin, which is sensitive to emotions.

Hull performed hundreds of experiments on hypnotic suggestion and waking suggestion, and he investigated commonly observed hypnotic phenomenon such as catalepsy, unconscious muscle movements, heightened sensitivity, recovery of memories, and post-hypnotic suggestion (Hull, 1933).

Hull tested and compared many of the conflicting theories that attempted to define hypnosis as a type of dissociation, sleep, habit, or suggestion. Hull's work led him to draw the conclusion that hyper-suggestibility explained hypnosis best. He translated William James's ideomotor theory into the learning theory ter-

Figure 2.2. Clark Hull.

minology of stimulus-response (Triplet, 2006). Hull believed his research proved that hypnosis was neither a form of sleep, nor a pathological condition related to hysteria, nor a state of dissociation.

Hull's research did not really disprove other theories, but his experiments were indeed innovative. He was one of the first to enlist the latest technology to investigate the effects of hypnosis. Of course, in his day the equipment only recorded outer physical measurements, such as body movements or galvanic skin response, measuring skin conductivity from a finger or palm. Modern neuroscientific tools such as fMRI and PET scans have allowed us to look inside the brain to gather even more information. In this respect, hypnosis research continues to follow Hull's lead in applying technologies to help better understand the physical underpinnings of hypnosis. In addition, Hull's finding that hypnosis is best defined by its reliance on suggestibility has been integrated into the American Psychological Association's (APA) definition of the procedure: "The hypnotic induction is an extended initial suggestion for using one's imagination" (Green, Barabasz, Barrett, & Montgomery, 2005, p. 263).

The Work of the Hilgards: Using Our Multi-Processing Brain

Ernest R. Hilgard, (1904–2001) eminent professor of psychology at Stanford University and prominent researcher, devoted himself to hypnotic research since 1957. He headed a prominent laboratory called the Stanford Laboratory of Hypnosis Research, and he performed experiments with his wife Josephine R. Hilgard, MD, PhD, who was a professor of psychiatry at Stanford (Figure 2.3). The Hilgards worked with a number of well-known collaborators who went on to make significant contributions in hypnosis and related fields. They used more than 1,000 college students as subjects. Like Hull, they based their experiments on normal human capacities.

Hilgard is well known for his development of the Stanford Hypnotic Susceptibility Scales. The relative susceptibility of individuals to hypnosis can be determined based upon their suggestibility test scores. Hilgard believed a certain percentage of people have a genetic predisposition toward hypnosis, and that this talent remains relatively constant, just as some people are athletically, musically, or artistically gifted. The Hilgards were strong advocates of hypnosis as a distinct state that differed from everyday consciousness. They responded to those who saw little difference between responsiveness to suggestion in hypnosis and responsiveness in the waking state by showing that there are wide individual differences in susceptibility. They believed that if these differences are not taken into account in the research design, they interfere with accurate results.

Figure 2.3. Ernest and Josephine Hilgard.

Divided Attention and Neo-Dissociation

Based on Janet's dissociation theory, described during the early period of hypnosis research discussed in Chapter 1, Hilgard developed a neo-dissociation theory. Expanding the boundaries of Janet's theory further, Hilgard believed all people, healthy and neurotic alike, always experience more than one thing at a time. "We do not choose simply to attend to something while neglecting everything else, for our attention may be divided among two or more streams of thought or courses of action" (Hilgard, 1977, p. 1). Hilgard's insight has proven to be true of many functions and structures of the brain, in conjunction with attention. For example, we have two pathways for processing visual stimuli: the ventral pathway and the dorsal pathway (Squire & Kandel, 2000). *What* something is and how it is represented in form, such as its color or shape, is processed with conscious attention through the ventral pathway. *Where* something is and how to move to its location in space is processed without conscious attention, or unconsciously, through the dorsal visual-motor pathway. For example, you can see the page you are reading now. You may even be aware that you are seeing it while you read, but nevertheless, you will probably reach out to turn the page without giving it much thought. Both processes can and often do occur at the same time, even though you are only paying attention to the act of reading, rather than seeing the page, because different areas of the brain are activated for different purposes. We will discuss these two types of processing in depth in Chapter 6.

Hilgard believed that in hypnosis, this natural dissociation stands out clearly, presenting itself for observation. Therefore, when observing hypnosis, we can deepen our understanding of the workings of attention, memory, perception, creativity, and imagination. He illustrated this view with examples of hypnosis-induced acts such as automatic writing, pain reduction, involuntary movement, amnesia, and age regression.

Hilgard theorized that we all have a "hidden observer" (Hilgard, 1977, p. 209). Even though hypnotized people may think they do not recall anything about their trance experience, the hidden observer recalls everything and understands what is happening. Here again, neuroscience research reveals some clinical evidence for this claim. Michael Gazzaniga has performed extensive studies on the unique functions of the two brain hemispheres and has proposed that we have a left-hemisphere interpreter that "allows us to construct theories about the relationship between perceived events, actions and feelings" (Gazzaniga, 2000, p. 1293).

Through many years of innovative experimental research, the Hilgards influenced the course of hypnosis in a positive way. Their rigorous research on hypnosis encouraged a revival of the scientific study of consciousness. The Hilgards' research, with its useful models, furthered the field of hypnosis. In addition, these models translate well into broader contexts of motivation, learning, memory, and perception to foster modern understandings of how the mind–brain system functions.

Milton Erickson's Naturalistic Research and Indirect Hypnosis

> By naturalistic approach is meant the acceptance and utilization of the situation encountered without endeavoring to psychologically restructure it.
> —Milton H. Erickson, *"Naturalistic Techniques of Hypnosis"*

Milton H. Erickson (1901–1980) was one of the foremost twentieth-century practitioners of hypnotherapy (Figure 2.4). He was an innovative medical doctor who devoted his career to hypnosis. Although he was very knowledgeable in traditional hypnotic theories and methods, he was able to think beyond previously established categories to create original and highly effective hypnotic methods. His research, theories, and practice took hypnosis in completely new directions.

Figure 2.4. Milton H. Erickson

Erickson's theory of hypnosis was based on a firm belief that the unconscious mind is a reservoir of potential. People think that they function best by being completely rational and consciously aware of their motivations and beliefs, but Erickson believed that a large part of our intelligence comes from the unconscious. In fact, the conscious mind often holds us back, through deeply ingrained learning about what we can and cannot do. Many abilities are already present in the unconscious mind, just waiting to be mobilized to help us learn and grow. Recent neuroscientific research shows that the brain does have many unconscious pathways that are indeed intelligent. Hypnosis enlists the unconscious to break through barriers and discover new possibilities—and we will utilize these pathways in this book. By going into trance, you can tap into latent potential. Erickson found creative ways to help people get around the barriers that held them back, so that they could make positive use of the vast reservoirs of potential for change and growth that were just waiting to be enlisted for their benefit.

Erickson's Research

Modern research is usually performed in a laboratory, but Erickson believed that there was another way to do research, which he called the naturalistic approach. His naturalistic research allowed him to observe phenomena in the midst of their interrelationships without intruding artificially upon those relationships. As a result, naturalistic research could monitor subjects as they reacted spontaneously, in ways that might not emerge in the artificial laboratory setting.

Erickson firmly believed that researchers, like therapists, should not impose their will on subjects, but instead should just set the stage for subjects to be able to respond as they would naturally, without any input from the researcher. From working with hundreds of subjects, Erickson found that "The simpler and more permissive and unobtrusive is the technique, the more effective it has proved to be, both experimentally and therapeutically, in the achievement of significant results" (Rossi, 1980, p. 15).

Erickson began demonstrating this idea in his early psychological research, to understand how important the hypnotist was for producing a deep, productive trance state. Subjects were told that they would be trying to observe their own inner thought processes. They were to sit comfortably and imagine that they were moving imaginary fruit, one piece at a time, from one imaginary bowl to another. With no mention of hypnosis and no interference from the experimenter, the subjects were free to carry out the instructions in their own way. As a result, those subjects who completed the task spontaneously went into a deep trance, demonstrating that when asked to turn focus inward and then left alone, people tend to have a deep self-hypnotic experience. This capacity is very useful for clinical work and can give you confidence in your own natural abilities to perform self-hypnosis.

Erickson developed designs to study hypnotic effects as they appeared in their natural setting, or as close to the natural setting as possible, so as not to interfere or influence the results. He often preferred to perform careful, deep studies of one subject at a time, rather than apply an artificial, standardized condition to numerous people. The uniqueness of the individual was not subtracted from the experiment and so could be studied. Erickson firmly believed that suggestion always takes place in a context. His early in-depth experimental work strongly influenced the development of his ideas about the nature of hypnosis and would influence his therapeutic work in years to come (Erickson & Rossi, 1980a).

Erickson spent many hours training subjects to develop the ability to go into deep trances. By working with individual skilled hypnotic subjects he could learn more about complex relationships between factors affecting hypnotic phenomena. Standardized laboratory studies, which by their very nature need to restrict and isolate variables, risk producing findings that do not reflect the complexity of the actual phenomena outside of the laboratory. Erickson's naturalistic research showed him that "Psychopathological phenomena cannot be understood in terms of the modality of their expression and manifestation alone, but rather that an understanding must be looked for in terms of their fundamental interrelationships and interdependencies" (Erickson, 1943, p. 58).

Empirical research in experimental situations often requires isolation of the dependent and independent variables, which may lead to overlooking important, subtle interrelationships. Naturalistic research allows the experimenter to discover subtle and important interrelationships, interrelationships that might not have been known beforehand. By including discoveries from the naturalistic method, traditional empirical research can use its own methodology to learn more, and naturalistic research can take the findings of empirical studies and expand them. The two methods can supplement each other.

Mobilizing Expectancy

Erickson pointed out that just as an attitude of expectancy can influence the results of an experiment, the attitude taken toward our capabilities in ourselves can influence what becomes possible for us to do in hypnosis, in therapy, and in life. Therefore, you can use your expectations, hopes, and attitudes to assist in your self-hypnosis therapy.

Erickson not only used expectancies to facilitate the therapeutic process; he also upended expectancies in order to assist his patients in reorienting to what was possible for them. Often therapeutic change requires that people alter their view of themselves and their resources. Erickson was fond of presenting puzzling cases in his teaching seminars. Students found themselves thinking of new, creative ways of understanding patients and problems. A wide range of techniques can derive from the use of expectancies, hopes, and attitudes, and we will guide you in altering expectancies when they interfere with your progress.

Erickson's View of Susceptibility

Erickson believed that anyone could be hypnotized who sincerely wanted to be, so long as he or she was willing to put in the time and effort to do so. According to Erickson, the variability in results of hypnotizability studies derived from individual differences between people. One important variation is in how quickly people respond to hypnosis. As he liked to tell people, one of his best subjects required only 30 seconds to develop a deep trance, while another one of his best subjects required 300 hours. Both subjects, when given the time they needed, developed deep, responsive trances. Experiments that used a standardized 20-minute induction would not be able to account for deep levels of responsiveness obtained from subjects who needed more time for trance induction. Yet these subjects, once well-trained, could produce all the phenomena on the hypnotic scales.

Erickson believed that, in order to understand the true nature of hypnosis and hypnotic phenomena, it is necessary to take time and care to hypnotize each subject deeply and completely. By working with every individual carefully and deeply, he could help all his subjects to bring about the best possible results. Similarly, you can develop your self-hypnotic skills, if you are willing to give it the time you need.

Therapeutic Trance and the Unconscious Mind

Erickson used hypnosis as the primary mode of therapy. He believed that hypnosis allows therapeutic work to proceed effectively and efficiently. He often said that the trance facilitates learning that would take a much longer time in conventional therapy. He also believed that altered states of consciousness were the key to creative learning. Erickson felt that all of the major breakthroughs in his own life came during hypnosis.

Erickson distinguished between trance induction and trance state. Although some therapeutic work can be done during induction, the main work in hypnotherapy takes place through the *therapeutic trance*, as he called it with Rossi (Erickson, Rossi, & Rossi, 1976). The trance is a state of focused attention and active unconscious functioning. This unconscious functioning tends to be uniform and universal in its features, even though each person is a unique individual. Erickson was interested in unconscious understanding, and spoke directly to the unconscious whenever possible. This gave him an uncanny ability to sense and activate the very thoughts of his patients and students. In every seminar we attended, most of the members of the group believed and found that Erickson's stories were meant for them personally. Erickson's trance work permitted patients' unconscious minds to be dissociated from their conscious minds, so that they could work on therapeutic matters without interference from conscious resistance. Through the therapeutic trance, the unconscious can be appealed to directly. In keeping with life's mystery and wonder, changes in behavior, thoughts, and feelings take place by themselves.

The Use and Development of Indirect Suggestion

In keeping with his general problem-solving approach of stimulating the patient's own inner resources, Erickson developed a special form of suggestion: the indirect method. The more traditional direct form of suggestion tends to use specific statements. These statements rely upon the motivations and voluntary cooperation of the patient to do what is asked. However, many people who come for therapy have found that their motivations and personality do not allow them to voluntarily resolve their difficulties. Erickson's indirect forms of suggestion help the patient become capable of accepting therapeutic suggestions necessary for change. Indirect suggestions explore and facilitate what the patient's response system can do on an autonomous level, without really making a conscious effort to direct it (Erickson & Rossi, 1979). Indirect suggestion uses the subtlety and complexity of patient responsiveness, especially when tackling the thorniest problems that brought the patient to therapy. The patient's motivations and personality, along with the natural mechanisms of the mind, are used in formulating indirect suggestions. The best discoveries in therapy are those that occur to the patient spontaneously. Indirect suggestions offer hints of certain possibilities without filling in the details. Erickson would tell patients, "Healing takes place in your own way and your own time," and he believed it. A cut heals naturally of itself so long as the wound is cleaned and covered. Similarly, mental difficulties can be healed if circumstances are arranged so that constructive mental processes can take place in and of themselves. Therapeutic trance allows natural healing capacities to occur. Therapeutic change takes place when people undergo an alteration of their internal world of experience: a change in their meanings, assumptions, and beliefs. This change involves reorganization and re-synthesis of abilities people already possess.

Utilizing What Is Already There

A proper therapeutic goal is one that helps people to function as adequately and as constructively as possible, to use their tendencies in positive ways and while meeting their needs (Erickson & Rossi, 1980b). Your own memories and sensations are the best place to start for bringing about and using trance. Erickson believed that by turning attention inwards, people would find a wealth of experiences from their past and present to draw on. Erickson viewed the life cycle as a continuum, with certain skills to be drawn on and challenges to be met at each phase. He looked for what was preventing his patients from flowing with the natural cycles of their lives. Then he applied his knowledge of human nature in creative ways to help patients solve problems, resolve conflicts, and move forward.

Part of Erickson's understanding derived from his own work with self-hypnosis, using his own memories in coping with joint and muscle pain. Erickson knew that he could exercise until he was tired to reduce his physical pain. But when physical exercise was not an option, such as late at night, he used self-hypnosis. He began to realize that he could vividly remember exercising, becoming fatigued, and relaxing while in trance, and thus feel relief from his pain. By using an intense memory of exercising he derived many of the same benefits as actually doing it. We now know that intense visualization in trance does activate the same neural pathways that engage during the actual experience, which helps to explain why his methods were so helpful for his physical rehabilitation. This and other findings led Erickson to utilize people's personal experiences, through memories, sensations, and perceptions, to help activate responses using hypnosis.

The idea of using personal experiences evolved into a method to facilitate trance inductions even when people had difficulty going into trance. Erickson found ways to help people enlarge on what they were already doing, thinking, perceiving, or remembering, even if they seemed to be resistant. You will find that even if you have failed to be hypnotized in the past, you will be likely to develop a trance using this approach.

Erickson's Contributions

Milton Erickson's contributions to the field of hypnosis continue to be influential. Today, there is a large global foundation, the Milton H. Erickson Foundation, devoted to continuing, disseminating, and developing his work. His innovative and creative approach to hypnosis has encouraged many professionals to integrate hypnosis into their practice. His methods are now being merged with other forms of hypnosis, helping to enhance the overall effectiveness of hypnosis in general.

Ernest Rossi and Mind–Brain Unity

Ernest Rossi worked closely with Erickson for decades and was one of the pivotal figures in bringing Erickson's work to the attention of the world. But he has also made significant contributions to neuro-hypnosis with his own unique, integrative approach to mind–brain healing using hypnotherapy (Figure 2.5). He has explained how neurogenesis and neuroplasticity are stimulated by novel experiences, drawing upon research that has shown how enriched environments literally stimulate new neuronal growth. He uses the naturally occurring ultradian rhythms of the body (60- to 90-minute cycles of attention and inattention), which we all experience throughout the day and night, to better facilitate change. He has researched his ideas in several controlled studies and shown how hypnosis leads to neurogenesis (Rossi, Iannotti, Cozzolino, Castiglione, Cicatelli, & Rossi, 2008).

He believes that hypnosis does far more than simply repair disturbed thoughts. He is searching for the molecular-genomic mechanisms that fuel the problematic thoughts that are found when people are suffering from stress, trauma, PTSD, and other common psychological problems. He and his research team have found that hypnosis has an ideo-plastic quality that brings about a significant change in the genes, which leads to stem cell growth, reduces inflammation (thus reducing pain), and reduces cellular oxidative stress, which is part of the healing process (Rossi & Jensen, 2010).

Figure 2.5. Ernest L. Rossi.

How the Mind and Brain Co-Create Each Other

Rossi has devised a model for how the mind and brain influence each other during hypnosis and through interactions with the environment, by picturing the entire process as a circle (Figure 2.6). The cycle begins when consciousness observes. This observation of others in the world activates the mirror neurons in the brain. Mirror neurons interface directly between the observing consciousness and the outside world by firing in response to intentional movement observed in other people. This firing of neurons moves the cycle forward to turn on gene expression, which is the synthesis of new proteins. Protein synthesis then fosters the formation of new synaptic connections in the brain, or neuroplasticity. Now the cycle begins again, by creating a new observing consciousness that incorporates the added potentials resulting from new neuronal growth and connections. Through this process of interacting with others in the environment, the mind and brain are co-created (Rossi, 2007).

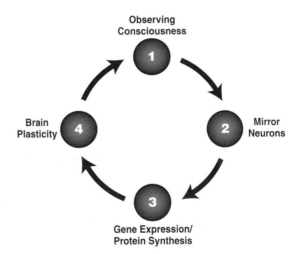

Figure 2.6. Co-creation of mind and brain. Courtesy of Ernest L. Rossi.

The Four-Stage Creative Process

Mobilizing all the findings about the natural mechanisms of this mind–brain cycle, Rossi puts clients through a four-stage creative process using hypnosis to stimulate natural mind–brain–body healing (Figure 2.7). The first stage prepares the client to have a novel experience with the recognition that neurogenesis (the

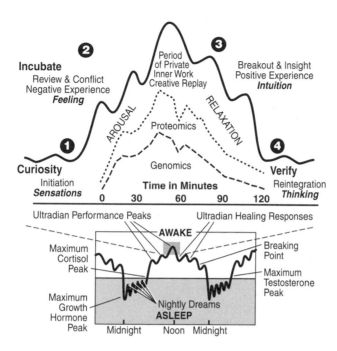

Figure 2.7. The Four Stage Creative Process. Courtesy of Ernest L. Rossi.

growth of new neurons in the brain) will be stimulated. This preparation helps the client to break out of the usual limitations, and feelings of boredom or inadequacy.

The second stage is incubation, a time for turning inward. People suffering from problems like depression are incubating, but they rarely conceive of it as part of a creative process. Rossi shows how this is an opportunity for people to deal with the conflict between their rigid and limited conceptions and feelings and new potentials, to break out of these patterns. Often at this stage people feel threatened by the new potentials, but this is just part of the process. When this stage is successfully navigated, this well-focused arousal brings a crisis, and people break out of their old patterns to stimulate a process of gene expression and neurogenesis (Rossi, 2002).

Stage three, illumination, comes in a flash of insight. What characterizes this stage is the recognition that something new has happened. People often have new ideas, hunches, and glimpses into the possibility of a more positive future.

This is a stage of transition, so people often have a sense of unreality, as if these changes could not possibly be happening to them. But it offers novel experiences that had not been permitted to emerge before, and here is the stimulus for neurogenesis to occur.

Stage four is verification, when people test their new orientation to help integrate it into real life experiencing. It involves an active cultivation of the positive understandings to make lasting changes. "Having survived the breakup of the old world and the precarious task of finding and facilitating the new, we are now truly launched on a path of self-actualization that may be experienced as a spiritual transformation" (Rossi, 2002, p. 282).

Rossi continues to teach around the world and to carry out research that will continue to show how hypnosis can stimulate neurogenesis and neuroplasticity. His research suggests that we have great potential to enhance our brains for happier, more fulfilling lives.

The Social-Psychological Approach to Hypnosis

Most of the researchers we have been discussing thus far have tried to investigate hypnosis by searching for what hypnosis is or what its key elements are. But a different approach has been to ask, what is hypnosis like? From this perspective, hypnosis is more like a sociological interaction, and can be modeled as a sociological role. Theodore Sarbin (1911–2005) was the founder of a sociologically based model that conceived of hypnosis as taking a role. Sarbin believed that a theory of hypnosis must account for four major phenomena: dissociation of behavior, automatic response, magnitude of response from spoken instructions, and individual differences in response. Role-taking theory, enacted at a very high level of organismic involvement, explains these hypnotic phenomena as a social drama. A successful hypnotic subject is highly motivated, has a clear perception of how he or she should act as a hypnotic subject, and wants to be deeply involved in this role. The depth of hypnosis can also be explained, not as a matter of trance or a state of consciousness, but rather as the degree of involvement or absorption in the hypnotic role. Analyzed in its sociological context, hypnosis becomes explainable, measurable, and understandable. Thus, hypnosis is best explained as "contextually supported, goal directed action" (Spanos & Chaves, 1991, p. 44).

This model draws upon a larger sociological perspective that looks for the cause of behaviors, thoughts, and feelings by considering the social context. Most of our life's activities involve acting out a socially defined role such as being a parent, a student, or a friend. Each of these roles has certain norms and standards for how to behave which help determine how we act out these roles. Hypnosis is just another role we can take, with certain rules that help shape our behavior. Subjects learn to act out the role of a hypnotized person.

Another social–psychological perspective comes from Theodore Barber (1927–2005), who defined hypnosis not as a state or a trance, nor as hypersuggestibility. Instead, Barber considered hypnosis to be a special interaction between hypnotist and subject, where expectancy, motivation, and belief explain the phenomenon. Subjects' hopeful and expectant attitude toward hypnosis opens them to being led in a structured experience. Barber called this interactive process perceptual-cognitive restructuring.

These social views are often characterized as non-state theories, which might seem to leave out any account of the nervous system. However, one of the founders of this sociological perspective, George Herbert Mead (1863–1931), explained how the nervous system is always engaged, playing its part in the larger sociological context. "The mechanism of the central nervous system enables us to have now present, in terms of attitudes or implicit responses, the alternative possible overt completions of any given act in which we are engaged" (Mead, 1934, p. 117).

In this sense, then, the meaning of things and our ideas about them, always in response to the social context, involve patterns in our central nervous system that make it possible for us to test out and chose our actions. "The central nervous system, in short, enables the individual to exercise conscious control over his behavior" (Mead, 1934, p. 117). Furthermore, the central nervous system is at the basis of society itself. Mead said, "These higher levels of the brain make possible the variety of activities of the higher vertebrates. Such is the raw stuff, stated in physiological terms, from which the intelligence of the human social being arises" (Mead, 1934, pp. 240–241). Thus, the social-psychological role of hypnosis engages the nervous system in the role-playing process. Expectancy and belief involve neurological processes, which can provide a fuller account for how we enact our roles. In Chapter 4 we will discuss how the brain changes from expectancy and belief, lending even more evidence for how intimately linked our mind and brain really are. We should not forget Mead's claim that these actions we take within the social context are made possible by the responses in the central nervous system, so that we can understand the social role theory as playing an important part in our neuro-hypnosis account.

The role theorists aptly pointed out that everything we do in life can be viewed as role-playing: as parents, sons and daughters, brothers and sisters, workers and students. This is not to say that when we play these roles, we are not these roles, because when we are fully engaged in the role of parenting, for example, we truly *are* a parent. Similarly, when playing the role of a hypnotized person, we *are* in hypnosis, with certain accompanying brain changes that inevitably occur.

Conclusion

Whether hypnosis is a brain state or a role is a secondary level of explanation. At a more primary level of understanding, we can see certain processes occurring in the mind–brain system. Experts in hypnosis through the ages have noticed the importance of the nervous system in hypnosis, but have often tried to look beyond for alternative, more abstract explanations. Hypnosis can be understood at different levels, such as the social context, the language level (suggestion), the body level (a form of sleep), or the quality of mind or consciousness (state). But the thread that weaves all these levels of explanation together is the mind–brain system, with its ever-changing processes that bring a new clarity to the many enigmas surrounding hypnosis.

3

Integrating Hypnosis Theories with the Mind, Brain, and Body Connection

While each method possesses certain unique and distinctive characteristics, they are not mutually exclusive. Within the framework of each distinctive therapy, certain features of other methods are utilized.

—G. Wilson Shaffer & Richard S. Lazarus, *Fundamental Concepts in Clinical Psychology,* p. 376.

THROUGHOUT the history of hypnosis, there have been many different theories of what hypnosis is and how it works. Liébeault, Bernheim, the Nancy School, and some twentieth-century researchers considered hypnosis to be mainly induced by suggestion. Pavlov believed it was a kind of sleep. Janet and Hilgard thought that hypnosis was a form of dissociation in the normal consciousness. Erickson believed hypnosis involved unconscious trance, which could be utilized for therapeutic change. And Barber, Sarbin, and Coe held a social psychology-based view that hypnosis involved taking on the role of a hypnotized subject.

Today, thanks to our new understandings of the mind–brain system, we can have a unifying framework for hypnosis that draws all of these theories together into a meaningful whole.

An Integrative Theory of Hypnosis

Research on hypnosis and the brain is based on various theories. To use findings from these often conflicting theories, you can think of hypnosis as being an integration of all of them. In general, brain–mind processing is an ongoing part of daily experience. In hypnosis, the use of the natural capacities of the mind and brain may be increased or decreased, by either focus or dissociation. And because the brain has the capacity to alter itself at any point in life, via neuroplasticity and neurogenesis, the hypnotic experience can foster real mind–brain change.

This chapter will show how these theories come together as part of the mind–brain system, and can all help us to better understand hypnosis. Each hypnosis theory points to the potential of different techniques and methods to enhance certain types of skills. Try to be open to many possible ways to experience and utilize hypnosis when you are making your real and positive changes. At one time, one of the theories may be more useful; at another time, another theory may offer a more useful map for your particular needs.

The Neuroanatomy of Hypnosis

Neuroscience is the new frontier. Modern imaging technology allows us to enter the previously unexplored territory of the brain in action. Imaging the hypnotized brain offers important means for understanding hypnosis from a new perspective. The historical theories of hypnosis combined with neural imaging research have led to new ideas about the effects of hypnosis. Furthermore, hypnosis research offers some new insights into how the brain works. By providing a means of comparison between how the brain functions in hypnosis and how the brain functions when fully awake, we learn more. "Neuro-imaging techniques offer new opportunities to use hypnosis and posthypnotic suggestion as probes into brain mechanisms and, reciprocally, provide a means of studying hypnosis itself" (Raz & Shapiro, 2002, p. 85). Research using electroencephalography (EEG), positron emission tomography (PET) scans, and functional Magnetic Resonance Imaging (fMRI) provides helpful data to answer age-old questions and to clarify some of the mysteries of hypnosis.

Evidence for Hypnosis as a Unique Brain Occurrence

In general, brain researchers currently believe that hypnosis can be clearly distinguished from the normal waking state through distinct, recognizable changes which consistently take place in the brain during hypnosis. Hypnotized people have increased cognitive abilities such as more focused attention, better ability to be deeply absorbed in something (see Chapter 5), more effective information processing skills, faster reaction times, and better access to their imagination. Improved efficiency in brain activity can be observed in the unique patterns of activation and inhibition of different parts of the brain. The enhanced performance is likely due to more frontal to posterior connections, greater coherence between anterior brain regions, and faster neuro-electrical signaling (Ray, Blai, Aikins, Coyle, & Bjick, 1998).

Further evidence for hypnosis being a unique brain state comes from studies of ERP, or *Event Related Potential*, a measure used with EEG that gives a specific time interval between a stimulus and a response. The idea here is that the ERP might be a way of recognizing similar brain activities. Events that have the same ERP are identical—in this case, identical brain states. The hypnosis subjects in several studies were all found to have a characteristic ERP marker at P300, whereas the suggestion-only subjects did not. What P300 means is that the ERP for the hypnotized subjects registered a positive peak on the EEG machine 300 milliseconds after the stimulus of the hypnotic induction. These findings were repeated in several different laboratories, leading a number of researchers to conclude that induction of hypnosis produces a distinctive response at a characteristic time (Barabasz & Barabasz, 2008).

People have tried to understand what hypnosis is by investigating how it is different from something else, such as everyday consciousness. The difference has been addressed using modern EEG, combined with logic. The gamma frequency range of 40 hertz (Hz) has been considered one possible measure for the neural correlate of consciousness (De Pascalis, 2007). This 40-Hz ERP has been defined as a measure of focused arousal in specific sensory circuitry, and can thus be used as a measure of brain activity when thoughts and perceptions are integrated together, as they are in alert consciousness. So, if the gamma frequency breaks down during hypnosis, we might be able to conclude that hypnosis is different from normal alert consciousness. This is indeed what happens: In a number of varied studies, gamma oscillations of normal consciousness did break down during hypnosis in highly susceptible subjects, but did not break down in controls and less susceptible subjects (De Pascalis, 2007).

As we have noted, Pavlov compared hypnosis to sleep. This issue has also been addressed by EEG studies. Early EEG studies in the 1940s compared hypnosis to normal sleeping. These researchers found that EEG sleep patterns were different from EEG hypnosis patterns (Gordon, 1949). A contemporary researcher who has done extensive studies of the neurophysiology of hypnosis confirms that even though people feel very relaxed in hypnosis, their brains are active (Crawford, 2001). De Pascalis's EEG research on the brain hemispheres showed that when people first go into hypnosis the left hemisphere is more active, but as they go deeper, the left hemisphere is inhibited (1998). So, there is inhibition in hypnosis, similar to Pavlov's definition of hypnosis as partial sleep. But more important, these findings tend to support the idea that hypnosis works with the non-verbal, unconscious processes found in the right hemisphere of the brain.

EEG tells us when the brain is responding, but does not reveal where the brain is responding. Further research using PET scans and fMRI imaging has helped to locate changes and responses in the brain during hypnosis. The brain stem and thalamus alter as the hypnotized person becomes deeply relaxed. The anterior cingulate cortex (ACC) is also changed during hypnosis, similarly to the way this brain area responds when people are less vigilant, meaning less spontaneously attentive to external stimuli.

Hypnosis also brings about an inhibition of the left dorsolateral prefrontal cortex (Gruzelier, 1998). This part of the brain is activated when we engage in higher-level types of mental processing such as planning, organization, and regulation. We do indeed find that during hypnosis, people monitor themselves and their environment less. Deliberate, conscious thinking is deactivated, which probably makes it easier for us to make better use of automatic, unconscious processing. Erickson described this hypnotic effect when he said that hypnosis bypasses the conscious mind and frees the unconscious mind.

Dissociation

The new fMRI- and PET-based research presents evidence for a functional dissociation occurring with hypnosis, just as the visionary hypnosis researchers Hilgard and Janet believed. When people are hypnotized, they experience dissociation between different parts of the brain. Many studies show that hypnosis alters how parts of the brain communicate with each other, causing a disruption of communication between subunits that are responsible for conscious experience (Vaitl et al., 2005). In one study, dissociation was found between the anterior cingulate and prefrontal cortexes. The anterior cingulate cortex is involved in monitoring conflict, and the prefrontal cortex helps with cognitive control processes.

Another study used the Stroop, a test that measured what happened when two types of competing processes were paired together (1935). In the Stroop test, a list of color words (red, blue, green, etc.) were shown to subjects. The no-conflict situation was when the word *red* was colored in red ink, and the conflict situation was when the word *red* was presented in a different color, such as green or yellow. Subjects were asked to state the color of the letters and disregard the meaning of the word. Highly hypnotizable subjects who were simply told to relax performed more poorly than the control group on the conflict situation. The researchers concluded that these results indicated a functional dissociation between conflict monitoring and cognitive control processes (Egner, Jamieson, & Gruzelier, 2005). But subjects who were directed through suggestion to disregard the meaning and just see the color of the ink performed much better than the controls, indicating that hypnosis combined with suggestion made it possible for people to disregard the conflict altogether, and thus produce superior conflict resolution, to bring about a higher level of performance (Raz, Shapiro, Fan, & Posner, 2002). Thus, we see the integration of dissociation and suggestion with the altered state of consciousness that brings about superior abilities. Combining these aspects of hypnosis will help you use your capacities to their fullest.

Pain research has offered further evidence that dissociation occurs during hypnosis. It has long been known that hypnosis focuses attention, and this ability to distract attention away from pain sensations is used as one method in pain reduction. But newer studies add another dimension by considering dissociation. Hypnotic pain control may also come from the dissociation between the brain areas that are responsible for sensing pain and those that are responsible for evaluating pain (Miltner & Weiss, 2007). The disconnection between different sub-regions of the brain once again seems to be encouraging something that is normally difficult to do: expanding human potential in positive ways.

Hypnosis and Suggestion

We might wonder, then, if hypnosis is a different state from waking consciousness; is it simply due to suggestion, as many of the traditional theories claimed, or is it something else? And if it is something else, how is it related to hypnosis? These questions have also been explored experimentally. Based on evidence from EEG, some researchers believe hypnosis produces measurable and distinctive changes that differ from suggestion or imagination, and these differences occur from the very beginning with induction. When subjects enter hypnosis, they show a corresponding change in their brain activity which differs from subjects undergoing suggestion alone (Barabasz, 2000; De Pascalis, Magurano, Bellusci, & Chen, 2001; Oakley, 2008). And yet, we know that suggestion is a vital tool of hypnosis, helping to bring it about during induction, deepen it during trance, and foster the direction that changes take. Used in combination, hypnosis and suggestion bring the most powerful results.

Whether hypnosis is just suggestion or something else has been addressed by many experimental studies. One study combined EEG and PET scans (Rainville et al., 1999), and measured cerebral changes between three different conditions: relaxation, hypnotic relaxation, and hypnosis combined with suggestion for pain relief measured when one hand was immersed in unpleasantly hot water. Activity in the brain was different in all three cases, and hypnosis alone differed from hypnosis combined with suggestion. During the hypnosis alone condition, subjects measured increases in the (visual) occipital region and in delta activity, similar to the kind of brain waves found when sleeping. They also had decreases from the right interior (sensory) parietal lobe and bilaterally in the inferior frontal areas. But when hypnotic suggestions were added to control the pain from the hot water, brain activity was different. These subjects showed increase in the frontal lobe predominantly on the left side. In fact, the suggestion-related increases were in the very regions of hypnosis-alone related decreases. The researchers stated that their results demonstrate distinctive patterns of cerebral activation between hypnosis and hypnotic suggestion.

Some people have wondered whether hypnotic hallucinations are the same as acts of imagination. PET studies offer an answer to this question. The brain activity of highly susceptible subjects was observed during the production of hypnotic hallucinations. PET scans were compared for subjects under hypnosis with subjects having the same experience (i.e. visual or auditory) in the normal waking state. For example, in one experiment, highly susceptible hypnotic subjects listened to an audiotaped voice while a PET scan measured the brain's response. Next, these subjects were asked to imagine the voice while a measurement was taken. Finally, they were told that the tape was playing when it actually was not. The PET scans showed that the auditory area of the brain (the right anterior cingulated cortex) was activated when the subjects heard the tape and when they hallucinated hearing the tape. But interestingly, this area of the brain was not activated when the subjects imagined the voice. Researchers concluded that, "Hypnosis is a psychological state with distinct neural correlates and is not just the result of adopting a role" (Kosslyn, Thompson, Constantini-Ferrando, Alpert, & Spiegel, 2000, p. 1279).

Playing the Role of a Hypnotized Person

The social role theory of hypnosis considers the mind and brain in their social context. You are always existing within a social context. Even when alone in your own home, you are actually still part of a social system: a citizen of your country, a member of a family, and one of the inhabitants of the world.

On a more personal level, whenever you think something, you do so through your body: You are embodied cognition. We know from neuroscience that every thought and feeling is experienced and processed through the nervous system. The mind, brain, and body function together as a unit. This ideomotor effect will be discussed in further detail in Chapter 7, and you will learn more about how your mind, brain, and body function as a unified system.

So, when you participate in hypnosis, you are offering yourself the opportunity for your mind, brain, and body to share in the experiences of a hypnotized person. Everything you do, every role you play, every experience you have, brings about a new brain state, a different set of physiological responses, along with corresponding thoughts and feelings. We have the power to influence what we think and feel by what we do. Your engagement with your world of interaction can become a resource for positive change. And by taking on the role of a hypnotized person, you can foster healthy new responses that will be helpful to you.

Contemporary Research on Hypnosis Effectiveness

The power of hypnosis has been used therapeutically to help people with many kinds of problems. Modern researchers have provided a large body of research showing widely varied areas where hypnosis is an effective form of treatment. All of the applications in this book are backed by research that supports the use of hypnosis either as a primary or adjunctive treatment for the problem or disorder in question. We will review some findings to show you that these methods have helped others, and thus may be helpful to you too.

A number of researchers have been exploring whether hypnosis can be used along with other forms of treatment. In a large meta-analysis which looked at a number of studies, Kirsch, Montgomery, and Sapirstein found that hypnosis increases effectiveness when combined with one of the most commonly used modern treatments, cognitive-behavioral therapy (1995). So, you can draw from cognitive-behavioral therapy for supplementary ways of working with your thoughts, feelings, and behaviors.

Researchers have also been testing very specific applications of hypnosis to control pain in a number of different fields, including medicine, dentistry, psychology, and even athletics. Miller and Bowers found that highly hypnotizable subjects had significant reduction of pain regardless of whether they also used cognitive strategies (1986). These findings suggest that hypnosis alone might be effective for pain control.

Many studies have investigated the use of hypnotherapy for chronic tension-headache pain, and have found that there was a significant reduction in the number of headaches and in their intensity when treated with hypnotherapy (Melis, Rooimans, Spierings, & Hoogduin, 1991). The treatment of the pain of childbirth with hypnotherapy has also been successful. Harmon, Hynan, and Tyre found that hypnosis helped reduce the pain of childbirth and control depression after birth (1990). Hypnosis can even alleviate the severe chronic pain associated with cancer. Cancer patients have been able to tolerate the discomfort of cancer with lower doses of pain medication and less anxiety and suffering after undergoing hypnosis (Chaves, 1993).

Hypnosis has been tested as a treatment for a number of psychological issues including anxiety (Kirsch et al., 1995) and depression (Yapko, 1995, 2001, 2006), with positive results.

We have included here a few samples of the types of studies being performed to show you that hypnosis is being tested in many areas and results are showing that it is as effective, if not more effective, than other modes of treatment. You can be confident that hypnosis stands along with many other modern approaches as a viable and effective form of treatment.

Conclusion

Hypnosis activates an array of neurological processes. During trance, the usual conscious processing in the prefrontal cortex is deactivated and separated from other processing. This releases the unconscious processes from conscious direction and allows for a more free flow in creative, non-conscious pathways. In hypnosis, attention is focused and absorbed, and often directed inwardly, without the usual monitoring and vigilance that we usually turn to the outside world when we are paying conscious attention to our surroundings. When combined with suggestion, attention can be directed in a particular direction, bypassing conscious limits, defenses, and problems, thus providing an opportunity for something new to take place. By playing the role of the hypnotized person, your mind, brain, and body unite in the act. With all these tools just waiting to be put to use, fascinating experiences await you.

PART II

Tools of Self-Hypnosis

4

How the Brain Changes the Mind and the

Mind Changes the Brain

The detailed structure and function of the brain can be modified by experiences
. . . Enriched experience leads to greater branching of axons and dendrites . . .
Specialized experiences can alter brain development . . . Extensive practice of
a skill expands the brain's representation of sensory and motor information relevant to that skill.

—James Kalat, *Biological Psychology,* p. 132

WE have described some of the ways that hypnosis changes the brain and mind.
But you might wonder, how can this help me? How would these mind–brain
effects fix my problem? The answer is found in the broader mind–brain system.
Neuroscientists now believe that the brain affects the way we think and feel.
Change can be elicited in both directions: The brain changes the mind and the
mind changes the brain. By taking advantage of the flow within and across this
mind–brain system, you can optimize your potential to bring about the kinds of
changes you are hoping to make.

Brain and Mind: The Interrelationship

You know that the mind and brain are related somehow. And with all the new findings about the brain, it makes sense to recognize that the mind and brain work together in a well-coordinated system. But how does this happen? Does the brain determine how you think and feel? Or does the mind influence how the brain functions? Or is the mind somehow separate from the brain, taking a nonmaterial form?

René Descartes (1596–1650) began the discussion by separating mind and body. When he wrote, "But what then am I? A thing that thinks." (Descartes, 1641/1968, p. 106), he set the mind apart from the body. Neuroscientific findings about the brain have convinced many philosophers that they are not separate, but instead that the material or physical brain forms the foundation for the mind. Certain brain structures and pathways influence how we think and feel, such as when we feel afraid and the fear pathway is stimulated. But new evidence also shows that the mind has just as strong an influence on the structure of the brain. Scientists call this *neuroplasticity* and *neurogenesis*. Findings from hypnosis research illustrate that a hallucination alters the brain just like a real experience, which suggests how hypnosis can be used as a tool to help foster neuroplasticity and neurogenesis and make real changes in the brain–mind system (Rossi, 2007).

There are important issues to ponder about the relationship between mind and brain. Some say that the physical reality of the world is the only true or actual reality. All that can be known is substance, and that substance is physical or material. The rest is speculation. We can understand the nature of something by knowing all about its physical properties and behaviors, and this is the complete reality of what things are. Thus, to know the mind, we only have to know the material brain. Some take the next logical step: If the brain and mind are inseparable, with identical qualities, they must be the same thing. The mind literally *is* the brain. This view is known as *identity theory*. A more extreme view is the eliminativist position, which holds that there is no mind, only the brain. A more moderate position is functionalism, which argues that the mind is a function of the brain.

Other positions favor the presence of a mind distinct from a brain, or even the prevalence of the mind over the brain. A nonmaterial or nonphysical perspective is found in Buddhism, which holds that the world is continually changing, and so there is no real, lasting physical or material substance: Everything is mind. Thus, to truly know anything, we should begin from the recognition of the impermanence of the world, and even of ourselves. By using methods such as meditation and trance, Buddhism suggests, we can discover our true nature.

You will have many opinions about these issues. In this book, we assume that the influence is mutual, and so all of these positions have something to contribute to our understanding of the closely related activity of the mind and brain together, functioning as a unified system.

How the Brain Influences the Mind: Begin with Neurons

The brain is made up of neurons. Neurons are the functional units found in the brain and throughout the nervous system. There are more than 180 billion neurons in the nervous system with at least 80 billion involved in cognitive processes. Each neuron connects with hundreds of other neurons, and so we have vast potentials for an enormous amount of interactions occurring simultaneously.

Neurons have two main functions: They process certain chemicals within themselves, and also communicate with other neurons. They have four distinctive parts that make these functions possible: dendrites, cell bodies, axons, and synapses (Figure 4.1). The word *dendrite* comes from the Greek word *dendron*, meaning "tree." Dendrites serve as input and output zones, taking in information from other neurons. They provide a source of experience-dependent neuroplasticity, with changes in the brain sometimes happening as quickly as in a moment, or evolving over a lifetime.

The *cell body* is where signals from the dendrites are combined, altered, packaged, and then sent out to the axon for communication to other neurons. Here is also where genes are processed and neurogenesis is initiated and sent out through the axons.

The *axons* are long strands that extend out from the other end of the cell body. They act as the conduction zone, transmitting through a single wire carrying an

Figure 4.1. The Neuron.

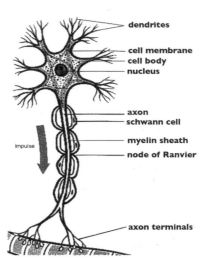

electrical signal from one neuron to the next. Finally, we have the output zone at the ends of the axons, the axon terminals.

At the terminals are the *synapses*, where important communication between and across cells occurs. The Greek word *synapse* means clasp together, which is, in a sense, what the synapses do. This communication process of inputs, integration, and outputs across the synapse involves a kind of computational procedure, such that when the connections between two neurons fire together often, they tend to become wired together. This firing and wiring process is ongoing, and helps to account for how neuroplasticity takes place.

Neurotransmitters at the Synapse

The terminal end of an axon makes a connection with a dendrite from another neuron by means of the synapse. The dendrites generally receive synaptic inputs and axons generally send synaptic outputs. When the synaptic gap between two neurons is close enough, the electrical signal can simply leap across and keep going. But more often, the gap is too large for this to happen. With the larger gaps, the electrical signal is converted into a chemical, known as a neurotransmitter, and the chemicals swim across the gap and then are converted back into an electrical impulse (Figure 4.2).

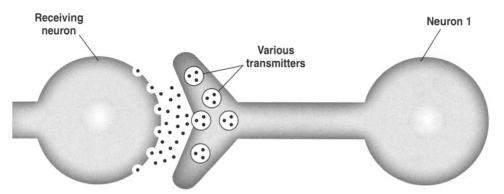

Figure 4.2. Neurotransmission.

We have a number of neurotransmitters that are manufactured inside the cell bodies of the neurons. They communicate different things to the body, such as to be alert, be calm, or not feel pain. When you take a medication, you might think that the drug is responsible for making you feel better. But in reality, the drug is stimulating the body to produce more of certain neurotransmitters or to block the action of other neurotransmitters. The neurotransmitter system usually has everything it needs already built in. But when the neurotransmitters are out of balance, drug therapies and psychological treatments (such as self-hypnosis and psychotherapy) can stimulate or inhibit processes to help find a better balance.

Types of Neurotransmitters

Neurotransmitters move through the autonomic nervous system and through many areas of the brain. Neurotransmitters communicate many different things. Glutamate is an excitatory neurotransmitter that is found throughout the nervous system. GABA (gamma aminobutyric acid) is inhibitory and, like glutamate, is also found everywhere in the nervous system. Certain neurotransmitters are more specific in what they communicate. For example, dopamine is related to a sense of pleasure and reward. Serotonin is involved in emotionality and sleep patterns, norepinephrine influences alertness, and endorphins are a group of neurotransmitters that alleviate pain.

The Central Nervous System and Peripheral Nervous System

All the neurons combined make up the nervous system, consisting of the central nervous system (brain and spinal cord) and the peripheral nervous system (autonomic nervous system, cranial nerves, and spinal nerves) (Figure 4.3). The peripheral nervous system extends through the whole body and communicates information to and from the central nervous system. The autonomic nervous system interacts closely with the central nervous system, often automatically and unconsciously. Hypnosis can tap into these systems by activating these involuntary, unconscious processes. You will learn how to work with the autonomic nervous system when you bring about changes using trance and suggestion.

The neurons of the autonomic nervous system include two key systems: the sympathetic nervous system and the parasympathetic nervous system. You can think of the sympathetic nervous system as an activation system. It prepares the body for vigorous action. The parasympathetic nervous system acts as an opposite to the sympathetic nervous system's activations. So, when the sympathetic activation constricts blood vessels or inhibits digestion during exercise, the parasympathetic activation relaxes vessel walls and stimulates digestion when the

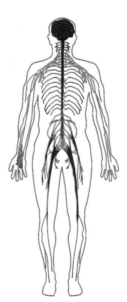

Figure 4.3. The Nervous System.

workout is over. We might understand the sympathetic and parasympathetic systems as interacting in a unity of opposites. Different experiences may excite or inhibit one system or the other, partly because these two systems use different neurotransmitters. Both systems work together to help foster appropriate responses. These systems of activation and deactivation are involved in emotions such as fear and anger, as well as in our responses to stress and feelings of enjoyment. Together, these two systems maintain the control that keeps the mind, brain, and body in balance.

Brain Structures and Functions

The brain orchestrates the nervous system. It is often described in terms of its structures and functions. By understanding both, we can gain a better understanding of the brain's diverse achievements. Unconscious processing tends to travel a short, subcortical path through the lower brain areas, known as bottom-up, without engaging the higher-level-processing cortex. When you are aware of your emotions, sensations, and cognitions, the information has usually traveled the long path for processing, sometimes called top-down, involving both the lower areas and relevant higher parts of the cortex. With hypnosis, you will learn to work with both types of processing, conscious and unconscious, to facilitate therapeutic change.

Lower Brain Areas: Brain Stem and Cerebellum

At the base of the brain is the *brain stem*, the transitional area between the spinal cord and the brain. This area plays an important role in regulating vital body functions such as breathing, heart rate and other automatic functions. These lower brain areas coordinate their action with many other regions of the brain (Figure 4.4).

The *cerebellum* (Latin for *little brain*), located at the back of the neck, contains more neurons than all the other parts of the brain combined, and yet only composes 10% of the brain's weight. It has two hemispheres, each of which contains

Figure 4.4. Lower Brain Areas:
Cerebellum and Brain Stem.

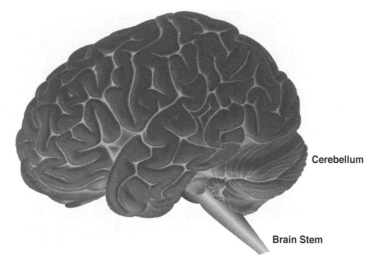

Cerebellum

Brain Stem

functional sections known as lobes, with connections between them. The cerebellum interacts closely with other parts of the brain, and serves a variety of functions, including the regulation of higher cerebral processes in motor planning, cognition, involuntary functions, and problem solving. It also regulates posture and the command of movement. We have all experienced the effort required to learn something new, such as a sport, dance routine, or instrument, and this is when the cerebellum is active. Once movement control is learned, the cerebellum becomes less active and other parts of the brain get involved.

Interior Brain Areas: Basal Ganglia and Limbic System

The region that spans the area from the brain stem to below the cortex in the interior of the brain is the *limbic system*, which regulates emotions, and the *basal ganglia*, which oversee voluntary movement and coordination (Figure 4.5). The basal ganglia form a C-shape of four interconnected structures: the *substantia nigra*, the *caudate nucleus*, the *putamen*, and the *globus pallidus*. These structures are also involved when we plan movement, do movements in sequence, and maintain learning. This area is also part of predictive control, attention, and working memory.

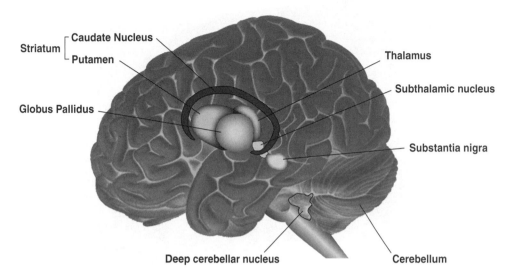

Figure 4.5. Basal Ganglia.

The limbic system has been paid much attention in the context of health and healing, since it is intimately involved in regulating emotion, fear conditioning, and fight-or-flight and stress responses, as well as learning and memory (Figure 4.6). Many structures that play a central role in the limbic system include the amygdala, hippocampus, cingulate gyrus, fornix, hypothalamus, and thalamus. Several other structures are considered important for emotion, and thus are included as part of the limbic system including the olfactory cortex (involved in the sense of smell), the pituitary gland (which regulates hormones), the mammilary body (which relays information from the amygdala and thalamus), the orbitofrontal cortex (part of the prefrontal cortex) and the nucleus accumbens (which plays a role in functions including reward, laughter, pleasure, addiction, and the placebo effect). All of these structures interconnect and interact together, although some contribute more to one function than to another. With so many varied brain structures all closely interacting functionally with each other as well as with higher cortical functions, it makes sense that emotions play such an important role in every aspect of living.

Figure 4.6. The Limbic System.

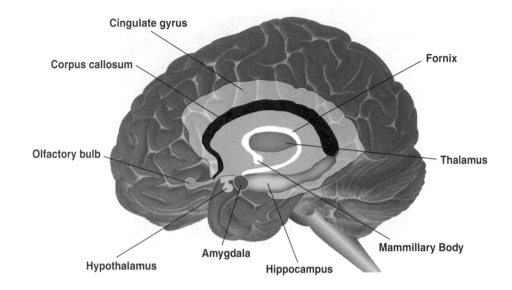

Higher Brain Areas: The Cerebral Cortex

The *cerebral cortex* is the outer layer of the hemispheres with many convolutions, or *gyri*, and folds, or *sulci* (Figure 4.7). Folding increases the surface area of the cortex, so that more than two-thirds of the surface is hidden from view. The cortex is sometimes referred to as the higher part of the brain. Having so much surface area allows for all the mental processing we are engaged in all the time. Each hemisphere is divided into lobes that are connected to each other through the corpus collosum, fibers at the center of the brain that help the two hemispheres to communicate with one another. There are four lobes on each hemisphere: frontal, parietal, temporal, and occipital. The lobes monitor different functions, although they are all interrelated, interacting together.

Frontal Lobes

The *frontal lobe* accounts for nearly one-third of the cerebral cortex. Located at the front of the frontal lobe, behind the forehead, is the prefrontal cortex. The prefrontal cortex areas follow a general circuitry connecting them to lower brain regions. The fact that the prefrontal areas have extensive links throughout the brain shows how interrelated brain functions really are. Areas of the prefrontal cortex are involved in executive functions, which include planning, higher-level decision-making, sequencing, and goal-directed behavior. Independent thinking is processed in this area as well. Another part of the prefrontal cortex processes personality characteristics such as empathy, socially appropriate behavior, and emotional control.

The primary motor area, located in the back (posterior) area of the frontal lobes, is important for control of movement. This area has a map of the body on it. Larger portions of the cortical map are devoted to areas that are used more, such as the hands and face. The non-primary motor cortex, located in front of the primary motor cortex, includes a pre-motor area and a supplementary motor area. These areas are involved with movement and coordination in general, such as stance, gait, and initiation of voluntary movement sequences. Mirror neurons are located in the motor area of the frontal lobes. These neurons are involved in understanding and empathizing with the intentions and actions of others and help with our comprehension of social cues.

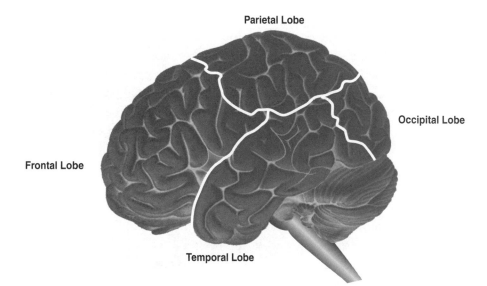

Parietal Lobe

Occipital Lobe

Frontal Lobe

Temporal Lobe

Figure 4.7. The Lobes of the Cerebral Cortex.

One other important area located in the frontal lobes is the cingulate gyrus, also called the cingulate cortex. This area is involved in motivated behavior, spontaneity, and creativity. Complex behavior, conflict monitoring, and attention are also processed in the cingulate gyrus. This area is primary during the emotional reaction to pain and in the regulation of aggressive behavior. It has also been found to play an important role in maternal attachment, as evident in behaviors such as nursing and nest-building in animals (Vogt, Finch, & Olson, 1992).

The Parietal Lobes

Behind the frontal lobe and close to the cingulate gyrus are the parietal lobes. These lobes are involved in sensation and perception of touch, pressure, temperature, and pain. Sensory information from the body is correlated there during perception or cognition of the sensation. The parietal lobes are used when locating objects in space and mapping the relationship of the body to the world. The back (anterior) portion of the parietal lobes are the sensory strip. The body is mapped on the sensory strip for sensations, similar to how the primary motor cortex is where movement is mapped for the body.

The Temporal Lobes

The temporal lobes are located near the temples. They are primarily involved with auditory information, and are where the primary auditory cortex is located. The left hemisphere side is where we find Wernicke's area, a region that plays a larger role in understanding spoken language. The aspects of visual processing that are located in the temporal lobes involve perception of movements and face recognition. Although some visual processing occurs near the bottom of the temporal lobes, the primary visual areas are located in the occipital lobes.

The Occipital Lobes

The occipital lobes are located in the posterior region of the brain. Axons gathered from visual input from the eyes pass through the thalamus and are directed to the primary visual cortex, located in the occipital lobes. The visual cortex is also sometimes called the striate cortex because of its striped appearance. Human beings rely on their vision quite heavily, and this is revealed in the complexity of this region of the brain. There are more than 32 zones for visual processing, involving such different aspects of vision such as recognition of color, texture, and movement. All 32 zones are located in the occipital lobes.

How The Brain Areas Work Together

So how do all of these brain areas function so that we experience other people, our world, and ourselves as we do? Our senses provide a window to the world. First the sensory receptors (eyes, fingertips, nose, tongue, ears) detect certain textures, temperatures, sounds, tastes, and visual stimuli. For example, as you touch the pages of this book, the receptor cells in your fingertips convert the energy into a change in the electrical potential across its membrane. The sensory signal travels from your fingertips through the touch sensory pathway to the highest level of the brain in the parietal lobe. The intensity and location of the stimulus influence the signal that is sent. Each sensory system has its own pathway, so as you look at the book, the signal goes to your occipital lobes. Within the brain, we find receptor fields of cortical maps for the particular sensory modality. Within the cortical maps we see the process of neuroplasticity, as the ones we use more often tend to grow larger. Attention, regulated in the frontal lobes, is what helps us to notice important stimuli and ignore others, such as noticing what you are reading while you ignore noise from the street outside.

Pathways

The central nervous system is a complex collection of structures and functions that are organized in pathways. Our thoughts, feelings, and behaviors are intimately involved in the flow of these pathways, which are dynamic systems of interaction between brain structures, and the flow of energy and neurotransmitters.

A number of pathways of signals sent through the nervous system regulate our mind–brain–body balance. One pathway processes sensory input and has a special pathway to process painful stimuli. A reward pathway regulates positive emotions and drives toward fulfillment, satisfaction, and enjoyment. Another dynamic regulatory system, the fear pathway (which becomes a stress pathway when overactivated), provides the capacity to respond to and cope with a threat by instigating a fight, flight, or freeze response if necessary, and then return to homeostatic balance. We also have regulatory systems of appetite and the sleep–wake cycle. When any of these systems are out of balance, disorders and problems tend to develop. Since all of these systems are intimately connected in their functioning, they can alter how we think and feel and are significant in psychotherapy. This book will help you to take these mechanisms into account to help make lasting changes, adding a neurobiological dimension that will strengthen the effects of hypnosis.

How the Mind Influences the Brain

Neuroscientific research has shown how the activation of certain brain pathways influences how we think and feel. But a growing body of research shows that the mind influences the brain as well.

The Power of Expectancy

Expectancy has been an important concept in psychology for many years; it states that what we think, believe, and expect has a profound influence on the brain and the body. Gustav Theodor Fechner (1801–1887) was a versatile individual: a humanist, poet, physicist, and philosopher who was ahead of his time. He wanted to show that the unity of mind and body is so clear that it can be characterized in a mathematical equation. He believed that the relative increases of bodily energy correspond in a fixed ratio to the measure of the increase of a corresponding mental intensity. He called his method *psychophysics*. He believed that psychophysics was the exact science of the fundamental relations of dependency between the mind and body. Today we extend that relationship to include the brain.

So, what influences this relationship between mind and brain? One factor is the individual differences between people. Another important determinant is the set or expectation of the observer. Expectant attitudes predispose an observer to react slower or faster, depending on how the expectancies are sequenced. Fechner demonstrated that muscles can be given a set which then persists in judging how heavy something is. He showed that once an expectation that a weight of a certain size looks a certain way is given to the muscles, another weight, identical in appearance, would usually be estimated to weigh just as much, even if in actuality it is heavier or lighter.

The Placebo Effect

More recently, placebo research has shown how a mental expectation is communicated directly to the body. Placebos are inert substances containing no active ingredients of any kind. In early studies, a control group was given placebos. The members of the control group believed that the placebo contained medicine to treat their condition. These subjects often improved as much as the group that received real medicine. What was learned from these studies is that positive expectations can influence a physiological condition, and contribute to increased health.

Researchers developed these concepts further, conducting experiments utilizing pure placebo response. In one experiment, subjects were told that they would be given a placebo, and it was explained to them exactly what a placebo is. However, they were also told that many people had been helped by placebos, and the researchers believed the placebo would help them too (Park & Covi, 1965). Most participating subjects gained dramatic relief from their problems. Some even requested refills! This unexpected finding was disregarded at first, but was later confirmed by other research (Frank & Frank, 1991).

The placebo effect is now well accepted. Comparison with placebo is an indispensible part of clinical-trial testing for modern medicines. In addition, we now know that even though the placebo is initiated by a mental expectancy, the effect is not just "all in the mind." Placebos have been shown to stimulate the same brain regions that opioid neurotransmitters do. Both placebos and opiate drugs deactivate the pain regions in the cingulate gyrus, an area that monitors the intensity of pain that we feel. This tells us two important things. First, there is a close interaction between mind and brain and body that is always going on. Second, expectations can be powerful forces for enhancing health. Suggestion is a method that can help to enlist expectations, and you will work with these forces in Chapter 7.

Directing Mental Powers through Attention and Absorption

Attention and absorption are another set of tools to use; they are described in more detail in Chapter 6. Directing attention to physiological responses can be very useful at times. For example, people can deliberately cultivate relaxation to reduce their stress response, perhaps helping to heal an ulcer condition. Calm relaxation has been used to help lower blood pressure. Controlled research using hypnosis, biofeedback, relaxation training, hypnosis, and meditation has indicated that there is good reason to accept useful links between mind, brain, and body. Correct technique can make higher potentials of functioning available (Simpkins & Simpkins, 2004, 2009, 2010). We will offer many ways to work with the suggestive quality of expectancy to foster the effects you are hoping to make.

Social Influence on Mind–Brain and Body

Feelings of hope and positive expectancy toward the future can have a dramatic influence on the mind and brain. Walter Cannon illustrated the effects of negative attitudes in the extreme case of what he termed voodoo death (1942). He described documented instances where a strong emotional shock brought on by fear or threat could lead to death. As one example, residents of islands such as Haiti, Jamaica, and the Bahamas, where voodoo is practiced, may have heard or seen instances of voodoo curses, with dire consequences following for the recipient. A shared world of beliefs and attitudes about the power of voodoo contributes to its devastating effects. Locals know curse symbols. When a curse is cast, there is fertile ground for the mechanism of self-suggestion to bring about the feared event. But voodoo death is not limited to any one culture. The effect of death from fearful expectations is also found in prison camps and other hopeless situations. This intense reaction shows the important role the mind plays in shaping physical responses.

How can thoughts and experiences that seem to be in the mind be brought to the level of the body? How can the mind–body gap be bridged, when negative expectancy interferes? Hypnosis works with both mind and body to help bridge the gap. Mind, brain, and body should not be separated because they interrelate in a pattern or unity, a gestalt. Mind is embodied in each individual's unique organism, in relation to his or her environment. The point of contact and natural identification is the boundary where interaction takes place. When you have conflict and consequent tension, you tend to identify with one part of your conflict and alienate yourself from the other. Which part you identify with depends on your needs, your sense of identity, and the demands of the situation. For example, if you are sitting in class, you probably will identify more with your mind, given your focus on ideas and concepts. Bodily concerns are in the background, unless an urgent need or interest begins to draw your attention. If a throbbing headache comes on, it draws your attention away from your mental activities. Suddenly body awareness becomes central, until you manage to either take care of what is bringing on the pain or else stoically accept it and refocus your attention on the teacher. Awareness of body sensations is a built-in part of the signaling system, intended to remind you to attend to what you need. This can start the motor for action, so to speak, encouraging you to do something about your needs. By getting in touch both consciously and unconsciously in hypnosis, you begin to find a healthy, motivated, creative adjustment.

Influence from the Unconscious

Many of the effects of mind on brain are elicited unconsciously; therefore, facilitating your unconscious is a valuable tool for hypnosis. There are many dimensions to unconscious response and these influences will be described in depth in Chapter 5 and throughout this book.

Neuroplasticity and Neurogenesis

Neuroplasticity, as we have discussed, is the ability of the brain and nervous system to reorganize its neural pathways, connections, and functions. Specifically, neuroplasticity involves a change in the connections between synapses. Neurons have the ability to modulate the strength and structure of their synaptic connections as a result of certain types of experience. Thus, plasticity happens at the neuronal level between neurons at their synapses.

It has long been known that the brain changes dramatically during certain critical periods of development, but brain changes can happen at any age. Neuroplasticity can occur from exciting and novel experiences. It can also be initiated after brain damage or even from physical dysfunction. For example, those who are deaf from birth become more sensitive in their other senses, because the parts of the brain typically used for hearing become adapted, somewhat, for other senses. We also find neuroplasticity in the hippocampus, the area involved in learning and memory. New measurable growth takes place in the hippocampus as a result of what we experience and do. For example, taxicab drivers, who must navigate their way through unfamiliar streets on a daily basis, show extra growth in their hippocampus, lending support to the idea that you can grow new connections as a result of what you do.

The brain has neurological stem cells that undergo neurogenesis, or the creation of new neurons. Although the majority of neurogenesis takes place during prenatal and early childhood development, it continues to occur to some extent throughout the life span. You can enhance or impede neurogenesis at any point by what you do and how you do it.

Conclusion

The mind, brain, and body interact together. You can intervene in many ways and at many levels, through the mind, the brain, or the body. Using hypnosis, you will learn how to work with all these natural capacities at different levels, to make the best use of the system you already have. In time, you may be able to turn the tide in better directions, fostering more of the best functioning for you.

5

Becoming Open and Absorbed

for Deeper Hypnosis

Swept in Fate's currents, swirling around
We seek an island of peaceful safe ground.
If we open our hearts we endure and transcend
Then Fate becomes destiny, to love without end.

—C. Alexander Simpkins

Absorption

WHAT is absorption? Absorption is the ability to fully engage mental and emotional processes in something to which you are paying attention. You have probably experienced moments of absorption, when you are so involved in something that time slips away and you forget everything else. Sharing an intensely happy experience with someone you care for deeply, reading a gripping book, or watching an unusually spectacular sunset can be an absorbing experience. What you may not have known is that your ability to be absorbed is a tool you can use for a fuller hypnotic experience.

Absorption has been known to be associated with hypnotic susceptibility since the 1970s, and so it is a well-accepted tool for developing a deep hypnotic experience (Tellegen & Atkinson, 1974). Absorption occurs spontaneously when you are interested in something, but it is also a skill that can be taught and learned. Since we all have the capacity to be absorbed in something, everyone can build upon this natural capacity and thereby improve their work with self-hypnosis. This chapter will help you extend and expand this important hypnotic tool.

The "object" of attention can take many forms. It might be interpersonal, such as a significant other, a loved one, or a really good friend. It can also be something found in your environment such as a piece of art, a game, or a beautiful flower. Another source for objects of absorption are sensations within you, such as a deep feeling of inner calm brought on by resting in a comfortable bed, or a peaceful feeling of warmth that occurs while sitting in front of a campfire. These inner kinds of "objects" are frequently used in hypnosis.

Recent findings show that absorption plays an important role in the psychobiology of self-regulation. This means that people who are able to become absorbed also tend to be capable of handling their emotional reactions well. Studies have discovered a correlation between high absorption and cardiovascular responsiveness (Vaitl et al., 2005), which allows for better handling of stress. Thus, absorption is an important skill with many benefits for healthy living.

Components of Absorption

Absorption includes two key components: openness and focused attention. These might seem to be opposites, but actually they are linked and enhance each other.

You will learn in this chapter how to approach hypnosis with openness and direct your attention, keeping it focused. Openness has been defined as a sincere involvement in experience, and alters how you feel and think across a variety of situations.

Attention is the means for engaging your involvement and openness to situations in order to foster absorption. Attention is an important tool of hypnosis that can be developed with training. As Braid proposed, hypnosis is directed attention. You can train your openness and attention with exercises. Both skills can be enhanced if you decide to try. This chapter will help you foster these skills.

How the Brain Changes When You Are Absorbed

During hypnosis you are absorbed in the experience. Certain brain areas are more active, while others are less so. Absorption and attention have been measured using modern technologies, to give us a glimpse of how the brain is altered when we use these important tools.

Neurobiology of Absorption

Typical brain activations and inhibitions in the cortex have been correlated with high and low absorption, as measured by EEG. People who scored high on tests that measured their level of absorption underwent changes in the occipital region. These people were also able to use their attention more flexibly (Davidson, Goleman, & Schwartz, 1976)—a useful trait to foster for hypnosis. Modern researchers have found that hypnosis involves alterations in the brain that are associated with absorption and focus of attention.

Neurobiology of Attention

Attention has been modeled as taking place through several distinct systems in the brain. One component is in the front part of the frontal lobe, and involves the anterior cingulate gyrus. This part of the brain helps to direct attention like a spotlight, narrowing our focus on the object of our attention. A second component of focused attention is located in the right part of the frontal lobe and alerts us to respond to stimuli quickly. The posterior system is involved in orienting, and is found in the back part of the parietal lobe and anterior temporal lobe, with strong connections to the thalamus and an area involved in visual processing called the superior colliculus. All of these parts of the brain coordinate together to make up our attentional system.

Attention has three primary functions: orienting, vigilance, and action (Posner & Peterson, 1990) and we find that the brain areas that are activated in the attentional system help us with the functions of attention through the brain's visual, auditory, and movement pathways.

Hypnosis is a special kind of attention. On the one hand it is similar to how we focus our attention in everyday life, by activating the anterior attentional system, especially the anterior part of the cingulate cortex that is involved in narrowing of attention. We feel very relaxed when under hypnosis, which is different from when we are vigilantly paying attention, for example, when driving a car. Instead of activating the posterior attentional system, which moderates vigilance, this area is deactivated during hypnosis (Spiegel, 2008). These brain changes help to explain why, during hypnosis, you will feel relaxed, yet still responsive. It also helps to explain the tendency during hypnosis toward inner focus rather than outer scanning of the environment.

Fostering Openness

Openness can be developed in many ways. You will find some ways discussed here and others throughout the book. As you become familiar with your own responsiveness, feel free to make your own creative adaptations, to help you approach self-hypnosis in your own way and in your own time.

Begin with Sincerity

Hold faithfulness and sincerity as first principles.   —Confucius

The first step in developing absorption is to sincerely want to do so. Confucius wrote about the importance of sincerity in helping to bring about wisdom. In fact, he believed that sincerity comes first. He encouraged curiosity and the willingness to search deeper. His teaching method instilled the motivation to learn how to be curious and open for learning. As he wrote, "When I have presented one corner of a subject to anyone, and he cannot from it learn the other three, I do not repeat my lesson" (Analects 7-7, in Legge, 1971, p. 61). This quality of searching deeper is an excellent skill to foster, and the following exercise can help you do so.

Exercise in Searching for the Other Three Corners

As you read the each exercise in this book, can you be curious about the effect it will have on you? Can you wonder how it will put together new patterns in your brain–mind system? Is there a willingness in your body to begin to relax? And if so, can you be curious what it would be like for you to have this experience of relaxation, and what new potentials of underdeveloped, natural resources can open up? Do this as you approach any of the exercises and trance experiences and your effects will be stronger and more beneficial.

Develop a Non-Judgmental Attitude

Being sincerely curious is the first step toward developing openness. But what if you find that you stop yourself from doing so? Often people feel like they can't be open. They have their reasons: Perhaps such openness seems naive or even stupid. These judgmental tendencies are a misuse of higher-level processing ability. The human cortex has the most highly evolved frontal lobe, and here we find many fine-tuned cognitive skills that have helped to produce many great human achievements.

The ability to make judgments, to decide what is good or bad, better or worse, comes in handy every day. You will make a better decision if you carefully judge the merits of the situation at hand to determine what best suits your needs. However, when applying judgment to yourself for the purposes of being open to hypnosis, judgment may get in your way.

One way that people may prevent themselves from being open to an experience is by passing a quick judgment, almost without thought. Another is to come to a new experience with a preconceived judgment that it is bad, stupid, or not for you. Be willing to question negative preconceived attitudes about hypnosis in order to be open to the experience.

If you can keep an open attitude as you make discoveries about yourself, you will be more able to permit the experience to happen. Maintaining an open attitude will also allow you to make constructive use of what you learn from those new experiences and integrate the findings into your life. The story that follows shows the value of developing a nonjudgmental attitude that is balanced and thereby open to all possibilities.

Who Can Say If It's Good or It's Bad

Once an unhappy farmer went to the village Master to complain about his plight. He told the Master that his farm was failing, and he believed everything about his situation was terrible. The Master replied mysteriously, "Who can say if it's good or it's bad?"

The farmer returned to his farm somewhat puzzled. That night a wild stallion appeared on his farm. The farmer captured the stallion and harnessed it for work. He invested all his money in seeds, expecting that at last he would make great profits. Then he returned to the Master. He told the Master how overjoyed he was that the stallion had come. Now he could plow twice as many fields. He expected the Master to agree. But instead, the Master again responded, "Who can say if it's good or it's bad?"

The farmer returned to his farm even more puzzled than last time. He planted the seeds and worked very hard during the following weeks. The plants grew well. He looked forward to harvesting the crops soon. Then, one night, the stallion disappeared. The farmer was crestfallen. He had spent his last dollar on the seeds. All the fruits and vegetables would rot without the horse to help him harvest. He returned to the Master lamenting the loss of the stallion.

The Master replied, "Who can say if it's good or it's bad?" The farmer returned to his farm feeling dejected. But the next morning, to his great surprise and joy, the stallion returned and brought with him a mare. Now the farmer was elated! Not only would he have plenty of labor assistance from both horses, he would also be assured of his future prosperity, because they would probably mate and produce more horses. He rushed to the Master to tell him the wonderful news and receive the Master's blessing.

But instead, the Master said, "Who can say if it's good or it's bad?" The next day, the farmer's eldest and strongest son was riding the stallion, harvesting the crop. Suddenly the stallion reared and threw the son off, injuring him. Now the farmer was very upset. His son, his best worker, would have to rest in bed for months. He told the Master that his grief was boundless.

Again, the Master replied, "Who can say if it's good or it's bad?" As it turned out, the army came around to all the farms, recruiting the first-born son of every family to battle at the front lines of the war. Because the farmer's son was injured, he did not have to go. And who can say if this was good or bad? It is possible that the son might have become a war hero and a stronger person from the experience, or perhaps he would have been killed.

Judgments often put people on a roller coaster of emotion. Interpretation given to circumstances can be viewed from many perspectives. Free yourself from limiting judgments, which hinder your positive potential to be open and engaged in what you experience. If you find that you have difficulty being open to this new experience of trance, turn to Chapter 10, on resistance, where you will find some helpful guidance in working with and overcoming what might be standing in your way.

Developing a Nonjudgmental Attitude Exercise

Mindfulness meditation teaches a nonjudgmental attitude. Mindful awareness is non-judgmental. Like a researcher who is gathering data, set aside judgments. Suspend judgment until more data is gathered. Trust the process of awareness and this will help you to cultivate openness. So, if you notice something that you do not like, instead of immediately taking a position against it, simply take note of it. People can be harshly judgmental with themselves, often quickly turning to self-criticism as a way to improve themselves. Being open can be a more effective way to bring about self-improvement than criticizing yourself. Self-critical judgments often work against you, leading to inhibition and slowing down the flow of improvement.

There is an important difference between simply observing something that may need changing versus evaluating whether it is good or bad. And this applies to working in self-hypnosis. Non-judgmental observation often helps lessen defenses as a more open attitude is cultivated.

Fostering Openness by Acceptance Exercise

To become mindfully aware of what is there, keep observations clear and descriptive. Learn to accept each experience, without making comparisons or criticisms. Then, the finer qualities of experience can be fully appreciated, just as they are. To apply this non-judgmental attitude now, turn your attention to yourself. Observe yourself from head to toe in a mirror, and recognize all the different parts. Describe each part. Notice your hair, for example; note the color, texture, style. Observe your eyes, your eyebrows, etc. But stay factual. For example, observe that your hair is long, dark brown, and curly. Try not to use evaluative terms, such as unattractive or attractive, too long or too short, or not straight enough. Notice what happens as you simply describe yourself without making any judgments. Even if you usually consider certain things about your appearance to be flaws or faults, remember the teachings of the famous Zen Buddhist teacher Linji (Lin Chi). He often told his disciples that, though they believed they were deficient, in reality nothing was missing (Watson, 1993). Problems occur when people step away from what is actually there. He believed that people get too caught up in judging themselves, and this puts them out of touch with what they really are. Open your mind to looking at things about yourself and your world just as they are. And if you are willing to truly notice without adding anything extra, you will find that your negative appraisals will dissipate as you become open to experiencing what is.

Developing Attention Skills

Another component of absorption is attention. Attention can be conscious or unconscious. You can deliberately and consciously attend to something, such as another person, an object in your environment, or your own inner functioning. But sometimes you do not notice things consciously, yet may still be attending to them unconsciously. Like conscious attention, unconscious attention is also a natural ability of all living organisms. Attention that is unconscious and "free-floating" can be useful in applying self-hypnosis for developing the openness component of absorption.

Learning to Focus Attention Consciously

Attention is needed for anything to be consciously noticed. As a variation on the old philosophical riddle, if a tree falls in a forest and no one is there to hear it, does it make a sound; we could add, if a tree falls in a forest and no one pays attention, does anyone hear it? Conscious attention helps us notice and respond appropriately to circumstances.

You can use an outer object or an inner object as a focal point for concentration. The wiring for paying attention is there in the brain. Train your attention and you will find that it becomes readily available to you when you need it.

Focus on an External Object Exercise

Pick a small object in your house: a plant, a picture, or even a technological device like a cell phone. Place it in clear view and sit down close by and look at the object. Focus on the whole shape, then begin to discern the different aspects of the object, such as its sub-shapes, colors, textures, or anything else that you notice. Look at it carefully, keeping all your attention focused on this object. If your attention wanders, gently bring it back as soon as you notice it wandering. Do this for one minute the first time.

Focus on an Internal Object: Breathing Exercise

In hypnosis you will often be focusing on objects of attention that are within yourself. One of the traditional and most accessible objects for internal focus is breathing. We all have to breathe, and so breathing is easily accessible for training attention. Begin by counting the breaths. People who have difficulty focusing their attention will find that this is an excellent way to stop attention from moving around. Close your eyes and turn your attention to your breathing. With each breath in and out, count one. Go up to ten complete breaths and then start counting again. Do this for about two minutes. With practice, you will be able to stay focused on breathing for a longer period of time.

Learning to Focus Attention Unconsciously

Human beings are not merely another form of biological machine, an organism that responds to a stimulus with a mechanical learned response. We are quickly bored when a situation requires us to be machinelike. We crave stimulation. We reach out for excitement and actively seek challenge, novelty, and problems to solve. Human nature is contrary and irascible. Something more is there, hidden in the wings, awaiting the call for its time to appear onstage. This is when the unconscious begins its positive work, resulting in the emergence of a new synthesis, one that is not limited to conscious boundaries.

Even daydreaming is not a waste of time. The daydream can be a doorway to deeper regions of your mind. You enter and find your way, through symbolism, to experiences that are important to you. Visual symbols give you an opportunity to react.

Unconscious Attention Exercise

Have you ever gotten lost in a moment of daydreaming or reverie? This is a doorway into unconscious attention. Have you ever spent a timeless moment deeply concentrating on something of inner significance, then suddenly snapped out of it, realizing you had not thought of where you were or what you were doing? This is a form of trance, spontaneously begun. Seek a symbol that has personal significance and the potential to fascinate you. A mandala, an Escher picture, or any visual aid that is meaningful to you will do. Do not focus on it directly. Instead, let your thoughts drift freely as you look at it, allowing whatever comes to mind as you contemplate and focus deeply, so that your own thoughts and feelings can be stimulated.

It is positive and beneficial to be flexible and focused, with the capacity to pay full attention. Different types of visual organization can affect attention: diagrams, maps, and graphs can be objects for concentration, evoking your personal interest. Experiment.

Developing Thinking Ability by Not Thinking

Most commonly if we try not to think, we find that we cannot stop thinking. Thought follows thought in an endless sequence, a flowing river of ideas. The use of the mind seems automatic, with no escape. When you try not to think, you inevitably focus your attention on thinking; and whether you intend to or not, you often begin an inner battle, a battle for control of processes that you cannot control. This exemplifies the law of reversed effort in hypnosis: The harder you try not to think about something, paradoxically, the more you think about it. The thinking process itself is the inroad into the opening attention for hypnosis. The first step is to turn your attention to thinking itself.

Attending to Thinking Exercise

Let us explore what we are doing at a particular moment when we think. Are we really thinking for a purpose, deeply contemplating? Or are we merely spinning our mental wheels? What are we doing? Focus your attention now on your own mind for a few moments. Consider whether you can instead embrace thinking itself, taking it seriously, permitting yourself to think. Contemplate thinking so that you are not really distracted by it.

Following a Thought to Its Roots Exercise

Observe each thought as it emerges, following it to its source, its logical assumptions, its roots. Try this with one idea or concept that matters to you. What is the origin of this thought? How do you know it is significant, of concern? Is there really a rational basis for this concern? Or is there instead no basis? What is the basis for it? What keeps it central to you? This is the general outline of the method of analysis of thinking that helps to dissolve it as a process. You may follow this through to a single, specific, individual basis, or you may discover a more general foundation. Both methods have their use and application. Your thinking processes may change once they are freed from faulty bases.

Following Thought Exercise

Follow each thought: Notice each thought as it arises, and then notice the next one. Try to maintain the vantage point like an observer at a riverbank, watching. Do not lose yourself in any particular thought, but pay close attention to the process of your thinking.

When you think deeply, clearly, and carefully, the thought ceases to be a distracting problem. Superficial thought leads to problems. Thinking will eventually slow down on its own, by reaching deeper thought. Sometimes we believe that we cannot think deeply at all, but it is really a matter of finding the natural brain–mind wiring that we already have within ourselves.

Conclusion

Openness and attention can be developed over time with practice. Don't be discouraged if you find these skills are slow to develop. You may not see results right away, but stay with the effort. Sometimes change is subtle and you might not notice it. Trust the process and continue working through the book. Your efforts will bear fruit later, perhaps as a pleasant surprise.

6

The Unconscious and Automaticity:

Using What Comes Naturally

Flow with whatever may happen and let your mind be free:
Stay centered by accepting whatever you are doing.
This is the ultimate.

—Zhuangzi (in Hyams, 1982, p. 57)

MYSTERIOUS, elusive, seeming to escape rational explanation, the unconscious holds a certain fascination. Today, thanks to the new technology available for studying the brain, we have mounting scientific evidence indicating that many vital brain processes are unconscious. The unconscious serves important functions of intelligence. Hypnosis works through these unconscious processes and allows you to draw from the great reservoir of brain–mind potential.

Evidence for the Unconscious from the Two Hemispheres of the Brain

At first, scientists believed that unconscious processes could not be intelligent. But brain research about the two hemispheres of the brain performed in the 1950s, '60s and '70s gave one of the earliest sources of evidence that this might not be the case.

Neuroscientists studied patients who had damage to one side or the other, as well as those who had the connecting tissue, the corpus callosum, severed during surgery to help stop the devastating effects of epilepsy. They discovered that many structures seemed to be repeated on both sides, offering different options for awareness.

Initially, neurologists evaluated that the left side, which seemed to control language and the complex cognitive abilities involved in careful thought, was the most important side for intelligent functioning. Rational, conscious, deliberate thinking was believed to be all we really needed. But evidence gradually emerged to indicate that the right hemisphere might be necessary for intelligent functioning as well. Research in England during World War II revealed that patients with right hemisphere damage were deficient in a number of ways. They had trouble finding their way back to their rooms on the wards and even had problems putting on their clothes. It became clear that the two hemispheres had unique ways of conceptualizing and responding to stimulation. "Each left and right hemisphere has its own private chain of memories and learning experiences that are inaccessible to recall by the other hemisphere. In many respects, each disconnected hemisphere appears to have a separate 'mind of its own'" (Sperry in Springer & Deutsch, 1981, p. 52).

We now know that each of the two hemispheres has unique cognitive properties with its own strengths (Sperry, 1974). The left hemisphere is specialized for language, speech, and problem solving, and thus sometimes equated with conscious processing. The right is specialized for visual and spatial processing; it also constructs a representation of the visual world. In some ways the right hemisphere is more visually intelligent than the left, but since the right hemisphere is not associated with language, we are often less aware of its workings. For example, people who are good at finding their way around, even in an unfamiliar city, often do so in an intuitive, somewhat nonrational way. This kind of knowing is intelligent, but differs from consciously known details (such as, that a place you are looking for is located 2.4 miles north on highway 5). So, memories of pictures and orientation in space are processed in the right hemisphere, while memories that call for language, meanings, and concepts are processed in the left hemisphere. Both ways of knowing are intelligent and helpful, but one is explicit and conscious, and the other is implicit and often unconscious. Clearly, human intelligence stems from multiple parts and functions of the brain. Hypnosis enlists both sides of the brain to activate more capacities than simple conscious, deliberate action might be able to achieve alone.

Brain-Damaged Patients: More Evidence for the Unconscious

The way our memory works has served as another source for understanding the unconscious. Henry Gustav Molaison (1926–2008), better known as HM, helped develop new neuroscientific understandings about memory, learning, and the unconscious. In 1953, HM underwent an elective surgery to deal with his epilepsy. His surgeon, William Beecher Scoville, had found the epilepsy to be located in the left and right medial temporal lobes. Based on the limited understanding of brain functioning at that time, he decided that the best way to prevent the epilepsy was to remove two-thirds of HM's hippocampus, parahippocampal gyrus, and amygdala. Nobody predicted the serious effects this surgery would have on HM's memory. The surgeon immediately recognized the deficits following the surgery and began testing his patient (Scoville & Milner, 1957). HM could not form any new lasting memories, suffering from what is known as *anterograde amnesia.*

Surprisingly, even though HM could not learn new facts or recall what he had already done, he could learn new skills. He was given a task called the mirror-tracing task, in which he was taught to trace a pattern. He did the task every day, and each day he had to be instructed anew, from the beginning, as if it were the first time he had attempted the task. But paradoxically, his skills improved, showing that some learning was taking place unconsciously. He could learn *how* to do something, even though he had no memory of *what* he had learned. Based on many years of study with HM, we have gained strong evidence for the idea that there are different functional areas in the brain, some operating with full consciousness as they occur, and others working intelligently and unconsciously, without any awareness of them on the individual's part. Learning *what* does indeed seem to be distinct from learning *how.*

Neuroscience now conceives of memory as two separate but interacting systems, each with its own neural counterparts. One system is conscious, declarative and semantic; the other is unconscious, non-declarative and implicit. These systems have their own unique way of processing: Conscious recall for declarative, and unconscious performance for non-declarative. Conscious declarative memory and learning occur in brain areas separate from those where unconscious procedural memory and learning take place. The quality of attention can influence how well we learn and remember, but sometimes learning can take place without any deliberate focusing of attention. Emotions also affect unconscious processes. Thus, unconscious functioning is complex, varied, and offers a wealth of skills and capacities to be utilized in self-hypnosis to help you foster change.

Evidence for the Unconscious from Studies of Perception and Attention

Our senses take in a great deal of information, but consciousness is limited, only registering a few bits of information at a time. Our immediate short-term memory capacity tends to be around seven bits of information at one time. Anything beyond this goes unnoticed consciously, but research shows that it is registered unconsciously. The unconscious continually absorbs much more information than consciousness perceives at any given moment. This ability is tapped into when, for example, a witness to a crime is hypnotized in order to recall details of the event. The witness might be unable to consciously remember certain specifics, such as a license plate number on a car, but under hypnosis the entire scene can be visualized or even imaginatively revisited. Although there can be errors in recollection, sometimes a memory retrieved in trance includes more than what was consciously recalled. More information can be perceived through the senses and stored unconsciously, outside of awareness.

Even when we do not pay attention to a witnessed event or stimulus, it has still been perceived. If we do not interfere consciously, we will perceive and remember even a single presentation of an item. These processes do not involve our conscious attention. In certain situations, we receive unattended information without registering it, especially when our attention is directed towards something else. And this unattended information, even though it remains outside of conscious awareness, can influence our behavior, thoughts, learning, and emotions (Posner, 1978). Researchers devised a way to test how unattended information is processed called *priming*. Priming research has shown how stimuli that are not deliberately, consciously attended to can enhance learning from unconscious processing. As noted neuroscience researchers Squire and Kandel stated, "Priming's key feature is that it is unconscious" (2000, p. 160).

Priming refers to improved speed, accuracy, or efficiency in the ability to identify words or objects after having a recent experience with them. People respond more rapidly and fully to stimuli previously experienced than to completely new experiences. This ability is called *implicit memory* and it results from priming. Implicit memories improve our performance of a task, without the need for any conscious or intentional recollection of those experiences.

The brain acts differently when exercising these unconscious processes. PET images of individuals doing a task following priming reveal a reduction in activity in the visual cortex, specifically in the posterior occipital lobe. When priming occurs, the visual system has already processed part of the information, so less higher processing is required. These processes occur more quickly and efficiently than those that use conscious thinking because the priming effect for visual stimuli is processed earlier in the visual pathway.

The effects of priming can last for decades. For example, Mitchell and Brown (1988) showed that normal subjects retained priming effects for one week, as might be expected. But seventeen years later they retested some of their 1988 priming subjects and found these original subjects did significantly better with the primed material, and also showed a significant improvement over controls (Mitchell, 2006). Amazingly, these subjects had retained their priming effects all those years! Thus, unconscious changes you make can be efficient, stable, and lasting.

Unconscious Input in Everyday Life

Like priming, all kinds of inputs are registered continually without our being aware of them during our daily lives. For example, as you read the words on this page, you are probably not aware of your foot. But now that "foot" is mentioned you might notice that yours feels cold or warm, light or heavy, or perhaps tingly. Sensation in your foot was always present, but when thoughts were directed elsewhere these feelings were unconscious. Attention makes your perception conscious, but the experience exists whether consciously perceived or not. We know that people can have experiences with thoughts about the experience, even though the experience is unconscious, because these thoughts can be recalled later.

Memories, concepts, and information learned over the years are retained unconsciously. As children grow they learn how to walk, read, and write. At each stage of development, certain skills and abilities are mastered, and earlier ones are incorporated or transformed. This requires applications of intelligence, emotional maturity, and body coordination.

Abilities are stored not only as the specific, actual learned skill, but also as a more generalized potential, of learning how to learn. For example, skills used to form letters of the alphabet in early childhood are taken for granted as an adult, yet the component skills in forming the letters of the alphabet—making lines, circles, and the spaces in between— may be drawn upon later, in a career as an architect, an artist, or a builder. These implicit processes comprise learning and understandings you may have applied in different contexts throughout your life. And for our purposes here, it should be noted that connections can be made in hypnosis without conscious effort.

Neuroscience of Automatic Habits

Daily routine becomes automatic, regulated by unconscious processes. The alarm on your clock goes off in the morning and you automatically shut it off. You walk so naturally and easily that you may never think about the complex links between mind, brain, and body coordinating unconsciously, unless something goes wrong, and you have a problem. Try to remember yesterday's activities. Some events are murky and difficult to recall. But after concentration you probably reclaim more and more details, as you bring automatic activities into your awareness. Once a habit is learned, it can be carried out by simply thinking about the goal of the habit in question. Then the whole set of processes is triggered as we carry out the action effortlessly. This is how we are able to leap ahead, without needing to think about the intervening steps.

The areas of the brain involved in carrying out habits are the cerebellum and basal ganglia, which are both part of subcortical motor processing. The learning of habits uses very different areas than declarative learning, such as the hippo-campus, the structure where new memories are stored. The performing of habits engages the caudate nucleus, one of the parts of the basal ganglia involved in learning movement.

The Neurobiology of Conscious-Unconscious Pathways in Vision

Vision affords another way for distinguishing between conscious and unconscious pathways. Visual information flows in two pathways: ventral and dorsal. These two pathways tend to process information differently. *What* something is and how it is represented in form, such as its color or shape, is processed through the ventral pathway; the "whatness" of the thing in question is seen consciously by deliberately paying attention to and understanding it. *Where* something is and how to move to its location in space is processed through the dorsal visual-motor pathway; the object's "whereness" is processed unconsciously, without explicit knowledge or understanding, but instead with a sense of its spatial relationships to the body. When the dorsal pathway is the dominant process, we can make an accurate response to an object without consciously understanding how or why, such as reaching a hand out effortlessly to catch a ball.

Both conscious and unconscious processing have their uses, and so it makes sense to develop both. Some tasks or situations produce better results if processed consciously, and others will get superior results with unconscious processing. Often the best results come from a combination of the two. Thus, in self-hypnosis you will find your own unique conscious-unconscious balance to utilize either pathway as an access point.

The Psychology of the Unconscious

Psychology has described and worked with the unconscious processes as tools for psychotherapy. Freud first made the unconscious famous as the repository of repressed memories, and this is still an important component for the psychology of the unconscious. But as neuroscience has shown, the unconscious serves many positive functions, adding to our intelligence and sensitivity.

Unconscious as Intuition

Intuition expresses the poetry of the unconscious. We can think of intuition as the psychological function that transmits perceptions in an unconscious way. Intuitive processing can be an intelligent pathway to sophisticated understandings, and thus it can be a valuable skill to develop.

Aristotle believed that intuitive functioning is an extremely complex process, based on our ability to sense and perceive at a basic level, retain sense perception, and systematize these sense perceptions. Thus, intuition intelligently synthesizes data. Since the synthesis occurs outside of awareness, people know something without knowing how they know it. Intuition appears to work backwards, with conclusions reached before premises.

People experience uncanny hunches, spontaneous familiarity, or insightful realizations. Intuitive truth is usually recognized, not learned. Most people are aware of having intuitions; some rely on them. Intuitions may be extremely clear for some people, and vague to others. Intuitions involve sensitivity to nonverbal, nonrational phenomena. Some believe this sensitivity is a more accurate way of knowing reality's truth. Self-hypnosis evokes the use of intuitive mental faculties, permitting them to develop.

Both consciousness (through awareness and rationality) and unconsciousness (through intuition and unconscious experiencing) are important.

Associative Qualities of the Unconscious

The unconscious synthesis often occurs within a stream of associations, a free flow of natural, active, creative processing that takes place without intervention of conscious purpose. The unconscious makes associations just outside of awareness throughout the day. This process is extremely useful in hypnosis and trance processes.

William James carefully defined and described associative principles. When two brain processes are active at the same time or in immediate succession, one tends to excite the other. This is basis for the law of association (James, 1896). On the neuronal level, when two things become associated neurons involved in both fire together, and as the association is repeated, the wiring between them becomes stronger.

Association by similarity occurs from the free flow of thoughts. Similar ideas become linked, forming compounds that link to other ideas. Seemingly dissimilar ideas can end up mentally connected. Learning influences some of these associative processes. For example, if told the word "swallow," ornithologists will think of a bird, throat specialists will think of throat disease, and thirsty people might realize how much they want a drink of water. Associations are also influenced by how recent, vivid, or congruent the ideas are. All in all, the process of association is complex and multifaceted.

Despite its complexities, the flow of unconscious associations is not random; rather, it evolves from your individuality. Patterns of association reflect your past, including your likes and dislikes, past conflicts and resolutions, and your needs and expectations. Many other external and internal experiences can be crystallized through associative metaphors.

Learning takes place in therapeutic trance, and sometimes this learning leads to an original discovery. Other times we assimilate, recombine, or restructure old understandings. New possibilities and changes follow from the recombining and interspersing of meaning into the associative processes of the unconscious mind.

Dreams: Free Flow of Images

Unconscious processing has been described thus far in terms of thought, but sometimes the unconscious is manifested as images or pictures. These images often reflect deep levels of inner experience, unknown to consciousness. A single picture can encode many possible meanings and learning. In dreams, a few images can symbolize a complex, detailed scenario.

Dreams occur spontaneously and yet meaningfully in trance. For example, a hypnotherapy client of ours had a vivid image in trance of a woman wearing a dark shawl. Upon awakening she felt puzzled as she described her image. Therapeutic exploration brought out the connection to her Italian background and her feelings about her mother, who had been sedentary and withdrawn. This client was involved in many community organizations, having decided early in her life to be different from her mother. The symbolic image brought forth associations that helped her to better understand and moderate her tendency to overcommit herself.

Sometimes dream images are misleading. One client had a recurring dream of a frightening monster chasing her. Night after night she was repeatedly terrified by the dream. She was a quiet, sweet person who always tried to be considerate, kind, and warm. She rarely got angry and found such emotions difficult to accept. As she worked in therapy she began to conceive the monster not as a foreign body attacking her, but rather as her own angry feelings. She had crystallized her conflict into a symbolic image. After she accepted this, she was able to include more of her personality into her everyday life, and she stopped having nightmares. This symbol from her unconscious, though feared and avoided, turned out to hold the key to resolving her difficulty. The unconscious can express a complex emotional conflict in a single image.

Dreams have also inspired great discoveries. The organic chemist August Kekulé's (1829–1896) breakthrough discovery of the benzene ring structure emerged from a dream. He was struggling day after day, trying to uncover a configuration to account for the unique properties of benzene. One night he fell asleep working on his calculations and had a dream of a snake twirling around, chasing its own tail. Eventually the spinning snake caught its tail and turned as a circle. When Kekulé awoke, he knew that he had solved the problem. Benzene arranges its molecules as a ring, a possibility he had previously overlooked! He returned to the data and was able to show empirically the validity of his insight, still accepted today. Kekulé's unconscious synthesized his intellectual understandings into a symbol he could consciously trace back to the data. Dreams can be a source of creative ideas and a means for working out difficulties and envisioning new possibilities.

Our approach to self-hypnosis uses this theory of dreams. Dreams may symbolically represent needs and concerns. You can utilize this valuable communication with your unconscious in trance to resolve difficulties and expand potential. Research has shown hypnotic hallucinations are similar in character to natural dreams, and so both are equally effective windows into the unconscious. Self-hypnosis can help to tap this potential.

How Assumptions, Beliefs, Attitudes, and Expectations Lead Unconciously to Self-Suggestions

People predict and anticipate events using assumptions, beliefs, attitudes, and expectations. Some assumptions are unconscious, taken for granted as true, without correction from awareness. Attitudes deriving from these assumptions remain relatively stable, coloring and influencing our interactions with the environment. For example, when people have catastrophic expectations, they may give themselves self-suggestions that they cannot handle such a stressful situation. This idea leads to maladaptive behaviors and failures. The process can work in a positive way as well, where self-suggestions associated with positive expectations help people take courageous actions to meet difficult circumstances hopefully and confidently.

Assumptions and beliefs, and the corresponding self-suggestions, may be learned from family and friends, religion, culture, or school, often without being consciously evaluated. Others evolve from the intrapersonal, that is, the interaction of one's own personality with the world. For example, most people think carefully about it and then choose a profession, but personal beliefs and attitudes about work are often taken for granted and unconsciously affect the decision. People who believe that work is a struggle and an uncomfortable ordeal will often end up being nonproductive at work, a negative byproduct of their negative self-suggestion. Those who treat work with personal commitment and devotion, deriving an essential meaning for their life from it, will often achieve more and feel happier working. These attitudes and values may have evolved from personal inner dynamics, from interpretations of how one's parents worked, or from response to external circumstance, like a devastating war. Whatever the origins, our beliefs, values, and assumptions influence the kinds of real-life actions we perform. Hypnosis allows us to modify our assumptions and form new suggestions, in order to make alterations for our benefit.

The Unconscious Quality of Emotions

Everyone knows what they are feeling to some extent, but emotional responses are also felt and registered unconsciously. One study found that subjects had a significant increase in their amygdala activity even when presented with pictures of angry and afraid faces. The increased emotional response in the amygdala occurred when the pictures were shown directly and registered consciously. The increased emotional response also occurred when subjects did not pay attention to the pictures, registering them unconsciously (Williams, Morris, McGlone, Abbott, & Mattingley, 2004). This study showed that the brain reacts in the emotional areas of the limbic system even without noticing.

Emotions, both conscious and unconscious, have a strong influence on learning and memory. Our evaluations of whether we like or dislike something, or whether an input is associated with a traumatic or uncomfortable past experience, will have a profound effect on how we learn and remember. Just having an emotional response can increase or decrease the strength of learning. Even when emotions are unconscious, they influence how well we learn. In one experiment, students were exposed to certain shapes too quickly for conscious recognition. When given a memory test later, even though the subjects did not recognize any of the shapes, they felt more positive about the shapes they had "seen" unconsciously, even though they did not know why (Squire & Kandel, 2000). Hypnosis can draw upon these emotional factors to facilitate therapeutic learning, and we will guide you to enlist your emotions as a way to help yourself.

Testing Hypnotic, Unconscious Learning

Without awareness, the mind can take in information unconsciously, process it and learn new skills, and retain the learning for many years. Unlike conscious processes, which employ aware, deliberate thinking, the unconscious performs cognitive processing without awareness or deliberate thinking. This processing does not need language and semantic processing, and does not need to rely on explicit sequential logic, and thus responds more quickly.

We decided to distinguish conscious from unconscious learning for therapeutic change by comparing a conscious, insight-based form of cognitive therapy with unconscious hypnotherapy (Simpkins & Simpkins, 2008). Before therapy began, each subject specified a psychological problem, the target complaint to work on. The subjects were divided into two groups: One receiving hypnotherapy where work was done unconsciously, without any mention of the problem directly, and the other group receiving a cognitive form of therapy where the problem was discussed and analyzed. All subjects were tested before and after the 6 sessions of treatment. We found that statistically, both groups improved equally well. But the closing interviews, where subjects were asked to specify what they had learned from treatment, revealed some interesting differences. Everyone expressed satisfaction that they had gained new psychological tools, but the two groups reported receiving different skills. As one might expect, the cognitive therapy participants felt that their awareness acted as a distinct guide to sense situations, notice reactions, and trace feelings and thoughts. "I'm looking at feelings as opposed to surface thoughts. I can examine them since I am aware of them," remarked one participant in the cognitive therapy. Another said, "It's the awareness: stopping, stepping back, away from being immersed in it all, to look at it from the outside. I'm noticing things more and making an effort to observe my surroundings."

The hypnosis participants also felt that they had gained a way to know themselves by trusting and using their unconscious processes as tools. Often they experienced this as simply happening, without quite knowing why. One participant said, "Things are just kind of happening; I'm not sure why, but I am more relaxed, and I can trust my intuitive self." Another said, "My unconscious has opened up more and it does more. This feels good." This group tended to acquire an intuitive ability to sense their inner needs and a willingness to listen to their inner voice.

Despite the differences in treatment methods, participants developed some similarities. Many hypnosis participants expressed the same ability to be objective as the therapy participants. One hypnosis subject said, "It feels like something, a clouded something in me that has helped me stand back and look at things more objectively and be more relaxed instead of getting freaked out. I can't pinpoint what it is." Both groups felt they gained objectivity, but they experienced it coming from different sources: the cognitive-therapy group from a clear awareness, and the hypnosis group from a supportive unconscious. Both groups felt they gained greater understanding of themselves and their problems.

Thus, unconscious processing can be individualized, intelligently oriented, and sophisticated. Becoming sensitive to its subtle facets is a key to building self-hypnotic skills.

Conclusion

Freed from the bonds of preconception, you have an opportunity to make new connections, leading to new potentials. Hypnosis can allow you to bypass limitations, in order to bring about something different. In an altered consciousness, you have opportunities for open, creative moments. Now that you have familiarized yourself with the positive potential of the unconscious, you can begin to make this potential truly useful in your life.

7

Suggestion: Enlisting Your Ability
to Respond

Suggestion, on the one hand, with the impression of the suggested idea on the mind and its acceptance by consciousness; this is the afferent, sensory side of suggestion; and, on the other hand, with the realization of the accepted idea; this is the efferent, motor side of suggestion.

—Boris Sidis, *The Psychology of Suggestion*, p. 21

WE have many built-in capacities that help us respond to things. For example, if someone tells you about a wonderful book they just read, you might feel moved to read that book yourself. The process at work is *suggestion*, which can be defined as the natural ability to respond to an idea. We say that suggestion is *natural* because everyone responds to ideas, to a certain extent. We call it an *ability* because suggestion is a skill that you can develop. Even though some people are more naturally suggestible than others, we have seen in our clinical practice that anyone can enhance their responsiveness to suggestions, especially when they are motivated to do so. Being able to respond to suggestions that are beneficial and not engage in suggestions that are detrimental can help you to bring about lasting change. So in this chapter, you will learn how to start where you are and build on your natural ability to be responsive to suggestion. With an open mind and a willingness to be imaginative, you can learn how to enhance your sensitivity to suggestions, when you choose to do so.

Sometimes suggestions happen deliberately, as when you read the book your friend suggested. But often you respond to suggestions automatically, such as when you hear an old song on the radio and it suggests a memory of a time long ago when you heard that same song. Even though we respond to some suggestions automatically, we always, ultimately, have a choice to accept or reject a suggestion. You probably can think of instances when you turned down a suggestion, such as not buying a product just because you saw a persuasive advertisement for it on television. All suggestion is self-suggestion in the sense that on some level, you decide to incorporate the suggestion or not. So if you receive a suggestion to relax and you find yourself relaxing, you do so because deep down, even if you are not quite aware of it, you want to relax.

Suggestion is an important component of hypnosis. Although trance and suggestion are separate phenomena that can each occur without the other, many believe that hypnotic induction and suggestion are the two main components of hypnosis. Being in hypnosis can improve your ability to work with suggestion. The main emphasis of this book is self-hypnosis. Therefore, we deal primarily with self-suggestion, or suggestions that you give to yourself. We will guide you in how to work with self-suggestions in positive ways—without trance in this chapter, and with trance throughout the rest of the book.

The Neuroscience of Suggestion: Top-Down and Bottom-Up Processing

Neuroscientific research has shown that measurable brain changes occur when people carry out a suggestion. One often-cited study compared responses to suggestions of seeing colors on a grayscale pattern (that is, a black-and-white image made up of shades of gray) with actually seeing a color version of the pattern. Subjects were also asked to imagine that a grayscale version of the pattern was actually in color. An earlier study (Howard et al., 1998) showed that when people imagine seeing color, only the right hemisphere, or visually-oriented, areas of the brain are activated. But in the Kosslyn study, when subjects were given the suggestion of color during hypnosis, both the left and right hemisphere color-oriented areas of the brain were activated, just as they would be when subjects actually looked at the colored pattern (Kosslyn et al., 2000). The brain responds to suggestions by seeing, hearing, or feeling in the same way as if the stimulus was really there. Thus, working with suggestion can stimulate real responses in your brain and body.

Modern neuroscience can explain why suggestions have such a powerful effect. When you sense something, such as touching the page of the book you are reading now, sensors in your fingertips send a signal up through your nerves to your brain; this is known as a bottom-up process. Some suggestions come through a bottom-up manner, beginning with a sensation. For example, when you smell the fragrance of a freshly baked pie and you then suddenly feel hungry, a bottom-up suggestive response has occurred unconsciously. You were not thinking about eating or about pie, but smelling the aroma automatically brought about the thought and feeling.

The brain also has circuits devoted to higher-order processing in the cortex of memories, ideas, and beliefs drawn from past experience, learning, and culture. So, we might accept a positive suggestion that exercise is healthy from a lecture given on health, and as a result, begin looking for a gym and plan to work out. This top-down processing is pervasive in the brain's many networks devoted to representing ideas in the cortex, and can explain why a suggested idea, once accepted, often goes through higher-order brain processing.

Our construction of everyday reality as we know it is an ongoing combination of bottom-up and top-down processes. Suggestions also combine bottom-up and top-down processing. By activating the brain, suggestions can become woven into the fabric of our daily lives as seamlessly as if we experienced something directly. Thus, learning how to work with suggestion can be helpful for changing how you think, feel, and behave.

Varieties of Suggestion

Fundamentally, suggestions can be either spontaneous or induced. Spontaneous suggestions are occasional, involuntary responses to a stimulus as if it was a suggestion. By contrast, induced suggestion occurs when you deliberately set yourself—using the techniques of suggestion—to have an experience or accomplish a selected goal. Another way to think of these two phenomena is as conditioning.

A spontaneous suggestion is like an unconditioned reflex reaction that happens automatically, or reflexively. An induced suggestion can be viewed somewhat like a conditioned response, where learned links are used to help accomplish goals.

Familiarize yourself with the different types of suggestion that are used in hypnotherapy. Suggestion is more understandable when felt, so experiment with the ideas and exercises presented in order to personally experience how to use suggestion. These exercises in suggestion will help you learn about your own individual parameters of suggestibility, which can be especially useful when combined with trance.

Spontaneous Suggestion

The easiest place to begin is by noticing spontaneous suggestions, since they occur without any effort on your part, automatically. We will show you how to incorporate this naturally-occurring device by placing yourself into circumstances that will tend to suggest something you are hoping to bring about. This kind of suggestion can be used as a powerful tool for making therapeutic change.

Exercise: Noticing Suggestive Qualities

Think of a time in your life when you sat around a campfire, watching the dancing flames, and listening with increasing fascination to a frightening tale of ghosts and spirits. Later, as you ventured back to your sleeping quarters, sounds had an eerie tone, and shadows appeared to move ominously, giving you a feeling of fear and foreboding. In this example, an idea and fantasy presented to you became a reality for you. You felt as if you were in the midst of apparitions, even if only for a few moments.

Now, think of a time when you might have been feeling a bit depressed. You met up with a good friend whose pleasant smile and cheery disposition seemed to magically lift you from your doldrums. In this friend's presence your own thoughts and feelings seemed unnecessarily glum. Suddenly you felt positive again. You were released from your negative mood. You may wish to recall other examples of your own.

A sensation can give rise to a spontaneous suggestion by interacting with a preexisting idea. For example, if we expect someone to visit, a telephone ring-ing may seem to sound like the ring of the doorbell. If your imagination is active enough, you may think you hear the telephone ring when the house is essentially silent. Ideas and expectations can bring about a spontaneous suggestion.

We interpret our sensations in part through the context of our beliefs and assumptions about the world. Consequently, experiences, ideas, and emotions may be spontaneously suggested. For example, even though there is no obvious emotional meaning connected to eating, some people often want to eat when they feel a certain way. For instance, they may experience a suggestion to eat chocolate as a result of certain cues, such as feeling sadness over lost love. The action of eating is in response to a spontaneous suggestion, and not, in this instance, just a simple response to the feeling of hunger itself.

Personal Spontaneous Suggestion Exercise

Not everyone responds to spontaneous suggestion in the same way. Learning to be aware of your personal spontaneous suggestion triggers can be helpful in bringing about therapeutic change. First, cultivate awareness of spontaneous suggestions, noting and observing them as they occur for you. As soon as you notice one, concentrate on the experience as it happens. This requires careful observation. Notice the sensory or intellectual modalities that are typically suggestive to you. As you become more aware of them, you will learn more about yourself.

For example, the sounds of someone cooking in the kitchen might suggest a pleasant family experience. The smell of food can suggest its taste and the wish to eat. People with a smoking habit often find the smell of cigarette smoke suggests to them the urge to have a cigarette. If they successfully quit smoking, they often need to stay away from the smell of a burning cigarette, until the smell no longer suggests an urge to smoke to them. You may respond to spontaneous suggestion in many ways. Your personal characteristic variations are important for observing your own patterns of response.

Induced Suggestions

Induced suggestions are what most people associate with the idea of suggestion. They are given deliberately to bring about an effect. These types of suggestions can take many forms, and we will work with them extensively in this book. Induced suggestions are often thought to be direct and specific, but a more powerful form of induced suggestion is indirect and general. The many types of suggestions that follow are all the induced type.

Ideas become a reality when we accept them, and suggestion often involves accepting an idea unconsciously. Then, a reflex response takes place, transforming the idea automatically to a corresponding action. Like a conditioned response, this responsiveness to an induced suggestion is an entirely natural process that activates mechanisms of mind and brain in order to bring the suggestion about.

The ability to accept suggestions is strongest when the tides of consciousness are low; at that time, associations are more likely to flow. There are times when the threshold between the conscious and the unconscious lowers spontaneously. At these moments, concentration can take place effortlessly and attention can be focused through involuntary processes. Hypnosis helps to lower the threshold, making suggestions easier to follow.

When working with self-hypnosis, suggestions can be given deliberately to bring about an effect. Recognize that even when you are deliberately trying to induce an effect, suggestions should never be forced. Self-suggestion enlists the natural processes of the brain–mind system. Induced suggestions work better when they are offered, and then patiently, expectantly, their acceptance is awaited.

The Anatomy of Suggestion: The Ideomotor Effect

Suggestion consists of two parts: a sensory experience and a motor action. Neuroscience traces the interaction between sensory inputs and motor outputs along with how the input–output process engages some brain pathways, as we discussed in Chapter 4. William James called the two-sided, input–output quality of suggestion the ideomotor response. The ideomotor effect proceeds from having an idea that is translated into a bodily response, from the top down. It can also occur bottom-up when it begins with a sensation.

Experimenting with a Top-Down Ideomotor Suggestion Exercise
If you would like to experience the ability of your imagination to bring about an ideomotor effect, close your eyes and imagine a plate of freshly baked chocolate chip cookies.

Think about the gooey chocolate, the sweet aroma. Then imagine placing a cookie in your mouth. Taste the warm, sweet flavor. Does your mouth begin to water? If so, you have experienced the ideomotor effect of suggestion: An imagined image becomes directly expressed in the body response.

Allow yourself the time it takes to have your reaction. Be sensitive and aware of subtle responses. Some people may find that the response is immediate and very distinct, while others may not have as dramatic and bold a reaction. But the smallest little sensation can be nurtured into a very useful skill to be applied when you need it, so accept whatever occurs, with the understanding that you will be developing new skills as you read further.

Traditional Ideomotor Exercise

This exercise uses the imagination of movement, which is translated into real movement in your hand. The French chemist Michel Eugène Chevreul (1786–1889) is credited with first discovering this effect, known as the Chevreul Pendulum.

Get a plumb bob or any small, heavy object. Attach it to a string. Hold the string from the top and let the object dangle freely. Support your elbow on a table so that you are comfortable as you hold the string, but leave your arm and wrist free. Now close your eyes. Imagine that the pendulum begins to swing back and forth. Picture it vividly in your mind. Do not deliberately move or interfere with the hand that holds the string. Instead, focus on your imaginative image of swinging. Visualize the rhythmic sweep of the swing becoming longer. After a few minutes, open your eyes and look at the pendulum. Most people will find that it is swinging back and forth.

Close your eyes again. Imagine that the object begins to swing in the other direction. Exaggerate the image so that the arc becomes larger and larger in the new direction. Picture it as vividly as possible. Once again, do not disturb the hand that holds the string. Simply focus on your visualization. After a time, open your eyes. Is the pendulum swinging in the new direction?

Close your eyes one last time. Imagine that the pendulum swings in a circle. Allow the circular orbit to become larger and larger. Open your eyes to check. This may take time and practice to develop further. Some people can do it almost immediately. Others expand their abilities over time.

Bottom-Up Ideomotor Effect

A feeling or sensation in the body can also suggest an idea (bottom-up, as we described) with spontaneous suggestions. The mind, brain, and body work together, back and forth, naturally and effortlessly. But you can learn to work with this bottom-up process to induce suggestions. For example, you may feel heaviness in your limbs, which suggests to you that you are tired. Sometimes when engaged in exercise, people interpret certain body sensations, such as tone in the muscles, in such a way that inspires them to work out harder: "I'm feeling great today!" A feeling in the stomach may be interpreted as hunger even though one has recently eaten. Dieters often struggle with these kinds of implicit hunger suggestions, but they can learn how to turn the process around to help resist overeating and create better habits. With practice you can use both your body and your mind to help broaden your use of suggestion in helpful new ways.

Try turning your attention to your body now. Notice a sensation in your body. What does it suggest to you? Search for the implicit meanings you may be giving your sensations, suggesting you are tired or sad, comfortable or content, etc.

Ideomotor Relaxation Exercise: Enlisting Top-Down and Bottom-Up

We use both bottom-up and top-down processes for suggestions in this book. These processes can be used simultaneously as well as separately. The ideomotor link shows you how your mind can create effects in your body just as your body affects your mind. You can cultivate the link to bring about positive results, such as relaxation. We will often encourage combining both types of processes together. Then, when used with hypnotic trance, you will be able to enhance your responsiveness further than you were before.

Now try to use the ideomotor effect to bring about your own relaxation and calm. Sit in a comfortable chair or lie down on the floor or a bed. Close your eyes. Vividly imagine that you are relaxed. Imagine yourself completely at ease and comfortable. Picture your muscles relaxed, your breathing calm, and your thoughts quiet. You may like to remember a time when you were relaxed, such as on a vacation or in the company of someone you care about. You may prefer to think about someone else being relaxed; for example, you might picture a young child peacefully sleeping. Imagine relaxation as vividly as possible. Wait for your response. If you hold the image in your mind, your body will naturally respond by letting go of tension. You will become calmer, similar to your image, without trying to make it happen.

Suggestion as Focused Attention on an Object of Interest Exercise

Braid considered concentration of attention to be essential for successful hypnosis and a prerequisite for the acceptance of suggestions. By narrowing your attention, suggestions are met with little or no competition.

If you would like to experiment with this approach, find a sensory experience that has a naturally captivating quality, such as glowing coals in a fireplace, a full moon over a body of water, or a quiet field in the evening. Ensure that you have no external demands requiring attention, and can be undisturbed as you watch. Then, let your attention be drawn exclusively to the scene you have chosen. Permit your thoughts to dwell on nothing but the coals, the fire, the moon, or whatever you have chosen. In time you may have an experience of drifting into a state of deep absorption. At this point you can experiment with self-suggestion. Suggest that you see an image in the coals, or patterns on the water, for example. Try inviting a corresponding relaxation of your arms and legs, or perhaps all your muscles, while you watch. You might suggest heaviness, lightness, warmth in your arms or legs, or coolness in your forehead, to name just a few examples. Each successful response to self-suggestion tends to reinforce the general tendency of responsiveness.

Fixation on Eye Closure Exercise

In this classic exercise used by Braid, focus your attention by looking upward until your eyes become tired. Then give yourself this suggestion: "My eyes are becoming heavy and want to close." Wait for your response. Often the eyes water and even flicker as they begin to close. Follow and appreciate the individual and unique responses you might have. You can learn about yourself by observing your tendencies. If you find yourself somewhat unwilling or unable to open your eyes, you have had an involuntary level of response to suggestion. Not everyone experiences this at first, but with practice you will improve. With a further suggestion you can release your eyelid muscles by suggesting, "Soon I will once again be able to open my eyes." Rest a moment, then stretch and reorient, awake and refreshed.

Different Forms of Suggestion: Direct and Indirect

As noted earlier, suggestions can be direct or indirect. Direct suggestions are those that specify what you are going to experience, such as "Your eyelids will grow heavy," or "You will feel relaxed." In direct suggestion you know what the results should be and for many people, the suggested results occur. Some people are very responsive to direct suggestions and can use them to guide their experience in positive and helpful directions.

Direct suggestions are different from everyday commands or requests. For example, if we gave the instruction "Please close your eyes," you would probably do so as a deliberate and voluntary effort, to be cooperative with the process. Direct suggestions are different. Even though they offer a straightforward statement about what you will experience, they are an appeal for a response. So when you work with direct suggestions, set your deliberate actions temporarily aside and wait for your response to happen.

Direct Suggestion Experiment

Try this direct suggestion as an experiment. Clasp your hands together with your fingers intertwined. Sit for a moment and feel your fingers intertwined. Then tell yourself that your fingers will begin to feel stuck together. Let the stuck-together feeling increase. Now try to slowly separate your fingers. Do you feel some resistance as you move your fingers apart? If so, you have responded to a direct suggestion.

If you were able to respond to this exercise, you will probably find that direct suggestion can be a useful tool for you to use throughout this book. If not, indirect suggestion may work better for you. But even if direct suggestion is effective in your situation, you still may also want to make use of indirect suggestions.

Indirect Suggestion

There are many forms of indirect suggestion: open-ended suggestions, compound and contingent suggestions, acceptance sets, and binds, to name a few. Some of them can be creatively adapted for self-hypnosis as you develop an open attitude toward your inner self. Using indirect suggestion in self-hypnosis requires that you set the stage for yourself with the general concept of suggestion. You can create both the specific description of the suggestion and the expected response, outside of awareness, intuitively.

Indirect suggestions tend to be subtle. An indirect suggestion does not tell you exactly what to experience, but gently guides and activates a response. For example, this is an indirect suggestion: "As I focus my attention on my eyelids, I wonder if they might get heavy and want to close?" Notice how the indirect suggestions can bring about the same kinds of responses as the direct suggestions you did earlier, but in a more permissive and open-ended way. This allows your unique personality to express itself and make the effect even stronger. Creative responses can come up that may turn out to be specifically what is needed. For example, you may find that your eyes feel watery and close at just that moment, coincidentally.

Indirect Suggestion Experiment

Clasp your hands together again. Notice the sensations of your hands intertwined. As you sit comfortably noticing your hands, you might enjoy feeling uncertain of which finger goes to what hand. You could wait for any interesting sensations that occur naturally such as a stuck-together feeling, warmth or coolness, tightness or looseness, or anything else that you spontaneously feel. When you are ready to separate your hands, let them come apart as slowly as they would like. What do you experience? Some people will feel like their hands became stuck together and that separating them is difficult, but this is just one of many possibilities. If you had any kind of experience in your hands, you have felt a response to indirect suggestion.

With indirect suggestion, you may not do exactly what has been suggested, but you will respond somehow. Also, you may not always respond immediately to the exact suggestion. You can feel confident, however, that you will respond in your own way and with your own timing.

In our many years of work with hypnosis, we have repeatedly seen the powerful effects of indirect suggestion. This form of suggestion allows you to work with and develop the best reactions from your unconscious. Indirect suggestions activate nourishing and healing responses.

Varieties of Indirect Suggestion

Suggestion uses the imagination and focus of attention to enhance ideomotor suggestive responses. You can activate these natural mechanisms of your brain and mind creatively, trusting that unconsciously, you will find your own best ways to free yourself from problematic difficulties and discover new ways of coping. Each person has his or her own individuality, and you can learn to work with yours in order to help yourself most effectively. Indirect forms of suggestion utilize your tendency to actively construct your own hypnotic responses from stimuli and suggestions. As you develop an open attitude toward your personal style, indirect suggestions can be adapted well to self-hypnosis.

Open-Ended Suggestions Exercise

Open-ended suggestions are an easy form of indirect self-suggestion to use. Try using open-ended suggestions with and without trance, to learn what your natural preference is.

Offer an open-ended suggestion to yourself with many possible responses. For example, "I wonder whether I could have an experience in my hand. It could become light, heavy, warm, cool. I don't know what I will feel, but will wait for my response."

Compound and Contingent Suggestions Exercise

In their simplest form, compound suggestions are made up of two statements connected by "and." Contingent suggestions involve two usually unrelated suggestions, which you relate together, one dependent on the other, for hypnotic experience.

Experiment by holding your arm out and suggesting to yourself, "As I hold my arm out it becomes heavier and heavier." In this experiment, a contingent link is made between holding out the arm and a suggested effect.

Bind Suggestion Exercise

Bind suggestions are numerous and potentially complex in their nature. For self-hypnosis some binds can be used, but others are difficult to place on yourself. The following bind exercise can be helpful in learning to apply binds in self-hypnosis.

Sit comfortably and place your hands on your knees. Pay careful attention to your right hand, then your left hand, and ask which one will be lighter, which heavier. Wait for your response; wonder which one will do what. You should not attempt to guess or anticipate. Just let it happen.

Posthypnotic Suggestion Exercise

Suggestion can also be applied post-hypnotically, intended to take effect after the trance is terminated. Posthypnotic suggestion is a field of application that derives naturally from trance work, allowing unconscious factors to take effect. When you act on a posthypnotic suggestion, you might spontaneously induce a brief trance, linked to the performance of the suggested action. After a posthypnotic response, you can go into trance quite easily. Posthypnotic behavior can be used in self-hypnosis to enhance what you have learned in trance. Various factors may affect how you respond to posthypnotic suggestions. Experiment to discover the most effective ways for you to respond. Start with a simple posthypnotic suggestion that permits time and individualization of response, using open-ended suggestions. Then experiment with varieties of posthypnotic suggestions. As response to one posthypnotic suggestion is gained, try several suggestions in succession.

Try to give yourself this posthypnotic suggestion: As you work through this book, you will experiment with trance using the self-hypnosis methods in later chapters. Suggest now that when you try to produce self-hypnosis in yourself, it will be easier for you to go into trance. You can also suggest that following trance, you will feel more relaxed and calm. As your ability to respond evolves, try other positive and useful suggestions.

The Use of Waking Suggestion for Change

You can use the tendency to set situations to your advantage by enlisting the help of self-suggestion. Since suggestion is not the same as trance, you can use waking suggestions—given when you are fully alert, going about your life—to help reinforce the process of change. Émile Coué encouraged his patients to say to themselves: "Every day, in every respect, I am getting better and better" (Coué, 1923, p. 22).

The use of a strong, direct suggestion that encourages you in the direction you want to go may be helpful. When making a waking self-suggestion, vividly imagine it filling your thoughts. The force of the imagination is far greater than the will, so do not will yourself to accept the suggestion, simply vividly imagine yourself doing it.

Also, try some open-ended indirect suggestions to stimulate more responsiveness by inviting and allowing an interesting experience. Here are a few direct and indirect suggestions that you could try. You may think of others that are specific to you and your situation. Be flexible, open-minded, and positive with yourself.

- I have overcome difficulties at times in my life and I can overcome this difficulty now.
- I can change a little bit every day.
- I have a great deal of positive potential and untapped resources.
- I am gaining new skills that can begin helping me now.
- I'm okay. I accept myself.
- I can do this!
- I don't know how long change will take, but I open myself to it and await change hopefully.
- My unconscious processes are a positive resource that are there to help me, and even though I may not understand just how the change will happen, I welcome the changes that will take place.

Regularly suggest the one or ones you choose at various moments over a period of time, not just once. It may take time to affect you, and even more time to reach awareness. Allow the time for change that it takes. There is no set external standard that you can use as a criterion of progress, only your own inner cycle.

Noticing Negative Self-Suggestions

Try to become aware of subtle, inner discouragement that you may be giving yourself. Pay attention at various times during the day to catch any subtle, negative suggestions you might be giving yourself without realizing it. Now that you have some sense of how suggestion works, you may recognize how dwelling on negativity can also fill your imagination.

As you begin to notice negative suggestions, be careful not to get annoyed at yourself. Keep an aware, but nonjudgmental, attitude. Recognize that you are on a journey of discovery and sometimes you may find areas that you do not like, ways that you need to change. Be patient with what seem to be shortcomings, because they may be the seeds of undiscovered potential. You will make changes that are needed, but the first step is becoming aware of how you are preventing yourself from changing.

Going from Negative to Positive

Buddha told his followers that change is always two-sided: first, it involves doing what is right and second, it involves *not* doing what is wrong. When making a change, it is essential for you to stop doing unproductive, unhelpful things that hold you back. This wisdom is very applicable to self-suggestion. You may be finding it helpful to give yourself positive suggestions, but you will have an even stronger effect if you can also stop giving yourself negative ones. So if you suggest to yourself, "I can do it!" you must also stop suggesting, "I can't do it!" This may seem obvious, but negative self-suggestion often sneaks in, unnoticed.

Enhancing the Success of Suggestions

An important factor affecting whether a suggestion is accepted or rejected involves the mental mindset of the person at the time of the suggestion. If people expect the worst to happen, they may unintentionally tend to bring it about through unconscious ideomotor mechanisms, paradoxically confirming their belief. Therapy entails altering expectations in a positive direction, so that people develop hopeful and positive expectations toward the future (Frank & Frank, 1991). Then the ideomotor mechanism works in their favor. Negative expectations lead the imagination away from the positive potential in a situation. Instead, people with negative expectations may feel discouraged from tackling challenges wholeheartedly, given that they perceive themselves to have only limited resources. Suggestion aims at these expectancies, to turn them around. Positive expectations encourage the transcendence of mediocre functioning, to open the door to unrealized potentials. With a positive attitude, adverse circumstances transform into challenging invitations to outgrow narrow boundaries of adjustment. Positive expectations are therefore useful.

Suggestion takes effect within the total context, the suggestion situation. The boundaries are the person giving the suggestion, the person receiving the suggestion, and the circumstances at the time (Weitzenhoffer, 1957). Many factors affect how we respond to suggestions. Suggestibility is primarily a function of your perceptual field, influenced by the setting or circumstances. We understand simple, clear circumstances and therefore can react to simple problems with our cognitive faculties. But increases in ambiguity and complexity may lead to failure to understand things consciously. If your situation is filled with unknowns or ambiguity, you don't tend to respond rationally. Complexity and ambiguity lead to scanning for parameters to help interpret matters. We grope for cues, and in this state of indecision and frustration there is a tendency to become more open to suggestion. Consequently, complex problems may be better helped by the therapeutic use of suggestion, which activates the wisdom of unconscious processes.

Conclusion

Throughout this book you will experiment with many forms of suggestion. These are tools intended to facilitate your work with self-hypnosis. Some readers may find that they respond best to direct approaches, while others may prefer subtle, indirect methods. Try various methods, and take note of what happens. What works best for you? Try to notice subtle, slower effects as well as the more obvious, immediate ones. Accept what your individuality gives you. Hypnotic learning takes place in your own mind. Associations to a suggested idea can be as helpful as your overt response to the suggestion at hand. Observe your reactions and tendencies. With time you will know your patterns, so you can elicit the responses you need, and expand upon them.

PART III

Experiencing Self-Hypnosis

8

Entering Trance

Floating like a white bird on the water. Floating on a great river of life—a great
smooth silent river that flows so still, so still, you might almost think it was asleep.
A sleeping river. But it flows irresistibly.

—Aldous Huxley, *Island*, p. 29

In the 1950s, the famous author Aldous Huxley learned to enter hypnosis under
the guidance of Milton H. Erickson (Erickson, 1965). The passage above describes
a trance induction given to one of the characters in Huxley's book *Island*. The felt
experience is vividly expressed. We invite you now to make a shift, from explicit
to implicit, from conceptualizing to sensing, from theory to practice. Experience
is ultimately the best teacher of hypnosis; as has been shown, unconscious understanding is nonconceptual, procedural, and involves visual, motor, or sensory
knowing, which is often best learned through personal experience. Everyone has
individual talents—some are good at dancing, others can draw accurately, while
others are adept at calculations. Similarly, we also have unconscious talents we
may know nothing about. We take these abilities for granted, as we just express
them, without thought. Some people are naturally able to relax, and some can
easily develop visual hallucinations (such as seeing colors when they close their
eyes), while others can forget or remember readily. Unconscious tendencies are

not always recognized as potential talents, and may even be considered problems or shortcomings. For example, forgetfulness might seem to be a difficulty, but sometimes forgetting clears the way to remembering what is important. Properly applied and worked with hypnotically, unconscious tendencies can be useful talents that lead to change and growth.

Approach these exercises with an open mind. You may find some exercises easier than others. Consider your efforts to be like an exploratory scientific experiment. You begin with the gathering of data to be analyzed at a later time. Then you will observe and notice thoughts, experiences, and reactions. These will become individual building blocks for trance. Do not pass judgment or draw conclusions while still collecting data. Allow time for them to be viewed as meaningful parts of a whole.

Do one exercise at a time, followed by reading of commentary. If you prefer, read ahead, then return to the exercises. Do not overload yourself, as there is no advantage to be gained from hurrying through the exercises. Cultivate sensitivity to your personal rhythms and timing.

Read the entire exercise several times, then set the book aside. Make yourself comfortable and try to do what you can remember from the exercise. Do not be concerned with what you may forget. Encourage yourself to have positive experiences with the exercises, and then trust the process. Discontinue any exercises that elicit discomfort. Check with your doctor or psychologist if in any doubt about the suitability for you. Go to a comfortable, safe place where you will not be disturbed, perhaps with a trusted friend, partner, or family member, to experience and experiment with phenomena.

Preliminary Exercises

When readying yourself for your first hypnotic experience, you may wonder if you are going to experience something utterly new, something you have never done before. The answer is yes and no. We all experience fluctuations in consciousness, such as when you discover that you have been daydreaming while idly waiting for someone. You might feel somewhat inattentive, quietly relaxed without really noticing anything in particular. You might have a quite different experience when waiting, for example, for a plane to land or a car to arrive, marking the beginning of a long-awaited vacation. At that moment your consciousness might be sharply focused and engaged in excitement and anticipation. Everyday consciousness can vary a great deal, and you can learn to use any of these experiences to help you alter your consciousness deliberately, in order to enter hypnosis. The best place to start is where you are, and so you can begin your trance experience with what you feel right now.

Exploring Everyday Awareness Right Now Exercise

Find a comfortable position to sit or lie down. Allow your breathing to be comfortable and just sit for a moment. As you do, let your thoughts drift and your attention roam wherever it likes for several minutes. Try not to get lost in any one thought-path; simply notice associations and let them go. After several minutes, reflect gently on what you are experiencing. Do you feel calm and relaxed? Do you feel tired and vaguely inattentive? Or is your awareness heightened in anticipation? Whatever the quality of your attention, allow yourself to sit quietly for a moment.

Exercise in Everyday Out of Awareness Unconscious

To explore the varying qualities of awareness as it manifests itself in everyday life, turn your attention to your hands. You probably were not thinking about your hands, but now that we mention them, you become aware of whatever sensations you are having. Perhaps your hands feel cold, tingly, or maybe light. You cannot accurately guess what you will experience without simply paying attention and waiting for the response. The experience occurs in its own way and in its own time. Sometimes it is interesting to place one hand on each knee and pay attention to the weight of each hand. You might find that one hand feels immediately lighter or heavier than the other, or that at first they seem to feel the same, but as you pay attention one becomes heavier than the other. You may be surprised by your response. While you are waiting for one hand to start feeling lighter, you might discover unexpectedly that one hand becomes cooler, or maybe you have a new experience of your hand feeling very far away, or growing larger. You will respond in your own unique way, and you will not know ahead of time how you will respond. As you learn to allow and be attentive to your spontaneous responses, you will become acquainted with your natural tendencies, often not consciously known, which you can then learn to develop.

Exercise in Peripheral Associations

Relax once again. This time try to recall how you felt after you completed the previous exercise. Picture yourself sitting or lying comfortably and remember how your hands felt. As you focus on remembering, you will probably find your body beginning to relax a little. While thinking about the previous experience, fleeting thoughts probably flicker in the back of your mind. Shift attention to one of these peripheral thoughts or experiences. For example, as the dinner hour approaches, notice if a vague thought or image is present about food. Perhaps you realize you are thinking about a pleasant moment. These less obvious thoughts are present just outside awareness, but you usually do not bring them into consciousness. In this exercise, try to mentally reach for those flickering thoughts as they appear briefly in the stream of awareness.

To work with this, let your thoughts drift for a moment. If you notice a flicker into awareness that you cannot quite recognize, invite yourself to have a feeling, an image, a thought, or a clue. As you become more at ease with your unconscious, you will be surprised to discover that your unconscious will supply you with a relevant thought or image even if the direct connection is not obvious.

For example, a client came for hypnotherapy to help her cope with feeling stressed and uncomfortable about her marriage, job, and family. During therapeutic trance, we suggested that she have a meaningful image, something that could help her understand and outgrow her problems. First, she saw lights, mostly white streaks. Then she felt an intense nauseous feeling. After she awoke from trance, she described this with dismay. She thought that she had not been able to produce an image, as requested. She worried that she was incapable of imagery. She did not realize that her unconscious actually was very responsive, expressing meaning in a way personally meaningful to her, using vague rather than obvious symbolic analogy. Later she discovered her feeling of nausea had a hidden significance that she worked through in therapy.

Discovering Your Perceptual Mode

People tend to perceive in one perceptual mode more than another. For example, someone might characteristically say, "That feels right," or "I want to get in touch with that." This person tends to orient kinesthetically, that is, through feelings and sensations. Another person might say, "I see your point. That looks good." This is a visual orientation. A third type will use metaphors like, "Did you hear about this?" or "I hear that." These people usually can clearly recall the sound of someone's voice. They tend to use their auditory sensing to orient. These are the three main perceptual systems of orientation. Taste and smell can be used to orient at times, but they are relied on less often. Combinations and individual variations are also possible.

Some people do not orient perceptually, but tend to orient conceptually. Those who conceptualize will say, "I think this is a beautiful day." Their thoughts about their perceptions are most central.

You will use all of these modes at various times, but you typically use one mode more than another. The exercise that follows will familiarize you with your own spontaneous mode of choice used for perceiving and processing.

Perceptual Mode Exercise

Sit quietly and relax, as in the other exercises. Now recall the moment when you first opened this book. Think about it for a moment, remembering as much about it as you can. Notice how you recall: Do you see a picture of the pages or your hands opening the cover? Do you remember how you were feeling—maybe tired, sore, wide awake, happy, or curious about the content? Perhaps you remember the sound of the pages as you turned them or the song that was playing on the radio at the time, or the noise from the street outside. Or you may recall what you were thinking about, such as your plans for the day or your ideas about hypnosis. If you saw a picture, you probably tend to orient visually. If you felt sensation, you may be more kinesthetic. If you heard sounds, you probably tend to orient through the auditory mode. If you experienced a series of thoughts, you are probably more conceptual. You may have combinations of these as well. Try this experiment a few times during the day using different memories and different tasks to double-check your results. Look for consistent patterns.

Once you determine your favorite mode, use this in the early exercises when there is a choice of modes given. Later, you will be encouraged to develop other modes. Each mode offers richness in experience and alternative inroads into the unconscious. You may be surprised to discover that you have been inadvertently limiting yourself to only one. Other modes of experience can also become comfortable and natural. We use our favorite mode as our map, for orienting in new territory. After you become familiar with your unconscious, you will not need to be restricted to this one mode.

Body Image Alterations

People take their body image for granted, as a fixed reality. Unless we have a change in our usual body experience, our general sensation of body image often goes unnoticed. Hypnosis can allow you to experience and work with changes in body image, and creatively apply what you learn to related problems.

Preparation for Body Image Alteration Exercise

Sit or lie down quietly. Let your muscles settle. Recall whether you had a stronger visual (seeing), auditory (hearing), kinesthetic (feeling), or conceptual (thinking) response in the previous exercise. You can use your preferred mode to achieve maximal relaxation for you. Your unconscious will regulate the level. Try not to prevent your natural response from occurring. Honest curiosity about what this experience will be like will help you. Wonder how you will feel. Wait for your response.

Getting Ready for Self-Hypnosis

You have done a number of preliminary exercises that developed some component skills for the hypnotic experience. Now you can begin to learn self-hypnosis.

Find a quiet and comfortable place where you can do this without pressure or interruption for at least 15 minutes. Knowing that you will be trying your first trance, you may feel excited or nervous. Glance inwardly now to note any attitudes you might have about doing self-hypnosis. Or, you may wish to pay attention to your feelings about trance, or perhaps listen to the inner dialogue of your thoughts. What are your reactions?

Sometimes people have superstitious ideas about the powers of hypnosis from television shows and movies, about how it can take control of the mind. Research indicates that no one has ever been harmed by hypnosis itself (Kroger, 1977, p. 104). Hypnosis allows you to be in touch with your inner needs and motivations. You will not do or experience anything that is inconsistent with your true nature, including your ethics and morals. It is reassuring to realize that personality remains constant. You nature does not change due to hypnosis.

Imagining Trance Exercise

Imagine for a moment what you expect trance to feel like. People sometimes say that they expect to feel relaxed or calm, to have their body become cool or warm, or to feel light or tingly. If you discovered in the earlier exercises that you tend to orient visually, try a visual image. Picture yourself in trance. Do you look relaxed? Are your eyes open or closed? Use your perceptual mode to imagine yourself in trance. Notice your response. Does it surprise you or is it consistent with your expectations? If you truly feel surprised, you have probably had a genuine unconscious response.

Now, you are ready for your first hypnotic experience, using your preferred mode. If you are curious, try all of these inductions at different times.

Trance of Listening Exercise

Recall a sound of nature, like the ocean waves, a bubbling brook, the quiet of a winter snowfall, the wind rustling through the trees, or any other sound which you have enjoyed. Focus your attention on this, but do not force or rush the sound. Simply wait for it to fill out, to become even fuller, or perhaps to alter in some way you do not expect. While you listen, your body can relax even more deeply. Your muscles settle, letting go of any unnecessary tension. Continue listening, allowing any other images, thoughts, or feelings to develop as well. Deepen the experience when you feel ready. Continue to relax deeply. Let your thoughts drift. When you feel ready, awaken from trance by counting backwards from five to one. With each number, as you approach one, you will become more alert, all your sensations returning to normal. If you finish but continue to feel unusual sensations, wait for a few minutes. Then, if you need to, close your eyes again and go back into trance for a minute or two. Suggest that your sensations will now return to normal and again count backwards from five to one.

Transitions in and out of trance become smoother and easier with practice. As you grow more familiar with hypnosis, you may not need to count your way out of trance. We may not explicitly tell you to count backwards after each exercise that follows, but use this technique if it helps make the transition to being awake easier. Alternatively, you may evolve your own way of awakening from trance.

Trance of Seeing Exercise

Recall an image or a place you have been and really enjoyed: perhaps a vacation spot, a hideaway in the mountains, a secluded beach, or a forest. Picture the beauty; look at the colors; walk around and reacquaint yourself with it. You would be relaxed if you went there, so your body can relax while you picture this place. You might see these images vividly, or they could be vague wisps of pictures and colors flickering past. However they appear, you can enhance the experience with a comfortable feeling of relaxation all over. Picture yourself relaxing even more as you wonder how deeply relaxed you can become. Let your thoughts drift. When you feel ready, bring yourself out of trance until you feel fully alert.

Trance of Feeling Exercise

You will probably find your attention wandering to the feeling in your body, and recall a very nice feeling of calm, both inner and outer. Ask all of your muscles to settle and relax. Can you silently recall a time in your life when you felt totally at ease, calm, and comfortable? Perhaps a clear memory will come to mind or only a vague recollection. Recall where you were, as in the previous mode exercises, but focus on the feeling you had in your body, of calmness or happiness. Fill out the details naturally with memories of the sensations, or other relevant feelings. You may be curious and interested in just what it would be like to relax deeper than you ever have before. Wait for the response as you continue to imagine that calm, comfortable feeling. Let your thoughts drift. When you feel ready, bring yourself out of trance until you feel fully alert.

In the exercises that follow, we may ask you to imagine an image. You might respond with a feeling, thought, a sound, or perhaps nothing at all. Keep in mind that these are all legitimate responses—your inroads into a working relationship with your unconscious. These links between conscious and unconscious are the keys to successfully learning and applying self-hypnosis.

If you have had difficulty thus far with the exercises, turn to Chapter 10, on resistance, then return here after you have experimented with defenses and resistance.

Trance Ratification

The trance experience is not always easy to recognize at first. You may have noticed that you were relaxed and calm but may feel that this is not anything unusual or different from ordinary waking. Confirmation that trance is happening helps to intensify the experience and leads to an increase in trance abilities. Erickson and Rossi refer to this as trance ratification (Erickson & Rossi, 1980a). Ideomotor signaling is useful for this.

Exercise in Ideomotor Signaling

Sit or lie down so that your hands rest either on your legs or by your side. Experiment with one of the previous exercises during which you felt responsive. Invite yourself to become even more relaxed than during that exercise. Once you feel comfortable, focus on your hands. Consider how frequently people move their hands in conversation without thinking about it. Sometimes the gesture is even more meaningful than the words. Do you talk with your hands?

Now, ask your unconscious a "yes" or "no" question. Designate one hand as "yes" and the other hand as "no." Choose a question for which you do not have the answer, such as: Would my unconscious like my legs to relax? Can I feel tingling in my fingertips? Can I have a pleasant memory? Can I see colors when I close my eyes? Now, wait and pay close attention to your hands. Do not try to move them, simply notice. Sometimes people feel the answer as tingling, lightness, or heaviness in one hand or the other. Sometimes a person will notice warmth or coolness. Still others will feel a finger lift up in one hand or the other, or maybe a feeling jumping from one hand to the other and back again. After a little while, you will know what your response has been, and in which hand. If you felt something in your hand, you unconsciously answered the question.

Conclusion

By using more of your potential, you open up to new possibilities for change. Entering trance may not be what you expected, or exactly as you thought it would be. These mysteries can make activating more of your mind and brain a fascinating exploration. Your conscious processes do not know what your unconscious processes already know. Conscious and unconscious, attention and inattention, thinking and sensing, movement and stillness—all can contribute in unique ways to deepen your hypnotic experience and offer a wealth of potentials for fostering the change you want.

9

Experimenting with Trance Phenomena

So I must become purposeless on purpose.

—Zen Proverb

THE experience of hypnosis can be enhanced by producing some of the classic hypnotic phenomena, such as automatic movement, vivid imagery, changes in sensation or hypersensitivity, or alterations in time consciousness. Experiment with all of the trance techniques in this chapter. You may find some are easier than others at first, but eventually you will probably gain skills in most of them.

Hand Levitation

Lightness and movement developing in a finger, hand, or arm are components of a classic hypnotic practice called hand levitation. The finger, hand, or arm feels as if it is moving by itself. You do not need to do anything in particular except to allow it to occur naturally. People who tend to use the kinesthetic mode may find this easier to do, but anyone can learn to experience it with practice. Hand levitation is done by following each successful action in sequence, which gradually gather momentum. Everything that you have already learned from this book will help to channel and shape your response. These exercises can be repeated as often as you like.

Exercise in Hand Levitation

Sit or lie down in such a way that your hands and arms are comfortable and free to move. If you are sitting, let a hand rest, palm down, on each kneecap. If you are lying down, place your hands down by your side, or fold them across your body. Do not restrain one hand with the other. Loosen your muscles, and focus attention on your hands. Notice any sensations you begin to have in your hands. One common feeling is a tingling in the fingertips. You might compare your two hands: Does one hand feel more tingly, or perhaps lighter, heavier, warmer, or cooler? Stay with the experience and ask your unconscious what it would be like for the tingling, warming, or whatever you are experiencing, to begin to lead to a feeling of lightness. You may feel as if something is tugging on your finger, thumb, or hand, like a helium balloon tied to your finger or wrist. You may begin to feel a pleasant lightness that grows lighter with every breath. Perhaps the tingling increases, bringing about upward movement. Do not inhibit the movement. Follow this experience sensitively, and let your fingers begin to raise. Stay with it and invite the lightness to increase, and your hand to raise even higher. If you like, suggest that your hand lift all the way up to touch your face. When it does, your relaxation in trance deepens more than before.

Give yourself time to allow these sensations to develop. You do not know which hand will respond and just what it will be like, but you can, as in previous exercises, become increasingly curious about how your unconscious will respond. Many creative variations are possible.

Hand levitation can be useful symbolically for overcoming problems. A client underwent hypnosis to learn to control his temper. He was an intelligent lawyer whose temper was interfering with his professional and personal life. His wife felt concerned as well because when he felt angry, he would throw things, breaking dishes and putting dents in the wall. His temper was not only emotionally disruptive, but it was also costing them money! Before the trance, we discussed hand levitation as one hypnotic method from which he could learn. He said he was curious about it but thought it would be very difficult to actually do. He developed a comfortable trance and even smiled as he entered trance. Hand levitation was suggested in a similar manner to how it was described in the above exercise. His hands barely moved, if at all, but his face became flushed and a few beads of sweat appeared on his brow. Upon awakening he recounted what he referred to as a "marvelous experience." He said that the levitation was so powerful that he was doing jumping jacks! The experience was vivid for him. He felt as if he had exerted tremendous energy. He was extremely pleased to realize that he could have such an intense experience in his imagination. This was pivotal in the moderation of his temper, teaching him that he could think an angry thought but not have to express it in action. He learned that control was possible for him.

Events that transpire during hypnosis do not always correlate with what they seem to be. An experience can become a metaphor, a symbol, or lead to something new—an inspiration for growth and learning.

Automatic Writing and Drawing

Another variation of automatic movement can be applied to writing. Automatic writing can be a way to express unconscious feelings or ideas that have not quite taken a verbal form consciously. For example, you have probably had the experience of talking on the phone or attending a boring lecture, and finding yourself writing or drawing automatically without thinking about it. This is a natural capacity and can be used in hypnosis to allow you to express yourself. Some people begin with just a small drawing or a few words, but with practice, automatic writing or drawing will flow freely. Figure 9.1 shows examples of automatic writing from clients in trance who were working on therapeutic change.

Exercise with Automatic Writing or Drawing

Sit upright with a well-supported piece of paper on your lap. Place a pen that has a sensitive tip that will not require much pressure, such as a rollerball pen, on the paper. You can also use a soft-lead pencil. Hold the pen or pencil as if ready to write, with the tip on the paper. Then, go into trance and suggest movement, similarly to how you did with hand levitation. Imagine your hand tingling, warm, or light and wanting to move. Use the

*Figure 9.1. Samples of auto-
matic writing.*

sensory experience that comes to mind, now, as you are allowing your trance to deepen.
Allow your hand to move, as it wants to.

Another way to do automatic writing is to distract your conscious attention as you allow your unconscious processes to flow.

Automatic Writing with Distractions Exercise

Sit as in the previous exercise, with pen or pencil in hand, lightly touching the paper. Before you begin, invite your unconscious processes to feel free to write or draw. Then, close your eyes and recite the multiplication tables or review a list of things you have to do, or any other well-laid-out, rational task you can think of. Keep going over the task until you feel ready to stop. Then, come out of trance and see what you have produced. You may want to sign and date your work.

Visual Imagery and Hallucination

Visual images often occur automatically in trance. Most people can learn to see visual imagery, even though it might be easier for some than for others. Vividness in mental imagery is a natural talent, but can be developed further with correct practice.

A classic method for entering trance is to focus the gaze on one object. The hypnotic subject is encouraged to look at an object that can fascinate, like a crystal, a lit candle, or a turning spiral. Use whatever interests you. We have often used wooden art, such as on the cover of this book. Milton Erickson had a beautiful quartz crystal on his desk for patients to look at. We provide an illustration here, but feel free to pick anything that interests you (Figure 9.2). Be imaginative.

Exercise in Hallucination

To begin, look at the object carefully. Study it, noticing all its components, the colors, and the shapes. Next look at the outline, then the interior. Watch very carefully, focusing all your attention on the object. As you concentrate fully on it, your thoughts can drift.

Figure 9.2. The Spiral. Wooden veneer art. C. Alexander Simpkins and Annellen M. Simpkins, 2006.

Think about the object, look at the object, and study it. As you gaze, you can let your body relax and your breathing rate settle. Let your eyes move around the object after you have studied all the different components. Can you see any alterations in the object as you look? For example, you may see blurring, a change in the colors, or an alteration in shape. Perhaps you notice aspects of the object you did not notice at first. How does the object appear to alter? Try suggesting a change in the object's appearance that you would be curious to experience, and wait for your response. Then relax your vision and let yourself return to normal seeing.

Interesting objects are often looked at as a hypnotic tool. However, since hypnosis is an inner experience, seek the image within.

Exercise in Inner Imagery

In this exercise, begin by relaxing your body as before. You might like to try this exercise after trying the previous one. As you are looking at your chosen object, imagine your eyelids becoming heavy. Suggest that your eyelids grow heavier and heavier. Wait for your eyes to feel ready to close. Then allow your eyelids to close. If they do not want to, after a long wait, close your eyes anyway. Relax your eyelids and allow your entire body to relax very deeply.

It is possible to visualize color in formless, abstract, or symbolic form. At first the color may appear as just one shade. Gradually it could alter in its shade or depth, or even change to a new color entirely. Sometimes people see a kaleidoscope of colors. Other times people see white or black afterimages, lights, or streaks. Experiment with offering a suggestion for a color you would like to experience. Wait for your response. Watch it evolve.

Anesthesia and Hyperesthesia

Anesthesia is a well-documented effect that can be produced during hypnosis. In fact, hypnosis has been used as the only form of anesthesia for surgery. For example, an educational film made in the 1950s shows a woman undergoing her fourth Cesarean birth under hypnosis with no pain. Hypnosis was used predominantly during surgery before the discovery of chloroform.

Classically anesthesia has been produced by direct suggestion, relying upon the subject's suggestibility. Hypnotic effectiveness does not only depend upon suggestibility; other factors play an important part as well.

Motivation can enhance the ability to produce hypnotic anesthesia. A client who was working on an intense personality change used hypnosis occasionally to relax. She did not think she was very good at hypnosis and even doubted its efficacy. She was an intelligent woman in her late 20s who suffered from intense anxiety. She felt stuck in an uncomfortable job and living situation. She tended to be judgmental, especially toward herself. During the course of treatment she had to get a tooth extracted, and she decided to give hypnosis a try, without the use of narcotics for pain during the surgery. She had no idea before the appointment how she would cope with only local anesthesia. She reported at her session following the dental work that she felt nervous at first, but that once in the chair she went into trance. She spontaneously imagined little creatures in her mouth with brooms, rolling big balls of pain away. While she viewed this amusing image, she became calm. She handled the procedure well and needed no medication afterwards. She had not expected to use an image, especially such a seemingly silly one, but it worked. Even her dentist laughed when she told him.

Hypnosis can affect pain in many complex ways. Prepare well before you attempt to apply these skills in practice. Do not substitute for good professional care; rather, enhance it with self-hypnotic technique.

Exercise to Practice Anesthesia with Direct Suggestion

Find a comfortable level of trance, suggesting relaxation and comfort of the body. Decide where you would like to produce the anesthesia: perhaps in your hand, head, or foot? Next, give yourself a suggestion in a mode that you have used successfully before—or you might want to experiment with something new. You could recall a time when you were outside in very cold temperatures, and after a period of time your nose and cheeks became so cold that they were numb. Recall the tingling, followed by a feeling of numbness. Suggest that the body part is tingling as it becomes colder and colder, until you can no longer feel it.

Sometimes you can produce anesthesia in a part of your body by dissociating from that body part. Imagine that your hand, arm, or wherever you have chosen feels far away from the rest of your body. You might feel as if your hand, for example, is growing in size at first, and then seems to take on an unreal or distant quality. Some subjects improve watching themselves from a distance. One client felt like he left his body sitting in the session and went to the beach. Some people feel a tingling or temperature alteration before the hand or arm begins to feel distant or numb. You can test yourself once you feel that you have achieved an adequate anesthesia by touching the anesthetized body part.

Hyperesthesia

Many know that hypnosis can reduce sensations, but few realize that hypnosis can also enhance sensations. This can be useful in some circumstances. A young woman in her 30s came for hypnotherapy. She owned her own tailoring business. She described herself as laid-back, but other people told her she was careless. She complained that sometimes she would miss a small detail during a sewing or altering job, which would cause her to have to redo the work. Even though she was a skilled tailor, her casualness was causing her to lose profits. She valued being a casual "beach person" by nature and felt reluctant to give up that identity. Yet, she knew she needed to improve in her work.

She enjoyed going into hypnosis. She especially liked what she called a "laid-back feeling of calm and relaxation" which occurred for her during hypnosis. We suggested that, during trance, she have an image of a place where she felt comfortable. She recalled a cottage where she had spent the summers during her childhood. She remembered many details: the sound of the lake water against the dock, the smell of the pine trees which surrounded the lake, the sparkle of the sun shining through the trees. She reexperienced the fine points of family events which she had long forgotten. She practiced recalling experiences during several sessions, and felt more confident each week. We also guided her in focusing on her body sensations, noticing how long her arms were, how far it was from shoulder to shoulder, the weight of her hands, and the temperature of her legs. This brought her deeper into trance. She became so sensitive that she could feel a whisper of a breeze or a minute touch to her hand.

During her fourth session she reported that she was experiencing some changes in her work without really trying. Seemingly automatically, she found herself paying closer attention, listening intently, looking carefully, and noticing exact details in her stitching. Her careful attentiveness resulted in a week with no errors or returns. At the same time, she was able to remain casual and laid-back, since the changes felt like they were happening automatically.

Hyperesthesia can be developed effortlessly in trance, and applied in useful ways in your life.

Exercise in Hyperesthesia

Begin with a memory, perhaps a place or an experience you enjoyed or one that happened very recently. Now consider what it would be like to recall details of the experience that you have forgotten. Concentrate on sense memories such as taste, smell, touch, or sound. Was there a bird or cricket chirping? Did the waves pound at the ocean? Can you recall the sound of a friend's voice? Wait for a memory to appear. Request that it become even clearer.

Time Distortion

Another natural ability of the unconscious is time distortion. Everyone has felt the minutes slowly ticking by while waiting in a long line at a store, sitting through a dull class, or enduring a boring dinner party. Conversely, there are times when the hours pass too quickly, and we wonder what happened to the day. These are both examples of the mind's natural ability to alter the experience of time.

If the average person were asked to define time, he or she would probably think of time as it seems on a clock. However, suppose everyone in a university course was asked how long the duration of a class session seemed. The answers would vary greatly. The interested, involved student would probably report a shorter duration than the bored, disinterested student. Time distortion occurs when the seeming duration of a time interval is different from the literal, clock-based time of that interval. Time can be distorted to appear to be moving either more quickly or more slowly than it really is, depending upon the experience. Both are natural and can be utilized for creative and therapeutic applications.

Milton Erickson and Linn Cooper did extensive research on this phenomenon (Cooper & Erickson, 1982, pp. 20–22). They carefully set up experimental definitions of time distortion to refer to the discrepancy between clock time and experiential time over a given time interval. During one experiment a trance subject was instructed to imagine going to a cotton field and picking four rows of cotton, counting the bolls as she picked them, one at a time. The subject was not to hurry. She was instructed to raise her hand when she finished. She raised her hand 217 seconds after she began and she reported picking 719 cotton bolls. She stated that she seemed to have been working for 1 hour and 20 minutes.

The second experiment involved the same task, except the experimenter put a time limit on the task. The time allotted was only 3 seconds. Amazingly, the subject reported an even stronger time-distortion effect. She had picked 862 bolls and it seemed like an entire hour and 20 minutes had passed! In both experiments, the subject had a time distortion experience, and by the second time, her skills improved dramatically.

The following exercises will illustrate both the experience of time speeding up and that of time slowing down. Each has its application and use. For example, speeding up the experience of time can be very useful for pain control, while slowing it down can make it possible to accomplish a task more thoroughly.

Preliminary Exercise in Time Distortion

Go into trance, relax, and be comfortable. Think about time for a moment. Picture the hands of a clock. Watch them move for a 5-minute period. Wonder whether you could tell the difference between 32 minutes and 33 minutes, or if you could distinguish an interval of 5 seconds from 6. Think about a time when you were very bored and time seemed to move very slowly. You may have felt this while waiting for something to happen. Next recall a time when the hours passed so quickly that looking back, the event seemed over before it started. Holidays often leave people with this experience. Let your mind drift and let associations flow freely. Relax very deeply. When you are ready, clear your mind of thought for a moment. Perhaps you would like to imagine a lake settling, where all the mud sinks to the bottom. The water becomes crystal clear, like your mind can be. When you are ready, wake up refreshed and alert.

Exercise in Slowing Down Time

You can give yourself a basic experience in time distortion. Find a safe, quiet place outdoors where you can walk comfortably with someone without speaking, for what feels like 15 minutes. Do not try to direct your attention anywhere in particular. When it seems like 15 minutes have passed, stop and check your watch. Immediately following, take a walk together in a busier place where you are comfortable, for what feels like 15 minutes. Again, let your attention float, unfocused. Do not look at your watch until you think you have walked for at least 15 minutes. Afterwards, note what you experienced, and return home. If you sensed a difference between experienced time and clock time during either walk, you have felt time distortion.

Imaginative Time Distortion Exercise

Allow yourself to go comfortably into trance. Once you feel that you have found inner calm, recall your two walks. Think back on the surroundings of each, one at a time, and try to visualize yourself there again. Some people will actually feel as if they are reenacting the walk. Assure yourself that you have all the time you need to take the walks again, and do not rush. Follow this procedure for each of the two walks. When you have completed one, wake up, noting how long the walk seemed to take. Check the time on the clock and compare it with your experienced time. Next imagine the second walk. Again, when you are finished with the second walk, check the time on the clock and compare.

Trance Time Distortion Exercise

Check the clock before you go into trance. Let an image occur to you—any image or scene. While you watch, other images may appear, one after another. Let these images become as vivid as they can until you feel as if you are right there in the scene. Follow the scene until you feel ready to clear your mind of all images. You might suggest a blank, a black nothingness, or a bright light. Play with the possibilities as you wait for your response and enjoy deep relaxation. When you are ready, awaken relaxed and refreshed. Note how much time you felt passed, then compare it to the actual time that passed. Repeat this exercise a few times at different sessions, attempting to make the images more and more vivid.

Trance Time Distortion Exercise II

Go into trance and visualize yourself doing an activity which normally takes a fixed amount of clock time to complete. You can choose from one of the following three examples, or choose one of your own: 1) swim laps, jog, or ride a bike, for 15 to 20 minutes; 2) cook breakfast, including all preparations, for 15 to 20 minutes (let someone else do the dishes!); or 3) watch the first quarter of a football game or any other favorite sport. Another possibility is to watch the first act of a play you enjoy.

You have practiced this kind of trance phenomenon several times. Make your choice as to what you will imagine doing. If you prefer another activity that takes about 15 to 20 minutes, use it. Try to perform this exercise for what feels like 15 to 20 minutes. Remember to note the time before you go into trance and when you awaken. When you have found a comfortable level of trance, begin the imaginative activity. Allow yourself to become intensely interested in performing it. Take your time and work to the best of your ability. Do not hurry. Try to be thorough. When you have finished, clear your mind. Wake up refreshed and alert. You can repeat this exercise a few times at various sittings. If you notice a discrepancy between clock time and experienced time, you have felt time distortion.

Frequently people will experience time expansion with these exercises. However, both time expansion and time constriction are useful tools. One of our clients had an experience with time distortion that clarifies its surprising benefits. She was working for a large company while she was going to school in the evenings to become a health care worker. She told us she disliked her job and felt like the time dragged by each day. She felt she barely had any time for herself or her homework. Some of her coworkers, who were also consulting us for hypnosis at the same time, reported that they experienced her as hard to get along with at work.

Throughout treatment she went into a very deep trance and always had total amnesia for her trance experience. We taught her time distortion like that found in the exercises in this chapter. Her unconscious spontaneously came up with a creative solution to her dilemma. At her next session she reported a surprising discovery. She found that work had changed: The day seemed to speed by. But strangely, after she got home in the evening she felt she had all the time she could need. Weekends went by slowly and leisurely, filled with extra time. As the weeks passed she found, much to her surprise, that work grew increasingly pleasant for her because it went by so quickly. She was happier and more relaxed, since she knew she would have plenty of time after work and on weekends to do her school-work and whatever else she wanted to do. Her fellow workers experienced her as changed: much friendlier and easier to get along with. By the time she finished school and was ready to quit her job, she felt sorry to leave. She even cried at the good-bye party for her. Her coworkers said they would miss their enjoyable friend! She applied her hypnotic skills when given the invitation to do so; great benefit for her and others resulted, helping her cope and transcend.

Regression in Time

Many know that, during hypnosis, people can recall past memories. Although they are not always found to be accurate enough for a court of law, working with memories can be a helpful tool for therapy. Even though age regression is a controversial topic, we have found that it can be helpful with clients, especially when they keep in mind that memories do not necessarily reflect real-life events, but instead can be used as a significant indicator of how they feel about that past event *now*. Hypnosis allows you to go back in time to reexperience an event from earlier in your life that has been encoded in memory; this process is known as age regression. In this way, you can help to change the future for the better.

Exercise in Regression in Time

Sit quietly and recall what you had for breakfast this morning. Then, as you allow your relaxation to continue, think back to your last birthday. Allow yourself to remember what you were doing, and how you celebrated. Can you reach back even further now, to a time when you were on a pleasant vacation, perhaps several years ago, or even your very first memory of a wonderful vacation? Allow yourself to remember some of the sensory details, such as what your vacation spot looked like, the temperature of the air, and the beauty of the surroundings. Let yourself recall how you felt, and what it is like to feel younger now during this memory, and the pleasant feelings of being on vacation. Think about the people you were with, the sense of being together or any other interesting emotions you felt. Let yourself reexperience, now, the enjoyment you felt on this very pleasant vacation. When you are ready, allow yourself to come out of trance, keeping some of the nice relaxation that you felt.

Conclusion

In this chapter you have experimented with many different hypnotic possibilities. Hopefully, you have approached the exercises with openness to your individual abilities, developing and enlarging upon these skills. Creative adjustments will help transform difficulties and resistance into assets. You can return to these basic exercises over and over, adding to the learning you have begun, until eventually trance becomes a comfortable and readily available tool.

Chapter 10

Overcoming Resistance

The water that fills the kettle is drawn from the well of the mind whose bottom knows no depths, and the emptiness, which is conceptually liable to be mistaken for sheer nothingness, is in fact the reservoir of infinite potential.
—D. T. Suzuki, *Zen and Japanese Culture*, p. 298

MANY people will find themselves naturally able to enter hypnosis to some extent. But some may feel like nothing happens when they try to enter hypnosis, even though they want to have the experience and are sincerely trying. If you find yourself resisting the process even though you would like to experience its benefits, you can work with your reactions to find your way into trance. Any response gives you a place to start. The beginning is emptiness itself. Experiment with the exercises and ideas in this chapter, and be willing to try different methods. You may find that some ways feel more natural than others. Learning to work with resistance will not only help you experience self-hypnosis, but it will also help you dip deeply into the reservoir of your own potential.

The Neurobiology of Resistance

The brain has many pathways, which tend to activate in patterned ways, a kind of conditioned response. So, when you smell your favorite food cooking, your reward pathway is automatically activated, expecting the delicious taste and enjoyment you have experienced in the past upon eating this food. If you eat this food often, neuronal connections become strengthened, and your reaction is likely to be stronger. Negative responses can also become ingrained, such as a fear of heights, or a tendency to become angry quickly and easily. On a neuronal level, the neurons that fire together, wire together, and so patterns are formed. But these patterns are not set like mortar between bricks. Many of the synaptic connections between neurons can be changed because of neuroplasticity and neurogenesis—and so, you can alter the negative patterns that may be interfering with carrying out your good intentions all the way down to the neuronal level in your brain.

Many negative patterns begin for positive reasons. For example, we had a client who had a fear of water that originated when she was a small child. She lived in a house with a large pool in the backyard. When she was three years old, she was playing outside and fell into the pool. No one came to her aid immediately, and she nearly drowned. After that traumatic experience, she avoided the water, as a way to keep herself safe.

As the years passed, she became more afraid of water. Each time she even thought about water, her fear pathways of the brain were activated, seemingly as a protective mechanism. As an adult, her boyfriend had invited her to go on a cruise. She wanted to go, but felt too frightened to accept the invitation. She recounted other times during her life when she had missed good experiences. She tried many types of therapy that are usually successful with phobias, including exposure therapy, but none of them helped her get over her fear. This client is just one example of the many people who become frustrated with therapy and cannot benefit from what it has to offer. The problem is more complex than it appears from the symptom, and thus the therapy does not seem to help.

Why do people resist change, even when it is for their own good? This may be due to a secondary reward of the resistant behavior. Although much is lost from not being able to get over the problem, something is gained, and thus a compromise is made. People find some pleasure in their adjustment, even though it is usually not fully satisfying. And so, the secondary reward motivates them to repeat the pattern in search of some happiness. Our client had found reward in being left alone during the family trips to the pool and the beach. She took on an identity as a socially independent individual, a loner with inner strength. She grew to depend on this concept of herself as a unique individual as central to her identity. Through hypnotherapy, she learned how to truly be an individual without relying on a lower level of reward. She could participate in activities and enjoy them—and she got over her fear of the water as well.

Drug and alcohol addictions are a common way that people settle for unsatisfying, often harmful rewards. With addictions, the rewards diminish over time, making the habit less and less satisfying, yet people often stay stuck in their pattern of addiction.

Once the reward pathways are disengaged from the negative pattern, rewiring becomes possible. Having novel experiences can help neurons to form new synaptic connections, and forming different habits can help to make these new connections stronger. You can then disentangle from resistance to change and find new opportunities to rewire with new connections. By immersing yourself in something different, you may be surprised to discover that you have more potential than you thought.

We invite you to enjoy these exercises and trust the process. Begin with where you are now, and learn how to know the present moment more fully.

Following the Flow of Awareness Exercise

Find an undisturbed place and relax for a few moments, but do not go into trance. Instead, notice what you are experiencing. For example, if you are sitting in a chair, do you start to notice how your body feels while you sit in the chair? Or perhaps you consider doing this exercise, and then wonder how you will do it. Observe and notice each thought, as your attention roams about. If you got lost in a particular thought, return to simply following your awareness. Stay with experiencing the present moment until you feel ready to stop. Do this exercise several times in different settings until you can follow your awareness.

You may feel that the previous exercise was easy, perhaps even a bit dull. But what led you to stop when you did? Did you run out of things to notice? When did this happen? What areas were you ignoring? For example, some people do well with pointing out every object around them, and then they stop when there is nothing else to notice. They may avoid or ignore inner experiences, reactions, and associations, attending only to the outer field of experience. Sometimes people avoid what is happening now by remembering the past, or anticipating the future. Try to explore your own reactions to the exercise you just did. Do not chastise yourself for not noticing certain areas. You can learn as much about yourself by considering what you did not notice as by considering what you did notice. All of this will be useful data. Everything has its place, a piece in the jigsaw puzzle of mind.

Opening Your Mind to Change

People develop habitual ways of doing things. Habits in action are often associated with habits in thought. Certain characteristic patterns of thought tend to go along with habitual activity. You probably have noticed this while carrying out your typical activities, such as washing the dishes or driving your usual route to work. Some habits discourage growth and development. Other habits encourage accomplishing meaningful goals efficiently and effectively.

Following A Habitual Experience Exercise

Choose a habitual activity to direct your attention to, a specific routine that you do regularly. Simply try to be aware of it while you are doing it. Do not interfere with the natural flow. Observe and notice, as you did in the previous awareness exercise, watching without censure or judgment as you carry out the activity. Be aware of the emotional content. Feel the sensations in your body and all aspects of the experience of doing the action.

Exercise in Exploring Your Experience

After you have chosen an activity and have been aware while doing it, try recalling the activity several hours later or the following day. Think back on what you experienced. Imagine yourself in action, paying attention as you did at the time. Did you have any difficulty staying with your experience at the time? If your answer is yes, you can explore that now. What thoughts or feelings floated through your mind at the time? Consider possible meanings. Do these accompanying thoughts or feelings have any conceivable connection to your experience? Follow your associations and the details of thoughts and feelings without interfering, while you carefully observe them. Sometimes associations are peripheral and distant, almost beyond grasp. Other times the connections are clear. Be patient and alert. Are there any other thoughts, feelings, sensations, or memories in the background, even for a moment? Follow these tiny cues down the interesting paths that open up. If you are touching upon a conflict area you may feel slightly nervous or uncomfortable. Rather than simply worrying about it, consider your feelings positively, as a possible indication that you are beginning to explore something important. Resistance may feel boring, uncomfortable, or sometimes embarrassing. You may lose your train of thought suddenly, or have even forgotten to concentrate. Take note if any of these things happen. You may be beginning to gain understanding about resistance to trance.

Preventing Yourself from Change

The brain has excellent built-in ways to help us protect ourselves. The hypothalamic-pituitary-adrenal (HPA) pathway (Figure 11.1, page 164) activates when we encounter something frightening, to help us take fast action and decide whether to fight back, run away, or freeze, so that the predator does not notice us (this is known as the "fight-or-flight-or-freeze response). In these and other ways, defenses can be helpful—especially when feeling the full force of an experience could interfere with competent action. Psychological defenses are often automatically adopted to protect against anxiety and threat. During a crisis, defenses can be invaluable in helping you cope well. For example, in job situations it is usually better not to tell the boss off just because you are angry.

But when used automatically, defenses may limit your options. Reactions to situations become too predictably patterned to allow for creativity, excitement, or growth. This can present problems when you are trying to make personal changes using self-hypnosis. Change is facilitated by freedom of choice. Learn to use defenses for defense, when necessary to endure or cope, but do not let them interfere with better functioning.

Working with Defenses

Hypnosis offers you new options. It is a chance to be free of unnecessary defenses, or an effective way to bypass defenses that interfere with healthy functioning. Trance works directly with the positive unconscious and bypasses conscious ego functions like over-reliance on defenses. However, if you have found that you are unable to go into trance, you may unintentionally be getting defensive, due to feeling resistant to trance. If you would like to explore and choose an alternative reaction, and if this seems to be possible, try the exercises that follow.

Identifying Defensiveness Exercise

Think about trying to go into trance. As you contemplate the possibility, what is your reaction? Do you feel vaguely uneasy, then immediately make a number of convincing excuses for not doing it? Do you think of countless reasons why you can't? Or maybe you feel like circumstances never allow you to sit down to do a trance. Do you believe other people try to prevent you from trance? Do you feel a vague, perhaps irrational fear of trance? Insight gained from self-observation may allow you to reconsider, so that you can experience trance.

It is difficult to diagnose yourself from a book, but viewing your reaction as possibly defensive may help you to question whether this reaction is the only possible reaction you could have. Perhaps you have taken it for granted that your defensive reaction is justifiable, a realistic response that happens naturally. A sense of free will or voluntary choice is not experienced. Believing that there could be another possibility can be the starting point for new options to appear.

Exaggerating Your Defensive Reaction Exercise

A day or more after attempting the previous exercise, try to go into trance. This time, if you feel the usual reluctance, try to exaggerate it. If your attention wanders, try to think of anything but trance. If you get bored, bore yourself further by deliberately doing nothing. After 15 or 20 minutes of this, once again try to enter trance. You may find yourself automatically going into trance at this point. If not, try shifting back to the defensive state and exaggerating it further. There is also much to learn from studying how you prevent yourself from successfully accomplishing your goals.

The Positivity of Negativity

Perhaps you have faithfully attempted to work your way through this book, performing exercise after exercise, but have found that, despite all of your efforts, you cannot achieve even the slightest semblance of trance. You might feel frustrated and angry at yourself, or start to doubt the efficacy and power of hypnosis. As we mentioned in Chapter 2, some equate responding to suggestion with weakness of the will. Have you considered the independence, strength, and self-confidence expressed in your resistance? This strength, when it matures, compounded with your whole personality, can actually become a driving force for resolving difficulties. Permitting oneself to respond to self-suggestion can lead to stronger willpower. Use the resistance in a more positive way, to resist the problem's grip on your life.

Lisa was a college-age woman who came to us for hypnosis, in order to lose weight. She also complained about being very forgetful: She forgot her keys, the date, or even her best friend's name! She learned to develop a deep trance. We invited her unconscious to work on these difficulties creatively, using her resources. She discovered, to her delight, that she could forget to overeat! She told us that at first, she forgot several meals, including her favorite desserts. She thought this was simply an isolated incident and could not possibly relate to her hypnotic work. But she continued to experience forgetting to overeat, coincidentally at useful times. Gradually Lisa began to recognize that what she had always considered to be a deficit and a problem could actually work to her benefit in another context. Concomitantly, her forgetfulness with keys and other things lessened, much to her surprise! Her forgetfulness had found a place. She had never thought her tendency could help her.

Once the unconscious is engaged to work in a positive way, problems can be not merely bypassed, but actually used as assets. This is another way to use resistance: to work for you, not against you.

Positive and Negative Exercise

If you sense that you have some negativity holding you back, invite your unconscious to make new connections for you. You may know things unconsciously that you do not know consciously. After all, you probably did not consciously or deliberately choose to be negative or to have problems. This changes naturally and automatically, when you permit unconscious resources within to work for you.

Prepare for this exercise by thinking about some of your talents and strengths. Describe them fully to yourself. Next, consider your weaknesses and faults. Enter trance if possible, otherwise sit quietly, wondering in general about the complex unity of the human body, and how the different systems are all connected: the skeletal system to the cardiovascular and muscle systems, the digestive system, and so on. Consider the interactions, the overlaps. After you have imaginatively gone through the body as best you can, relax and let your thoughts drift about whatever interests you. Then take a moment to pause and meditate on your experience.

Frames of Reference

You can accomplish amazing things unconsciously, without interference from consciousness. For this to occur, awareness need not be engaged in what you are doing. You have experienced this naturally when you are, for example, daydreaming. You may not have discovered how to use this natural talent.

Allow Unconscious Knowing Exercise
How do you go from the living room to the dining room? Think of as many ways as possible. Do not read on until you have given yourself at least 5 minutes to ponder this question. Jot down some answers. Now analyze your responses to learn about yourself and your limitations. Vary this creatively, with your own examples drawn from your own routines and situation.

Erickson used this exercise frequently. He would say that we could go from one room to the next in various ways. We can crawl, skip, run, or even do cartwheels, ride a bike, or roller skate. Or we can go out the door, get in the car, drive to the airport and board a plane for Hawaii. We could spend two weeks there, relaxing and enjoying the sights, then return home, and walk in the back door, through the kitchen, to the dining room. Did you get stuck after walking, running, or crawling? How many new ways can you think of now?

Figure 10.1. Shifting Blocks of Perception. Birch, walnut, and mahogany. C. Alexander Simpkins and Annellen M. Simpkins, 2000.

This next exercise shows how the frame of reference, as the context and starting point, affects experience.

Flexible Perception Exercise

Look at the figure above. Can you see squares leading in one direction? Look for awhile, and then start again from the other corner. Can you now see squares like steps, going in the other direction? Try to see the pattern in one direction, and then the other. You will only see one of these two directions at a time. In order to shift from one to the other, you must conceive of the background differently.

Perception is relative to context and perspective. We tend at times to take our own point of reference for granted, assuming everyone shares the same view. Our own meaning matters most, our perceptual anchor.

A favorite joke in experimental psychology centers on a laboratory rat who described the scientist overseeing the experiment, stating that he had trained that man so that every time he pressed the lever, the man gave him food (Watzlawick, Weakland, & Fisch, 1974). Is the experimenter conditioning the rat with food, or is the experimenter being conditioned to give the rat food by the rat's behavior? Interaction is reciprocal and can be viewed from either perspective!

Creative Thinking

Thinking can be defined as, "The deliberate exploration of experience for a purpose" (De Bono, 1976, p. 32). We are taught to reason with logic. A follows B directly; one fact builds upon the next. However, logical sequence can be limiting at times. Creative thinking, which encourages other possibilities and approaches, is a skill that can be developed. Obstacles to open thinking can be overcome. Defining a situation too early leads to narrow thinking from a limited perspective, or bias. You can learn to put things together in different ways.

Exercise in Creative Thinking

First, combine two triangles:

Did you think of a diamond or square? Can you think of other shapes? Now what do you have if you combine four triangles? How many shapes can you think of? This requires reorganizing and rethinking to come up with one or more larger figures made up of four triangles.

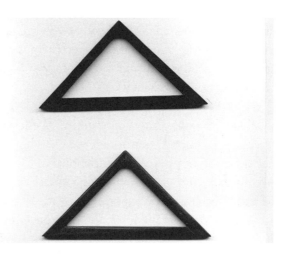

Figure 10.2. Triangles.

Figure 10.3. Creative combinations.

When working with yourself, you might unintentionally develop limited, redundantly patterned ways to interpret your situation. You may have one experience followed by another which always seem to go together in a certain pattern. Further experiences are dismissed as simply more of the same pattern. People inadvertently sort their experiences into restrictive, rigid categories, then feel bored or stuck as a result. Gabriel Marcel called this a "hardening of the categories" (Marcel, 1966, p. 41). An open attitude toward interpretation can help improve this type of situation.

Choosing a Hypnotist for Assistance

If you find that you still have not been able to experience hypnosis and accomplish your positive goals, consulting a professional may be a good idea. Therapeutic hypnosis ultimately takes place within the patient, but sometimes someone who is trained to recognize and guide hypnosis or hypnotherapy in others will make the difference. Often you can accomplish your goals by working on your own, but certain problems or circumstances may require a professional's input.

You might wonder how to know when to consult an expert. The answer lies within. You are obviously interested in hypnosis or you would not be reading this book. Experiment with the general exercises in trance and suggestion. If you find that you can readily experience trance, or that after practice you begin to find your way into hypnosis, then you know that you do have the ability to experience self-hypnosis without external guidance or someone to point it out to you. If you cannot make any headway with these techniques and have worked through this chapter as well, consulting a professional may help you. This does not indicate that you cannot ever work with hypnosis. If the motivation is present, you will be able to experience trance with proper guidance. You may find it helpful to work with a therapist if you feel stuck or threatened, to help get you back on track, to guide you in certain areas where you experience blocks or fears, or just for support and help with a stubborn conflict. You may only need to work with a professional for a brief period of time.

Choosing the right professional is a personal matter. Find a good match for you. Many professionals use hypnosis: hypnotherapists, psychologists, psychiatrists, social workers, and medical doctors. The ideal combination is a person with experience and dedication to hypnosis, as well as a background in one of the helping professions. It takes skill and professionalism: Hypnosis is both art and science. Learning to use your own unconscious to problem-solve and make changes is central. You should look for this to occur in hypnotherapy. An ally in your endeavors may be all you need for your journey to begin.

Conclusion

You can work with self-hypnosis as you learn to voluntarily allow the involuntary to occur. Limitations and conscious objections can be set aside temporarily for the purposes of self-exploration and personal growth. Ultimately, hypnosis is a personal experience. No one can force your experience to be a certain way. With time and regular attempts, you will be able to make the necessary discoveries that allow you to experience it. If you wait and stay with what you experience, it will eventually change.

Be patient and give yourself the time and space to evolve as you go along. Try to recognize your responsiveness, even if it is subtle. If the willingness is there, you can develop hypnosis and enjoy its benefits.

PART IV

Applying Self-Hypnosis

11

Balancing the Brain's Stress Pathway

Our lives unfold their beauty
Like the petals of a flower
In challenges from circumstance
We find our finest hour

—C. Alexander Simpkins

LIFE makes a variety of demands on us, to meet challenges, adapt, and satisfy our needs, as well as those of others we care about. These challenges, combined with an inclination to strive to achieve, engage a natural mind–brain–body process that we call *stress*. Stress is unique in being a generalized, nonspecific reaction to demands placed upon the body, as this chapter will describe. And although it can be the source of discomfort, it can stir you to greater achievements. By attuning to your resources within, you can become your best.

Stress research spanning many decades concludes that you can do something about how stress affects you. Hypnosis is one of the treatments of choice for stress management.

Selye's General Adaptation Syndrome

The Canadian physiologist Hans Selye (1907–1982) was the first to recognize that there could be a syndrome that was nonspecific to any one illness, but was nevertheless a component in all. He popularized the concept of stress as a distinct syndrome. Selye first proposed this idea when he was a medical student in 1926. He noticed all of the patients with different diseases shown to the students also seemed to share symptoms of a universal reaction to the disturbance of homeostasis, the body's internal balance, such as tiredness and loss of appetite. At that time, Selye tried to define this pattern of symptoms as "being sick," but he wondered if it might really be something more. Not until the 1950s did Selye's research bring him back to the implications of his early observations of a nonspecific reaction pattern. Whenever there is a continuous environmental stressor, people respond with the same kind of pattern. He called this reaction the *General Adaptation Syndrome* (Seyle, 1974).

The general adaptation syndrome has three stages. The first stage is the alarm reaction, when internal resources are mobilized in an attempt to return the body to its homeostasic balance. Second is the resistance stage, when the individual uses whatever resources are available to fight off the effects of stress. If the stressor persists, the resources become depleted and the organism experiences exhaustion at stage three. Selye believed that these three stages occur in any stress situation. This syndrome is a nonspecific reaction of the body as it adjusts to demands that are placed upon it, in an attempt to return to balance. This view is still widely accepted today.

New Theory of Balance: From Homeostasis to Allostasis

Homeostasis was the original conception of internal balance, but today, with a more integrative perspective, we know that environment and past circumstances all figure into a more dynamic balance known as *allostasis*. Allostasis takes into account an ongoing updating of your balance point, depending upon what you have experienced over time. So, for example, when you are stressed for a long period, your body will form a different equilibrium, adapted to meet the needs of the particular situation.

Neurobiology of Stress

Today, Selye's ideas have been expanded to include allostasis (Ganzel, Morris, & Wethington, 2010). We know more about how the stress syndrome comes about and is sustained in the brain. Several brain systems with a strong link to your thoughts and feelings are involved. On the neurobiological level, stress is a lot like the fear response, which comes from the autonomic nervous system (ANS) and sends a message to the muscles to fight, flee, or freeze. Your brain processes activate in this patterned way when facing danger, and so the first impulse is to take some action.

The ANS prepares the body for action by getting excited in some ways, but also by calming down at the same time. The excitation in the sympathetic nervous system response directs the adrenal glands to secrete hormones that cause the heart to beat more rapidly, muscles to tense, and blood pressure to rise. Breathing rate increases and pupils dilate. Blood flow is directed to the brain and muscles, away from internal organs and skin. The parasympathetic system helps maintain an internal balance by calming the emergency reaction and keeping the normal maintenance systems, such as digestion, going. These are all normal responses that ready the body to either confront or flee from an experienced threat.

The brain-to-endocrine system involves a reaction pathway that links the hypothalamus, pituitary gland, and adrenal glands together, known as the HPA (hypothalamus–pituitary–adrenal) pathway. Generally, the hypothalamus is important in maintaining the allostasis between your body and the environment, and it does so through the HPA pathway. The hypothalamus receives excitatory and inhibitory inputs from the ANS, along with inputs from the senses, which are related to what you are experiencing within your body and what you are experiencing in the external environment. The hypothalamus then releases neurotransmitters and hormones which are routed quickly into the circulatory system for a rapid response (Figure 11.1).

Several hormones are produced and released when you are under stress,

Figure 11.1. HPA Pathway.

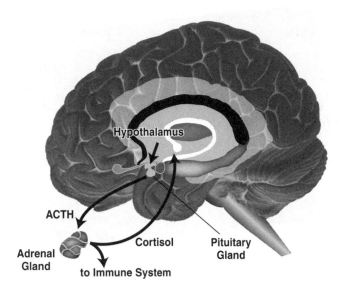

including corticotrophin-releasing hormone (CRH), and adrenocorticotropic hormone (ACTH). Production and release of another hormone, glucocorticoids, is fed back into the brain and pituitary to slow down the synthesis of CRH and ACTH. This circular process of activation and deactivation is usually kept in balance. But when there is a stressor, the system responds rapidly with a large increase in activity along the HPA pathway. Any increases are quickly brought back into balance when you are healthy. But long-standing psychological factors, illnesses, or difficult external circumstances (known as allostatic load) can create a balance that keeps the HPA pathway continuously activated. You experience this new balance as stress, similar to your car engine revving even when you are in neutral.

Thus, the generalized stress reaction adds extra discomfort to all kinds of problems. The positive aspect of this is that these processes are dynamic, always changing and responding, and so you can intervene at any point. By lessening your stress response, you will change the balance, like turning down the idle in your car's motor, to create a more comfortable allostatic balance. A nonspecific calmness and improved coping ability will enhance treatment of many psychological and physical problems. We encourage you to use the exercises in this chapter in conjunction with any of those in the other chapters. The generalized, overall rebalancing of your brain's stress reaction can be a powerful force for healing.

What Researchers Have Learned About Stress

A summary of the extensive research on stress can be helpful to you in learning how to deal well with your stressful situations. Researchers have investigated why some people cope better with stress than others. They found that how people handle stress is influenced by how they think about it. Expectations and self-suggestions play a large part in reactions to stress. People cope better when a situation is appraised as a challenge, rather than as a threat. Placebo research has shown how expectations and suggestions can literally alter the brain, and so taking a hopeful attitude can bring about real changes in the brain's stress response. People also do well with stressful situations such as surgery when they have realistic expectations. If you are properly informed and have realistic expectations, you will be better prepared and therefore cope better. A moderate dose of stress is not necessarily harmful. In fact, it may be helpful because it alerts your brain to be adequately prepared for challenges.

Stressors vary greatly, and require different coping approaches. For example, stress from your car not working when you need it is best managed by taking a problem-solving approach. The death of a close relative requires emotionally focused coping. Successful strategies can modify whether the situation or stimulus becomes helpful or harmful. Another surprising finding is that happy and exciting circumstances can also be stressful (anyone who has ever planned a wedding can probably understand how this could be possible!). With both pleasant and unpleasant challenges, the stress pathways are activated, putting the body on high alert. Both positive excitement and negative tensions can push us away from the balanced center. Restoring equilibrium is a helpful way to handle stress.

In sum, research clearly shows that you can have an effect on your stress. Even though you may not have a choice of the challenges you face, you do have a choice in how you handle them. This chapter will guide you in how to use self-hypnosis to deal with stress, working both consciously and unconsciously to change your brain's stress response.

First, Learn to Relax

One way of enduring stress is appropriate relaxation. We say *appropriate*, because stressful situations often require that you to be alert, work hard, and endure difficulties that are not going away. So simple relaxation alone—which could result in missing an important deadline, for example—may not be the most appropriate way to cope. But even when circumstances require more from you, there are always opportunities to include some relaxation. Just adding a few minutes here and there will make a difference.

You can learn to relax by using hypnosis and then call upon this skill when needed. The exercises that follow will help to develop a relaxed mind and body, which has a direct effect on your brain's stress reaction.

The approach to relaxation given here is *invitational*. You do not force a response, you simply invite it with a suggestion. Then step back, so to speak, and wait for your response. You cannot predict exactly what will happen, because you are opening yourself to the possibility of a new response. But you can trust that whatever response you have will become an important part of the process. So, when instructions are offered in the exercises, use them as potentials. Be sensitive to even the smallest response. Hypnotic response can sometimes be obvious, but more often it is subtle. During the first session, clients will often say, "I didn't feel anything." We guide them to turn to the subtle aspects of their experience: a slight tingling in one finger, a tiny temperature change in a hand, a flickering thought, or a minor shift in emotion, for example. When they take a moment to reflect on subtle responsiveness, they are often surprised to find more happening than they first noticed. With an open invitation that allows and waits, you too can begin to notice small changes. But keep in mind the words of the great Daoist sage Laozi, who noted that the journey of 1000 miles begins with one step (Simpkins & Simpkins, 1999a). Have confidence that you are initiating a process that will grow and develop over time.

Allowing Body Relaxation Exercise

Find a comfortable position, either sitting or lying down. Close your eyes and allow your breathing to be relaxed. Suggest that as you drift into trance you can become more and more relaxed. Offer yourself the possibility that you can let go of any unnecessary tensions, and then wait. As you feel ready, invite a deepening of your relaxation. Rest comfortably for 15 minutes or so, allowing yourself to remain very relaxed in trance. When you feel ready to return to full awareness, count backwards from 5 to 1, suggesting that you will become more alert and refreshed with each number until you are fully awake and aware. Relax as often as possible during times of stress. A few minutes spent relaxing consistently morning and night helps to counterbalance the brain reaction that adds more stress to the difficult circumstances you are facing.

Progressive Body Relaxation into Trance Exercise

Find a comfortable place to go into trance, perhaps in bed at night before sleep, or lying down on a comfortable couch, or even outdoors in nature. Let your attention scan through your body, noticing what you feel in your muscles. Tense all your muscles, tightening your face, including your eyes, nose, and mouth, your neck, shoulders, back, chest, torso, arms, hands, legs, and feet. Hold all your muscles tight, all the way down to your fingers and toes, for about 1 minute. Now let go and relax everywhere. Let go of all the tension and feel your body sink down. Lay comfortably relaxed for another minute. Then tighten again, holding tight all over for a minute, and then once again, relax deeply. Repeat once more, tightening for a minute and then relaxing.

Now as you allow your muscles to relax even more deeply, let your thoughts drift as you relax very deeply all over. Do you feel like you are floating? Sinking? You can become even more relaxed now as you allow the sinking or floating feeling to increase even more. And if you have a different sensation of relaxation, enhance that. Allow yourself to drift in trance, more relaxed than usual. When you feel ready, stretch your muscles gently as you become fully alert.

Relaxing Trance Imagery Exercise

Sit or lie down comfortably and allow yourself to go into trance using this relaxing image. Picture a beautiful sunset. You can remember a very beautiful sunset you have seen or perhaps a sunset from a movie you enjoyed. Or, if you prefer, create an imagined sunset now. The sun is sinking slowly down, down, toward the horizon. As the sun moves down, your body relaxes more. The sky begins to change from light blue to darker blue. Then gradually tints of color begin to appear: you might see pinks, reds, yellows or any colors you imagine. As the sun sinks down closer to the horizon, your relaxation deepens. As the sun reaches the horizon you see it gently disappearing—first the bottom is gone, now half-gone, and now just a glimmering speck of light remains until the sun is completely gone. Now your body relaxes as completely as possible. If you are watching a sunset over the ocean, can you see a flash as the sun finally slips down into the water? The colors in the sky darken into purple, deep red, and dark orange, and you relax even more. The whole sky is streaked with color. If you are watching a sunset over water, vividly imagine how the water reflects the color in the sky and let the relaxation spread all over. Enjoy the beauty of the image and the comfort of your relaxation.

Cueing Yourself for Trance

As you become more accustomed to trance, you can give yourself a cue that links to your experience of trance. One client we had used the word "snow" because it reminded her of a happy memory she had of visiting a cabin, nestled near a snow-covered mountain. She learned to sit comfortably, think of snow, and then enter trance. You can draw on a pleasant memory or on the enjoyable trance sensations you have been experiencing for your personal cue. You might need to wait quietly for your cue: It could be a word, an image, or even a feeling that will spontaneously occur to you when the time is right.

Cueing Yourself for Trance Exercise

Once you have thought of a meaningful cue and you have an opportunity to go into trance, sit or lie down comfortably. Let your body relax and think of your cue. As you hear or see your word, feel your feeling, or see your image, you will slip very gently and comfortably into trance. Your body becomes relaxed or alert, as you have practiced, and you can enjoy your typical feeling of trance. Allow yourself to go even deeper as you think about your cue. You don't know whether you will experience a light or deep trance. Just allow your natural capacities to express themselves as you enjoy your trance experience. When you are ready, come back to full awareness.

Use your cue to help you go into a comfortable trance whenever the time is right for you.

Stress Can Be Good for You

People often think that stress is a bad thing and should be avoided, but in reality, not all stress is bad. Sometimes stress can spur an individual on to better performance. *Hardiness* is a personality trait that you can develop from enduring stress well. It is fostered best when you can find meaning and challenge in difficult life situations. Viktor Frankl (1905–1997) not only survived a concentration camp during World War II, but also found meaning in the experience. He founded a method of analysis, logotherapy, which has inspired others to find meaning in even the worst situations (Frankl, 1988; Pattakos, 2008). There have even been cases where some illnesses have been lessened by stress. Even though war has a debilitating effect, during World War II, there were many documented cases of soldiers seeing their stress-related illnesses such as ulcers, migraines, and colitis disappear. Some of these people rose to the challenge of battle, discovering resources they did not know they had. In the process, they threw off conditions that had troubled them before the war (Whitehorn, 1956). You can probably think of a time when you rose to the challenge of stress and accomplished more than you thought you could. This quality can be developed to help you now in coping with stress.

We all need a certain amount of manageable stress for optimum functioning. Without the challenge from meaningful involvement and purposeful striving, people become unhappy and even may become ill. So, stress is not necessarily something to be avoided; sometimes it should be embraced. Manageable stress can be helpful—it is unmanageable stress that becomes detrimental.

Sometimes you can shift the balance from unmanageable to manageable, and thereby enhance the hardiness of your personality. You can begin by considering ways you might be thinking about stress that accelerate the brain's stress response. Some thoughts are conscious, and can be corrected rationally. Others are unconscious, occurring without any awareness. These exercises can help you to work with both conscious and unconscious thinking, to shift the brain's balance for the best possible response to difficulties.

Rhoda felt stressed. She blamed her husband. He had run off with his secretary and left her with their two teenage children and no income. She was desperately trying to earn enough money to support them, but having been a homemaker during the marriage, she had few marketable skills. She blamed her husband for that, too. She had trouble sleeping, and stayed up late at night, ruminating. This made things worse because her children complained that when she overslept in the morning she was not there for them. Then she felt guilty, because she was a good mom and knew she was letting them down.

She learned to do hypnosis and was encouraged to do self-hypnosis at home. And although hypnosis gave her temporary relief, she continued to feel stressed. We asked her to consider what she was telling herself about her stressful situations. She knew she was angry at her husband, and voiced it vehemently! But what she did not realize at first was the negative statement she was telling herself, over and over: This shouldn't be happening to me! The more she said it, the more she felt like a victim, and the more stressed she felt. We helped her to recognize the difference between what she could and could not change. She learned to stop expending energy on what she could not do and then to put her efforts into what she could change. She could not make her husband come back, but she could stop feeling sorry for herself. As she questioned the negative suggestions that followed from her poor-me attitude, such as "I'm helpless" and "There's nothing I can do," she began to have some mental energy available for more positive action. We encouraged her to spend more time thinking about her talents. She had worked in education before her marriage, and she used trance to reignite the motivation she had felt years ago when first entering this field. Gradually she turned her situation around from being a victim to becoming an achiever.

Conscious Attitude Change Exercise

Ready yourself for trance, but before you actually go into trance, think about your stressful situation. Consider what you feel and think about it. For example, if you are facing an exam, do you feel pessimistic? If your stress is work related, do you believe you have been unfairly burdened? If you are ill, are you also saying things like, "Why do bad things always happen to me?" Whatever the nature of your situation, try to become aware of your deeper thoughts about it.

Now that you know what you are thinking, ask yourself whether this thought is helping you handle the stress. Often people add to their stress by focusing on how bad it is, and deciding that they have little time or energy left for making improvements. But accepting the stress as it is and facing it courageously may actually help you grow as a person.

Review some of the creative problem-solving techniques in Chapter 10. Ask your unconscious if it can make some new discoveries. Are there other ways to think about your situation? Do you have any skills that might be helpful, even skills drawn from an earlier time in your life? Consider new possibilities.

Unconscious Attitude Change Exercise

Now, go into trance. Allow your thoughts to drift, without directing them one way or another. Simply remain curious about what potential understandings of your stressful situation can be discovered unconsciously. Change of thinking patterns may be subtle and slow at first, but keep inviting your unconscious to work on it. Change should be based in what can be, not what cannot be; a better understanding will follow. Remain in trance until you feel ready to wake up, refreshed and alert. Repeat this exercise daily over a period of time.

Dissociation

Some stressful situations—such as natural disasters, wars, physical pain, or illness—may be beyond your control. But your experience of these and other intense stressors is something you *can* control. Hypnosis can help you to alter the experience to make it less uncomfortable, using your natural hypnotic capacity to be dissociated. Developing dissociation may give you the capacity to face what must be endured with dignity. And your ability to dissociate hypnotically will lead to improved coping with difficult situations.

Trance Dissociation Skills Exercise

Sit in a chair, with your hands resting on your knees. Relax as you go into trance. Let yourself experience sensations in your hands, as you have in previous exercises. As you relax even more deeply, can you experience your hands as being far away? Or perhaps your unconscious mind would like to give you this experience with your foot instead. Can you see your hand or foot as being far away? Or is it a sensation of distance? Perhaps you imagine yourself looking down on your hand or foot from a distant vantage point? As you offer different ways to dissociate, wait for your response. Then, enlarge on that responsiveness, suggesting that you could feel further away, or feel less sensation. When you have had some success with this practice exercise, go on to the next one.

Dissociating from Stress Exercise

Close your eyes. Sit comfortably in one of your preferred positions. Let yourself go deeply into trance. Think of a time or place when you were not feeling stressed. Perhaps you were on vacation, or maybe you were having a lighter workload. Or if you are suffering from a prolonged illness, think back to a pleasant time when you were healthy. Vividly recall how you felt. Bring to mind any memories associated with that time or place in your life. As you think about this, you may notice that your body relaxes naturally. Your thoughts may become calmer as well. Enjoy trance. Suggest that when you feel ready to wake up, you can retain some of the experience of that other place now. You may find that the stressful feelings have decreased, as you are still enjoying the comfortable feelings from that other place or time.

Using Time Distortion to Cope with Stress

Hypnosis draws on the inner recesses of the mind, a timeless space of experience that does not rely on the ticking of a clock. Return to the time distortion exercises in Chapter 9. You can use this ability now to help in the midst of stressful situations. The ability of your inner mind to experience time in creative ways will allow a short trance to have long-lasting effects. This exercise can be done almost anytime: at your desk at the office, in your hospital bed, in the evening just before sleep, or during your child's nap. Making this exercise, or any of the exercises in this book, part of your daily routine can set the stage for a less stressful, calmer, but productive life.

Time Distortion Exercise 1

Take note of the time when you begin. Find a comfortable position, either seated or lying down. Close your eyes. Develop a deep, comfortable trance. Let go of any unnecessary tension. Imagine a favorite movie or book. Let yourself recall the story, from beginning to end. Imagine that you have all the time you need to review it. As you do so, enjoy the experience, feeling relaxed and entertained. When you have finished the entire story, wake up and check the time. You may feel as if a long time has elapsed, and yet, on the clock, only a few minutes have passed. Take some time here and there during your daily routine and do this exercise again. You will then be able to return to your efforts with renewed energy.

Some stress occurs from heavy demands at work or at home. With too many things to accomplish in too little time, people become stressed. Sometimes hypnosis can help you to literally work faster, thereby allowing you to accomplish tasks more quickly. Then the brain's stress pathways return to balance as the threat passes. Finishing earlier than expected can be a great stress reliever.

During graduate school, I (Annellen) had a paper due at a certain time on a certain day. Finally the paper was written, but it still needed to be typed. Unfortunately, there was not enough time to type the paper, given my usual typing speed. I decided to use hypnosis, went into trance and suggested that if I could find a way, I would type more quickly. Upon awakening, I began to type. Much to my surprise, the hands of the clock seemed to be moving more slowly as I typed at what felt like my usual speed. The paper was finished, but the clock seemed to indicate that plenty of time remained to get to school and turn in the paper. What I subsequently discovered was that my typing speed had increased markedly. This increase in typing speed has remained with me ever since, a useful enhancement of skill.

You can experiment with this for yourself. Practice some of the time distortion exercises in Chapter 9. Then try this exercise. Hypnosis is not magic, but you might be surprised how much latitude you have in accomplishing your tasks.

Time Distortion Exercise 2

As you are beginning to drift into trance, suggest that you would like to find a creative way to accomplish a certain task more efficiently and quickly. You do not need to make exact specific descriptive suggestions. Instead, invite your unconscious to find a way, perhaps a very unique creative way, to work rapidly. Hold your attention on the task and allow your attention to drift around it, wondering what your creative way will be. Then, when you are ready, go even more deeply into trance. Remain in trance until you feel ready to return to your normal, waking state.

Happiness and Well-being

You can discover happiness and well-being within, so that your life flows more smoothly. When you meet your circumstances with trust and confidence in your resources, you will feel better, and may master the challenges. Use this trance exercise to help you discover your own calm, confident center within, from your unconscious reservoir of potential, to help you enjoy well-being and happiness. If you cannot seem to feel positive after a reasonable time, turn back to Chapter 10, on resistance.

Positive Unconscious Exercise

Go deeply into trance, allowing your breathing rate to become comfortable, your muscles to relax, and a pleasant feeling to envelop you. Some may feel a comfortable warmth; others might feel a refreshing coolness, or maybe a sense of lightness or heaviness. Allow yourself to have your own response. Your unconscious response can be a positive ally in your life. You have felt confident in the past, at times. You did not do anything to make yourself feel confident, it just happened. Trust your response, permitting the time necessary. You have an untapped resource that you can be in tune with. As you relax even more, you can begin to feel your own deep calmness pervade your experiencing. This calmness will lead to a feeling of being centered and balanced. Let these feelings develop. Stay with this until you are ready to awaken, refreshed, with a feeling of well-being. Allow this experience to stay with you as long as you like.

Conclusion

The brain responds to what you experience. The brain's stress response can be eased by how you cope with the stressful situation. But making a change in a long-standing stress will take time, so be patient with the process. Try to be diligent in your practice of self-hypnosis. Make time to go into trance daily, even several times a day if you are working on a severe situation. You do not need to spend a long amount of time in each sitting, but do it often. As you continue to make the effort, you may begin to look forward to your self-hypnosis sessions. In addition, our clients have often found that they become an inspiration for others who are also suffering. So keep trying, and you will eventually enjoy the rewards of feeling more comfortable, coping better, and even helping others.

12

Regulating Emotions Consciously

and Unconsciously

It therefore seems that all the affections of soul involve a body—passion, gentleness, fear, pity, courage, joy, loving, and hating; in all there is a concurrent affection of the body.

—Aristotle, *De Anima*, p. 537

EMOTIONS are intimately related to your mind, brain, and body. In fact, emotions are not simply inner feelings. They are also embodied, that is, they manifest themselves physically. Emotions involve the physical movements you use to express them, such as smiling when happy, or stomping a foot when angry. They involve sensations such as butterflies in the stomach or warmth in the face. And they also involve your thoughts, concepts, and beliefs, such as when you look forward to seeing a loved one and feel happy, or remember a negative past situation and feel sad or angry. Emotions also involve patterns of activated brain processes that trigger the limbic system (See Figure 4.6), the emotional part of your brain. Just as cognition is embodied, so are emotions. And so, when you feel happy, your mouth moves into a smile, your thoughts are about a happy event, and the reward pathway releases dopamine in your brain. Thus, emotions are an integrated mind–brain–body experience.

All of these qualities of emotion are collectively referred to as *affect*, a term that includes the body, brain, and mind aspects of emotion all together, to bring about an emotional content to experiencing.

How the Brain Processes Emotions

The idea that emotions are an integrated mind–brain–body experience is clearly reflected in how emotions are processed in the brain. The central nervous system plays an important role in emotional responses, which are regulated through certain brain regions that function together as highly interrelated systems. These systems reach out extensively through the brain and into the body. Neurotransmitters and neurohormones are the messengers that send the signals through these areas to help regulate emotional experiences. The two key areas that are involved in emotions are the limbic system, including the amygdala and certain surrounding regions known as the extended amygdala, and the basal ganglia (See Figure 4.5), the four structures that are involved in movement. (Ganzel et al., 2010).

Since emotion is a mind–brain–body unity, you can change it with an intervention to any of the elements. Start a process by altering a sensation, moving your body, altering your thoughts, improving your interpersonal relationships, changing your environment, or having a novel experience. You can use self-hypnosis to alter sensations, movements, and thoughts. Through hypnotic visualization, you can have new experiences, alter feelings about relationships, and even gain a changed perspective on your outer circumstances.

The Short Path and the Long Path

Emotions are processed through the amygdala in two main ways: a short path and a long path (Figure 12.1). Often an emotional experience begins in the automatic systems in the body, arising from sensory experience, which is processed by the limbic system. The short path is fast, with signals traveling from the senses directly to the thalamus and the amygdala, bypassing the cortex. This shorter path accounts for the automatic, preconscious, or even unconscious quality of many emotional responses. If the emotional response travels this short route directly from the sensation to the limbic system, it arises before interpretation and is unconscious, outside of deliberate conscious control. If instead you think about the response, the emotion that occurs is consciously recognized, having traveled the long path. The long path sends signals through the cortex, thereby making emotions consciously recognized. When people over-think themselves into disturbance, the long path has been activated.

Here is an illustration of the two paths. If you are walking in a dark parking lot late at night and hear a strange noise, you might feel a stab of fear. The short path has been activated: Your heart rate increases, your palms become sweaty, and your face flushes, readying you to deal with danger. But then, if you see that the noise came from someone shutting a car door to drive away, all these reactions stop, and you become calm as you recognize that there is no danger. The long path has now been activated.

This figure illustrates the two pathways of fear:

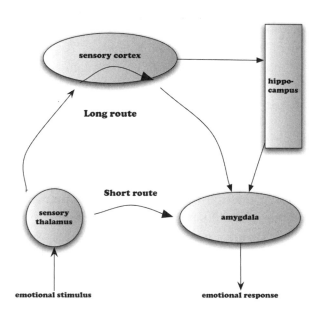

Figure 12.1. The two pathways of fear.

The two paths interact together. Sometimes one path can stimulate the other, such as during panic attacks, where a short path sensation in the chest promotes long-path worries about the sensations, leading to an increased short-path panic reaction. You can switch to a different path when necessary, for example, if, when considered in context, your quick, first reaction is not the best or the most mature response for the situation.

Hypnosis can offer methods for sensing and working with both paths to facilitate change. You can enlist all the tools of hypnosis, including suggestion, unconscious processing, and absorption to change these brain–mind–body reactions. We encourage you to open yourself to the possibility that you can influence how you feel for the better.

Working with the Short Path and the Long Path

You can learn to modify your emotional responses by working with short-path and long-path reactions. Begin by getting some cognitive control over those immediate, short-term reactions.

Often when one feels bothered by an emotion or mood, gloomy skies seem to fill the horizon. The experience clouds perception, and one feels as if their mood is not only their own mood, but how the situation actually is. Reactions seem immediate, coming from short-path processing. This is common with depressed moods, but can also be true with anger and irritability. So how do you find your way beyond a short-path reaction which feels out of control? One accessible inroad to changing an out-of-control reaction is to start from where you are.

You can begin to unravel the process by engaging your prefrontal cortex. Consider this: You might be quick to anger, but you were not born angry. You unknowingly have created your short temper yourself. Nor were you born depressed or irritable. Outbursts of temper, sad moods, and irritability are created from evaluative interpretations when the senses are stimulated by something external, such as "He shouldn't do this to me," or, "I can't do anything right." As you tease out the reasoning fundamental to the reaction, the short-path reaction can switch off, and the long-path response switches on instead.

Although many people turn to medication to calm them down, the brain at rest is calm and balanced. You can return to this natural center using hypnosis. It is *your* experience, and *you* created it using your own mind. Begin by returning your thoughts to your here-and-now awareness, and you will have an easier time working on your problems and enhancing your feelings of well-being. Knowing you can always return to this quiet moment, you may have the confidence to work through disturbing emotions.

Meditative Walk in Trance Exercise

Find a comfortable position for trance, either sitting or lying down. You might even enjoy doing this trance outdoors in nature. Go into trance and relax. Now imagine yourself taking a walk in a beautiful place out in nature. As you are walking, attend only to the experience. Pay attention to the feeling of your feet on the ground, the sights around you, the smells, and the sounds. Simply walk and be involved with the experience. Be fully present in each moment of walking. If you can stay with this relaxing experience in trance, you may feel yourself calming down just enough to feel some comfort. Turn to this trance as a resource when you need it.

How Emotions Influence Thoughts

Now that you are possibly feeling more comfortable, you may feel ready to start working on the problem. You can begin by exploring how your moods are influenced. Negative thinking plays a large role in depression, anger, and irritable moods. These negative thoughts are usually exaggerated, one-sided, or inaccurate because when people are feeling moody, they tend to interpret meanings from people and events more negatively. So, when you are in a positive mood you can experience someone's manner as cheerful and friendly, whereas when you are in a depressed or angry mood you might misjudge that person's same cheerfulness as annoying.

How Thoughts Influence Emotions

Negative thoughts can become a relatively stable, unconscious pattern of self-suggestions. Such a pattern casts a net over experiencing that may reshape or distort what is perceived, leading you in a certain direction and away from others. So, when you hear yourself saying, "I hate this," you are suggesting that this thing is bad, and should be avoided, causing you to ignore some possibilities it might hold.

"All human behavior reflects the need to make sense of the world" (Frank & Frank, 1991, p. 24). We create a meaningful environment as we navigate through our experiences. Emotions, along with behaviors and thoughts, both influence and are influenced by how we interpret our experiences. The theories and concepts we form about things lead to emotions, and our emotions lead to concepts and theories about our experiences. And then, self-suggestions arise from the interaction. Many of these self-suggestions are positive and helpful, but some can become limiting, and hold you back in life. They can interfere with relationships, achievements, and happiness, due to self-fulfilling negative expectations. In many chapters of this book, we have talked about the power of self-suggestion to influence you for better or worse. Brain changes occur from self-suggestion, so why not use this to influence your mood to feel better and do better?

Four-Step Ideomotor Change for Negative Thinking Exercise:
Observe, Question, Imagine, Allow

Here are four steps for changing your negative thinking using the ideomotor effect of self-suggestion to foster change: observe, question, imagine, allow. You will be better equipped to give up your unrealistic and inaccurate thoughts, which generate negative self-suggestions, and allow a change to automatically take place. The process requires some diligence at first to set it in motion. First, you start by consciously observing and questioning, and then allow your unconscious response to unfold.

Observe: Pay attention to what you are telling yourself when you feel depressed, annoyed, or irritable. For example, you may be dwelling on something that was said to you. But what else are you thinking? Dig deeper and you will hear some kind of assertion that you are making such as, "My mother [or father, sister, brother, wife, husband, child, or friend] is angry with me."

Question: Instead of simply accepting your negative thought as true, question it. Rephrase your worry as a question: "Is this person angry with me?" This should evoke your curiosity. Is he or she actually angry or not? There is a truth of the matter and you can find it out. Try to answer your question by looking for evidence. Perhaps you can find out by asking that person to clarify. But this might not be an option, so perhaps someone else could give you some information. Or you may be able to think of other situations involving that person. Is he or she chronically angry with everyone? If so, perhaps the comment was more a reflection of that person's disposition than of your action. Or is this person rarely angry, and perhaps you are projecting your own feeling? Are you perhaps angry with this person, and thus the anger actually is coming from you?

Imagine: If you discover that your negative thought is somewhat inaccurate—and many such thoughts often are—realize the discovery fully. Vividly imagine the new thought and all that it entails.

Allow: Allowing involves giving permission to have a change take place and then just letting it happen. Hold the idea, image, or feeling vividly in mind, and the natural ideomotor response will take place. Response builds over time, so be patient with the process.

Keep working with each negative thought, first becoming aware of it and questioning it, then imagining the truer thought or feeling, and finally allowing the new experience to take place. Do not blame yourself for having negative thoughts. Many people are overly hard on themselves, especially those suffering from depression. Once you commit yourself to changing your negative thinking, you may find that these ideas are not as intractable as you might have expected.

You don't need to rely on old patterns in order to be oriented, because your natural brain pathways are available for sensing and orienting. Trance exploration can help you to reexperience the roots of self-suggestion patterns that may interfere with present experiencing, and thereby open yourself to forming more realistic patterns.

Letting Go of Problematic Self-Suggestions Unconsciously Exercise

Close your eyes and relax for a moment. Let yourself drift into a light trance. As you feel yourself slipping into trance, wait for what thoughts come to you. Look behind the obvious, much like watching what passes by outside as you look out the window from a traveling car. Open yourself to any flickering thoughts that may be just beyond your view. Do you notice subtle, repetitive, or negative thoughts? Try to articulate what you notice.

Let your thoughts drift in this way and then try to look deeper. Ask yourself if something new can emerge in the flicker. Are there other ways to think about yourself that include your positive potentials? Let yourself enjoy a moment of calm and confidence, trusting that your unconscious processes are there to help, always a resource for you. You may not know what potential understandings your unconscious will discover, but know that these processes are intelligent and can help you find new options.

Shifting from thinking about what you cannot do or are not doing to what you can do and are doing may take time. Repeat this open-ended trance regularly. Be patient, because altering an emotional reaction may take some time to happen.

Even if you are successful with these exercises, you may have to wait for your emotion to change or mood to lift. You can help the process along with the next few exercises, which offer ways to foster a different reaction.

Regression for Unlearning Exercise

Most people think that learning involves acquiring new information, but sometimes before you can learn, you have to un-learn. We have all had the experience of first meeting a person and forming an initial impression of him or her and then later, after knowing that person for a long time, experiencing her or him very differently. As you go into trance, think about someone you know well. Think back to the last time you were with this person. Let yourself sense how you experience her or him. Now recall your feelings about this person last week, last month, a year ago, then several years ago, until you recall the first time you met this person. Let yourself reexperience your first meeting as vividly as you would like. Now compare that first impression with how you experience the person now. Have you taken on some limited attitudes toward this person? Next time you are together, can you experience this person openly, as if for the first time? Or perhaps can you reformulate your concept of this person and look for some of the better qualities you may be ignoring?

A Positive Use for Forgetting Exercise

Consider an opinion, belief, or attitude you once held about someone or something in your life which later changed. Many people have experienced loving a particular food as a child (pizza, cotton candy, etc.), but have found that later, as an adult, the food lost its exciting appeal. Or perhaps you used to be comfortable doing something but later, after having some negative experiences, you found yourself having difficulty doing or enjoying it. Recall vividly that early experience. Remember your enjoyment and ease. Your unconscious can recall the experience as if it just happened. The unconscious does not have a linear sense of time, so yesterday can be just as vivid as today. Take your time experiencing this memory. Can you allow your memory of this early experience to become more vivid as your present experience fades? Immerse yourself in the memory as you forget the more recent experience. When you feel ready, come out of trance relaxed and refreshed.

Accepting Emotions

All peoples of the world share in having certain primary emotions, and these are wired in: love, fear, anger, sadness, and happiness. The primary emotions give rise to the many varieties of secondary emotions, which are mixtures and shades of the primary emotions.

People often try to escape their feelings, change them, or avoid them. Paradoxically, one of the most effective ways to be more in touch with your environment and truly know yourself is to embrace your emotions, to feel them fully and become unified with them. In this way, you find out more about yourself and have the opportunity to learn from what you feel. And paradoxically, as you fully feel what you are experiencing, the emotion transforms and often dissipates into a feeling that is easier to handle, or even more comfortable.

In trance, you can experience your emotions from a safe, objective, unbiased vantage point. Perform this exercise at different times of the day, when you are feeling different emotions.

Accepting Sensations Exercise

Sit comfortably. Turn your attention inward, away from the outer world. Notice details of your physical experience, your sensations. Is your heartbeat gentle and comfortable, or is it quick and pressured? Does your skin feel warm, cool, or clammy? Where? How cool or warm? Are your muscles tight, sore, relaxed, or loose? Notice whether you feel any anxiety or tightness in your chest and stomach. What do you feel? Do you feel happy, content, sad, tired, annoyed? Link the physical components to the emotion. Do not attempt to alter your emotional state: Simply observe and wait for your feelings to emerge. Notice the experience, but try not to become lost in it; retain your vantage point of detached observer, sitting on the banks of the stream rather than being swept along with the current.

Emotions serve an important purpose in helping us to sensitively attune to the world. As has been described, our feelings of reward and happiness from the brain's reward pathway help to steer us toward health-promoting experiences. Our feelings of fear protect us from danger. Sadness helps us to mourn a loss, and anger spurs us to courageously face adversity. The proper use of emotions helps us to achieve our goals.

Accepting Feeling Exercise

Now that you have sensed your emotions, close your eyes again. Sit comfortably and relax into trance. Allow yourself to feel your emotion fully. If you are feeling sad, let the emotion spread through you. Let it be; do not try to alter it, but if the emotional tone spontaneously begins to change, allow it to. Embrace it and accept it. Thus, let yourself feel sadness if you are sad. Do not add to it or draw conclusions. Simply allow the feeling to be, and wait.

Accepting feelings can be especially helpful if you have lost a loved one. There is a natural mourning process. Somewhat like the labor of childbirth, if you endure and embrace it fully, even though it may be intensely painful, you gain from the experience and then move forward.

The meaning of emotions is often unconscious. Acceptance is an important step in coming to terms with what you feel and initiating a process that will transform your emotions as needed. Before passing judgment, learn to listen to what your unconscious has to say. One way to listen is inviting yourself to have a dream while in trance.

Accepting Unconscious Meaning Exercise

As you relax in trance, let yourself have a significant dream. You might suggest to yourself, "I would like to have a significant dream." Then wait for your response. You may not need to fully understand the dream. And even if you do not have a dream right away, accept that your unconscious is communicating with you. Trust the process as you continue to relax in trance. Hypnosis can help you learn to tolerate difficult emotions and learn from them. Trance is a resource for inner strength. Trust yourself and you may be surprised as your positive potentials for coping emerge.

Affect Regulation

As you accept your emotions, you may notice some imbalances in affect. Perhaps your emotions are uncomfortably strong, so much so that you have difficulty handling them. Or maybe you feel almost nothing, just a blankness or a feeling of fatigue. These imbalances lead to characteristic types of mental activity, along with over- or under-activation in the brain pathways as well. People suffering from too low an affect may have problems like depression, apathy, and chronic fatigue. Others whos affect is too high might be burdened with fits of anger or hostility. One way to help is by returning to a natural balance in trance, which will allow your brain to readjust. By using these exercises regularly, you can rewire some of your brain circuits for more balanced responsiveness.

Fostering the Opposite

Contemporary researchers are finding that restoring the balance of affect promotes health. For example, researchers at the Harvard Medical School used the balancing of opposites in treatment for explosive anger. Sudden elevations in blood pressure add to the release of adrenaline and other hormones that raise the heart rate and blood pressure. These researchers recommended relaxation techniques as an effective way to lower the energy level that is aroused by intense anger (Williams & Williams, 1994. p. 29). Hypnosis and suggestion can help restore the balance.

Calming to Find a Better Balance

Practicing regular calming can be very helpful in combating extremes of strong, disturbing emotions. It is best to begin at a time when you do not feel the uncomfortable feeling, when you are feeling fairly level. Once you have developed and trained your skills in the habit of calmness, you can call on your ability to be calm in the midst of a strong emotion or just before it erupts, moderating the course of your usual reaction.

In contrast, you also can identify when you are relaxed. People are more likely to notice differences. Contrasting the experience of loose muscles with that of tight muscles makes it easier to recognize when you are tense. This exercise may be especially helpful if you have had difficulty producing a deep relaxation in trance. Begin with this exercise and then, when your body is relaxed, try using a trance induction to go into hypnosis.

Warm-Up Body Relaxation Exercise for Trance

Lie down on your back on the floor, a firm bed, or a couch. Let your whole body relax as deeply as you can. Then tighten your whole body, from head to foot. Hold this contraction for approximately 30 seconds. Now let go and relax all over. Notice the difference in your muscles from when they were tight. Repeat three times. Try to deepen your overall relaxation each time you let go. You may rest awhile after producing this deep relaxation. With practice, you will gain greater control over your muscles to be able to relax more deeply at will.

Relaxation Trance Exercise

Close your eyes. Follow your breathing for a minute or so, letting yourself settle into trance. Scan through your body with your inner attention and allow yourself to relax as much as possible. Notice whether you are holding the muscles of your face, neck, shoulders, or back tightly. These are typical areas in which to hold tension. Can you release these areas? Do not think about anything in particular, except to be relaxed in the moment.

Now offer yourself a suggestion: I wonder how relaxed I can be? What will it feel like to be more relaxed than I have ever been before? You can then wonder if you will feel relaxation in your muscles, or whether it will be felt as a relaxing image, or even a sensation such as warmth or coolness. Sometimes people have a quick memory of a time when they were very relaxed. Do not force the experience. Instead, just wait with an open curiosity as to what will happen. You may be pleasantly surprised at just how relaxed and comfortable you can be. When you feel ready, open your eyes, stand up, and stretch.

Use these calming trance exercises or the calming trances from elsewhere in this book, and repeat them frequently. You will find that calming trances practiced here and there throughout your day will lessen extremes, so that you can moderate your moods and emotions more easily.

Raising Low Affect

At the other extreme, low affect can also present problems in your daily life. Depression is one of the most common mood problems, affecting at least 10% of the population from time to time, and twice as many women as men. The physical symptoms of depressed mood are low energy, apathy, loss of appetite, lack of interest in former pleasures, and disruption of sleep patterns. Doctors caution that when people are depressed, they are more susceptible to disease because of a lowered immune system response. If you have felt depressed for more than a few weeks, seek psychotherapy or hypnotherapy. Psychological treatment can make a difference!

Reduce Rigidity to Release Energy

People who suffer from low affect often feel stuck in rigid patterns. This rigidity can bring about fatigue and lower energy. The supple and flexible willow tree bends to weather powerful storms, whereas the rigid oak pits its strength against the elements. When the conditions are too forceful, extreme, and intense, the rigid oak breaks. When people take an inflexible attitude toward difficulties, they do not cope as well as they could. Learn to bend like the willow, and you will bypass many difficulties and not let circumstances take you to the breaking point. When the difficulty passes, you can spring back again.

Relaxed breathing helps you become less rigid, and more supple. As is written in the *Dao de Jing*, "By concentrating your breath until you become soft, can you be like an infant?" (Duyvendak, 1992, p. 36). When in trance, as you let go of tensions, your vitality can raise.

Whole Body Breathing and Visualizing in Trance Exercise

Sit comfortably, close your eyes, and breathe gently. Let yourself go into a light trance, relaxing all over as you focus your attention on your breathing. Follow the air as it goes in through your nose and down into your lungs. Imagine that with each breath in, the air penetrates through your entire body, softening and relaxing throughout. With each exhalation, tensions are released from head to toe.

Next, imagine that you raise your hands lightly over your head while you breathe in, expanding your rib cage slightly as it fills with air. Then imagine that you let your arms drop back gently to your sides as you breathe out. Imagine that you feel energy flowing through your body, as you become revitalized and energized. Repeat these visualizations several times.

Lessening Depression with Self-Hypnosis

One of the prominent views of mood today is the neurochemical theory. Depression has been linked to alterations in norepinephrine and serotonin transmission, two neurotransmitters that are important for arousal and attention (norepinephrine), and mood, pain, aggression, and sleep (serotonin). The norepinephrine system is one of the most global, traveling throughout the entire brain. Serotonin is made from an amino acid in the diet, tryptophan, so it is one of the few neurotransmitters that we have control over: the right diet leads to the right amount of tryptophan in the brain. Drug therapy uses SSRIs to block the reuptake of serotonin, thereby keeping it in the limbic system longer. We have seen that expectancy and self-suggestion have a strong influence on neurotransmitters, and so the regular use of self-hypnosis can alter your brain chemistry. Use self-hypnosis as an adjunct to psychotherapy or drug therapy to help you make real and lasting changes which will help you overcome the grip of depression.

There are also a number of new theories about depression that integrate well with the use of self-hypnosis. Some believe that depression arises from our interpersonal relationships. People who are married are 70% less likely to become depressed. Michael Yapko, an experienced expert in working with depression, tells us that depression is contagious (Yapko, 2009). How you think, feel, and relate to others will have a strong influence on how depressed you feel. You can take active steps to alter what you think and do, which will specifically change how you feel.

Using Hypnosis to Facilitate Your Interpersonal Relationships

You can apply self-hypnosis to improve your interpersonal relationships using the next series of exercises. Hypnosis is an interpersonal experience, because even during self-hypnosis you are in a relationship—a relationship with yourself. One key to having better interpersonal relationships with others is to have a good relationship with your own unconscious processes. So, begin by fostering a positive relationship with yourself.

Improve Your Relationship With Yourself Exercise

Enter trance in a way that you find most comfortable. As you allow yourself to go deeper, you do not have to think about anything or do anything in particular. Simply experience what is there. You have learned that you can trust your inner processing. Can you extend benevolence, to your own inner processes? Allow this suggestion to remind you how your thoughts, feelings, and sensations are your unique doorway to the world. Appreciate all that you experience as the seeds of your potential.

Now, can you extend this benevolence to the thoughts, feelings, and behaviors of others? Just as you can appreciate your own experiencing, you can also have appreciation for the experiencing of others. We all share in the capacity to develop our potentials, especially when we are encouraged and fostered. You can use suggestion positively to set this process in motion for yourself and the significant others in your life.

You can start with your intention of positivity toward each part of your self and toward your goal of being your best. Then this, too, will extend to your partner and other loved ones, as you begin to appreciate the good qualities in the other. Learn about yourself and appreciate your talents, however small they may seem right now, and you can project more love and compassion for your partner from that foundation.

Every interaction between people has an unconscious dimension. When you are relating to your partner, there is an implicit, unconscious element of trust, love, and caring. These qualities derive from your brain, which is wired for loving relationships as a way to perpetuate the species. When you are having problems in your relationships, these natural processes are disrupted, which puts even more pressure on the interaction. You can reclaim your natural capacity to love and be lovable by opening yourself to that possibility in trance.

Exercise in Attuning to the Unconscious Interpersonal Dimension

Go into trance and turn your attention to your experiencing as you visualize your partner and the interaction between you. How are you being affected by this relationship? Can you sense an underlying tone to the relationship, perhaps nurturing or maybe hostile? Do you perhaps wish the other well, but think he or she is wrong, mean, or domineering? The negative thoughts may be overshadowing a deeper feeling of caring that is unconscious. Your partner may also feel hostile, and yet on a deeper level, still care about you. This mutual caring is unconscious, but always going on. Vividly imagine the love and caring that is there, deep down. Allow it to develop naturally. By becoming sensitive and accepting of this level of caring, you can work with it and strengthen it using the many methods presented in this book, such as the 4-step method for altering negative self-suggestion. Just as you are critical of and hard on yourself, you are probably radiating negativity toward your partner. As you become more positive toward yourself, you will also find yourself naturally feeling better about others.

Depression may involve an inaccurate reflection of the positive caring that is happening on a deeper level, but may not be noticed. From moment to moment, there are varieties of unconscious experiences going on. A depressed mood overshadows the subtle qualities of ongoing unconscious processing. Depressed people usually withdraw, which leads to becoming even more out of touch with the rich potentials of their unconscious experiencing. Overwhelved by depressed feelings, people resort to a redundant state, filled with negative, self-deprecatory, and judgmental self-statements. By allowing your deeper qualities to emerge, you begin to have experiences that are positive and attuned, helping to lift your depression.

Exercise in Attuning to Your Positive Unconscious Potentials

Your brain has amazing capacities. Allow yourself to appreciate the fact that you can fall asleep when you are tired and wake up when rested. Your internal clock is wired in. You know when you are hungry and when you are satiated. Regulation is part of the brain.

And you can feel love for another and receive love. Loving attachments are wired in as well. You can also recognize that no two brains are exactly alike, and so you have features and qualities that are uniquely you. Even those who have achieved very little success so far in their lives have some wonderfully unique qualities to offer. Allow yourself to recognize these qualities, since they are already there, just waiting for you to discover them. This, too, is part of the brain's wiring. So, as you appreciate the natural built-in capacities of your brain, you can appreciate yourself. Allow that positive feeling to spread.

Use of Positive Self-Suggestion Exercise

You may not know just how you will express your positive potentials, and you might not know how, exactly, your negative worries will diminish. But you can open yourself up to the possibility that you are capable of more than you thought at the time you began to worry and feel negative. Even when depressed and unhappy, there are moments of feeling better—perhaps when tasting a food that you like or seeing a beautiful bird fly by. These moments are real and can be expanded. Trust your unconscious processes to help you now. Give yourself some open-ended positive suggestions that you can change, and you will open yourself to new potentials for a happier life.

Conclusion

Your emotions can lead you back to your natural center of balance. When the brain system is functioning well, your affect becomes an accurate doorway to your world, attuning you to situations. Negative self-suggestions can interfere with the responsive emotional system that nature has given you. As you accept yourself, you can begin to change. Move out of dark shadows and step into the light. Embrace your feelings fully in trance, and you will experience a transformation—at one with yourself, in harmony with your personality. Then, whether you are happy, sad, angry, or fearful, you discover an optimal balance, confident and centered, developing from your natural mind–brain resources. You can use trance to sense the natural caring and love for yourself and for others that is wired in. Return to trance regularly, and you may find that your affect can be steady and will guide you toward full engagement, in a satisfying and fulfilling life.

13

Addressing Substance Abuse and Other Impulsive Behaviors

The great thing then, in all education, is to make our nervous system our ally instead of our enemy . . . For this we must make automatic and habitual as early as possible as many useful actions as we can and guard against the growing into ways that are disadvantageous to us, as we should guard against the plague.
—William James, *Selected Papers on Philosophy*, p. 60

HABITS can be your best friend or your worst enemy. As James aptly points out, you should use your capacity to make the automatic abilities of your nervous system work for you, and guard carefully against letting your automatic habits lead you into negative patterns. You may have tried to change a troublesome habit, perhaps by making a new year's resolution, as people often do. The brain areas involved in habit-learning tend to work unconsciously, which helps explain why you may have trouble sticking with your deliberate plans to change a habit.

This chapter uses smoking as an example of a habit to change, but you can apply the general approach to different habits, by varying the relevant focus. Experiment with the exercises, invite unconscious learning, and trust your own individualized responses to occur. You do not need to know explicitly how it will happen, because unconscious learning takes place automatically, without conscious monitoring. You will feel the effects, when your habit fades away.

How the Brain Learns and Remembers Habits

Habits are learned and then stored in long-term memory. Long-term memory has been carefully studied, and we now know that there are two distinct ways in which the brain remembers and learns: information and facts are stored in declarative memory, while nonconceptual procedures and habits are recalled via non-declarative memory. Declarative memory tends to be conscious and deliberate, while non-declarative memory is unconscious and automatic. Thus, habits are formed as part of the unconscious, non-declarative memory system and are not directly, explicitly monitored by rational deliberate thought.

There are two distinct locations in the brain for these two different types of learning and memory. Habit-learning is processed in the cerebellum and basal ganglia, both part of subcortical areas involved with motor processing. In contrast, declarative memory and learning relies on the hippocampus and higher cortical areas.

Thus, because habits are unconscious, you will not affect your habit by using declarative conscious processing. A better way to change a troublesome habit is to work with it unconsciously. Hypnosis works directly through unconscious processing, and so it is one of the best ways to work with habits.

The Neurobiology of Compulsive Habits

Whenever people form a negative habit such as smoking, taking drugs, or drinking alcohol, it often begins with positive reinforcement from a reward associated with using the substance. The brain's reward pathway (Figure 13.1) gives you a good feeling when you do something that is necessary for survival such as eating, drinking, or having sex. Drugs such as cigarettes, alcohol, cocaine, heroin, ecstasy, and speed have a similar pleasurable effect at first, but not for long. The pathway begins in the midbrain, extends to the forebrain, and then goes back to the midbrain. In healthy reward processes, when the cortex receives and processes a satisfying sensory stimulus (such as drinking a cold glass of water when thirsty), it sends a signal activating a part of the midbrain known as the ventral tegmental area, which then releases the neurotransmitter dopamine through the reward pathway. Dopamine transmits the sensation of pleasure (the satisfying feeling of feeling refreshed after drinking the water). This in turn activates the attentional system, to focus attention on the water and the motor functions, so that you will keep sipping this life-promoting liquid.

The endocrine and the autonomic nervous systems interact via the hypothalamus and the pituitary gland to modulate the reward pathway. The body tends to self-regulate, so that we know, for example, when we have ingested enough water to quench our thirst. But when an addict abuses a drug or an alcoholic overindulges in liquor, he or she expends all the pleasure potential at once. The midbrain, forebrain, and neurotransmitter systems activate the positive sensation which results from taking the substance. The substance dramatically alters the action of the synapses, stimulating the reward pathway in a way that links the effect all the way down to the neurons. As a result, the reward pathway becomes compromised.

The body naturally attempts to normalize to homeostasis, but the drug presence becomes part of the balance. So the body adapts, and creates an allostasis

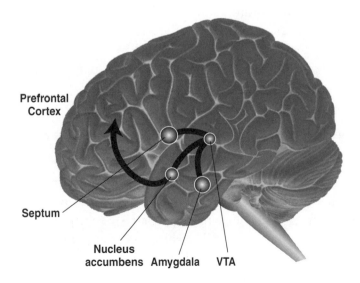

Figure 13.1. The Brain Reward Pathway.

instead, which incorporates the drug. The substance abuser's feeling of reward becomes rigidly intertwined with the drug use. The brain adapts to the continued used of the drug with habituation. More quantities of the drug are required for a change in feeling, as tolerance builds. Over time, the drug brings less pleasure and more restriction to a limited repertoire. Then the addict becomes stuck and unable to enjoy the varied pleasures life has to offer. Now, a new problem emerges for the addict to attempt to solve with the drug.

Withdrawal occurs when the user stops taking the drug. Withdrawal, marked by extreme physical and emotional discomfort, gives an opposite experience to the former seemingly positive effect of the drug use. The marked and long-lasting change in dopamine and other neurotransmitters is opposite to the effect when the drug was first taken, leaving the addict feeling depleted, anxious, and stressed. Withdrawal promises tremendous discomfort and for some drugs can even be life-threatening if not medically monitored.

Addicts feel compelled to continue to indulge in drug use, even though they sometimes wish they could stop. But research has shown that avoidance does not relieve suffering; it just perpetuates it (Domjan, 1998; Solomon, 1980). In this way, the dependency cycle continues. This cycle brings about a physiological change in the biochemistry of the reward pathway and the stress pathway. Hypnosis, by altering the neurochemistry, can help shift the balance back to the healthy, natural homeostatic balance that is wired in. After all, you were not born with this addiction, and so it is possible to return to your previous, normal ways.

Special Considerations for Impulsive Behaviors

Impulsive behaviors—such as nail-biting or obsessive hand-washing—work backwards, in the sense that the individual tends to feel anxious first and then uses the impulsive behavior to stop the anxiety. The same kind of loop is created as in addiction, but here the allostatic balance is altered to include the habit as a way of feeling normal. Unfortunately, just like substance abuse, the habit that might have helped to feel good at first becomes less effective over time. Furthermore, it is by its nature less satisfying than truly overcoming the anxiety. Similar methods for change can be used; therefore, many of the exercises in this chapter that use smoking as the example can be applied, with small variations, to other addictions, or impulsive behaviors. Also, turn to Chapter 16, on anxiety, for additional ways to address the anxious feelings that fuel impulsive behaviors.

Where to Begin

When people do not sincerely want to change their habit, they often find subtle ways to sabotage their efforts. Thus, the first step in changing a habit is to *decide* to stop. We have had clients come in because their spouse or parent wants them to change. But only when the client decides he or she truly wants to change, can the change process begin. No one else can decide for you; you must make your own decision to try and change your behavior. But a decision alone is usually not enough to break a long-standing habit, except in unusual individuals. In this sense, your decision is a *necessary* but not *sufficient* condition for changing a habit. Even though it may only be a first step, it is an important step to take.

However, even with sincerity, an opposite reaction may still take place. Quitting becomes difficult, due to the law of reversed effort. Paradoxically, the more smokers, for example, try not to smoke, the more they start to think about smoking. They are giving themselves a self-suggestion that brings smoking to mind. We see similar reactions with other substances, such as alcohol or drugs, or with impulsive behaviors or troublesome habits such as nail-biting or even playing too many video games. People will often try to stop, and even do so for a brief period. But then, as the cravings increase, they become bombarded with fantasies and beliefs about how good it will taste or feel to indulge in the behavior, or how much relief they will feel from performing the habit, and so they eventually return to it. They are trapped in a repeating loop. But through hypnosis, new understandings and possibilities emerge that can help to alter self-suggestions, which will then help to shift the brain pathways in a more positive direction.

Enlisting Unconscious Processes

As the neuroscience indicates, simply trying to force yourself not to engage in a poor habit will probably not be enough to change your behavior. You need something different. Enlist the help of your non-deliberate, non-declarative unconscious processes. This case example shows how these unconscious processes helped someone to stop smoking.

Jen came to us to quit smoking, knowing she would have difficulty doing it. She knew a great deal about quitting smoking—she had done it hundreds of times! She always gave in to the craving. Before the session, we led her to a beautiful area at the edge of the ocean. She got out of her car and followed us, with a puzzled look on her face. We demonstrated taking a number of deep breaths of fresh ocean air. She did the same. Then, we asked her to throw her entire package of cigarettes into the smelliest, dirtiest garbage can we could find, filled with vomit, dog waste, rotten food, and putrid decaying garbage. Jen said, "I might return to get them." We gestured toward the can and said, "Would you?" She answered, "I had better dump my ashtray too, because I might try to smoke the butts." We urged her to memorize the smell and appearance of that disgusting garbage can, and remember it whenever she felt tempted to smoke. Then we went to the office and began the session. She experienced a deep trance.

Jen quit that day, never to return to cigarettes. She came in for one more session about a week later. She told us that she was surprised that she had lost her urge to smoke. She realized that the function of cigarettes was important. Without her cigarettes, she needed to find a new way to relax. She learned to do so with hypnosis. A negative experience associated with a habit can facilitate letting go of it or changing it.

Getting Ready to Quit

Read and study as much as you can about the hazards of addiction. For example, learn what smoking actually does to your lungs and body, and how smoking can affect your health. Or look into what alcohol does to the brain—it actually shrinks brain mass over time. Consider how much money you spend on your habit and what you could do with the extra money if you quit. List all of the reasons you can think of not to continue with your poor habit: for example, probable harmful side effects, unpleasant odor, or how it affects those close to you. View YouTube videos that show the horrors of a cancerous lung, or the details of a slow death from emphysema. Your doctor's office may have more information and visual aids. Try your library. Becoming better informed might help you reinforce a decision to stop, if that is your choice. Learn what you can about physical consequences, to help you make a wise choice.

Uncovering Your Motivations

Uncovering personal motivations for your habit can also be helpful.

An alcoholic man had been drinking excessively for all of his adult life. He had started drinking when he was working in the entertainment business. His friends drank, and even his wife joined him in drinking. But he came to a point in his late forties when his doctor warned him, stop drinking or die. He did not really want to stop, but felt he had to. He knew all the reasons why he should not drink, how harmful it was, and that, in fact, it was killing him. But what he did not know was what his drinking did for him.

His therapeutic work involved uncovering the deep emotions and meanings he had given to alcohol. He learned that drinking helped him to connect with his friends and his wife, sharing in enjoyment together. He also felt, as many people do, that drinking was intimately linked to all his close relationships. He started to disentangle alcohol from relationships when we suggested that he try being sober while sharing an experience with friends. He decided to go golfing. Usually he and his friends started drinking at the first hole, and continued through the whole course. Needless to say, they would usually be quite drunk by the 18th hole! Our client found that he could share in a good time with his friends even though he was not drinking.

What surprised him even more was how much pleasure he felt in playing golf! He played much better while sober, and realized that he liked many aspects of the game. He found enjoyment in focusing on his swing, working on his accuracy, and feeling his strength when he connected with a drive. He also took pleasure in the beauty of nature around him, something he had never appreciated before. He told us that he could not remember ever enjoying golfing this much.

Gradually, he came to enjoy many aspects of his life. He saw that he had attributed most of his enjoyment to alcohol, and in disentangling his feelings of happiness, he found less of an urge to drink and more enjoyment in everyday living.

A popular misconception is that cigarettes, alcohol, or certain drugs are physically relaxing. But in reality, nicotine has a stimulating effect leading to increased heart rate and blood pressure. Alcohol may initially produce relaxation, but in permeating cell membranes, alcohol can quickly cause blurred vision, coordination problems, and eventual unconsciousness. Narcotic drugs such as heroin and depressants such as barbiturates are highly addictive, causing serious physical as well as emotional problems in their continued use.

People endow their habit with personal meaning. The substance becomes symbolic in the mind of the user. Actually, self-suggestion gives the substance its seemingly powerful effect. We have often told our clients who want to stop smoking, "You were not born smoking a cigarette. Whatever cigarettes do for you, you can do for yourself without them. You knew how to relax as a child and you can be comfortable without cigarettes now." The same logic can be applied to any problematic substance use or troublesome habit. The exercise that follows is written for smoking, but please substitute whatever habit you are working on changing.

Exercise to Disengage Habits from Self-Suggestion: Apply the 4-Step Method of Habit Change—Observe, Question, Imagine, Allow

Here is how to work with the typical self-suggestions that cigarettes are relaxing. Other typical misconceptions are that cigarettes help you look "cool," and stay thin. You will undoubtedly have your own self-suggestions to put through the 4-step method.

Observe: What is it like to smoke? How do you feel? What does smoking do for you? Do you think it relaxes you? Notice how your muscles and lungs feel. Smell the smoke. Feel the heat of the cigarette on your fingers. Observe anything else related to smoking.

Question: Does the act of smoking really relax you, or are you simply taking some time while smoking to relax? Perhaps you are attributing more power to the cigarette and less power to your own capacity to relax. Question whether cigarettes relax you by gathering information about the effects of cigarettes. Cigarettes do not have that kind of a physiological effect.

Imagine: Contemplate the situation as it really is: The source of relaxation is within you. Now, vividly imagine relaxing without smoking. Picture yourself in a situation when you usually smoke, without a cigarette and feeling fully relaxed.

Allow: Give yourself permission to relax without cigarettes. Allow the relaxation to spread, as you become free of illusory dependence on this outside stimulus to elicit your own response.

Drawing on the Unconscious for Change

Melanie was urged to seek treatment by her boyfriend, who was seeing us to help him overcome his heroin addiction. He was committed to the process and was making good progress. He cared deeply for Melanie and could see that she was hurting herself, and so he strongly urged her to come see us. Melanie was a tall, thin girl in her mid twenties with striking features and long blond hair. She was intelligent and college-educated, and came from a prominent family who provided her with an ample trust fund, paid to her each month. So, she lived very comfortably for a young woman who was not working. She seemed to have everything that could lead to a happy, productive life, but here she was, addicted to heroin and bereft of any motivation to do anything other than get high.

At first, she sounded like a person who wanted to make a change. She had an uncanny sense of what people would likely to want to hear, and since we were obviously on the side of sobriety, she told us that she was trying to quit. But as we all got to know each other better, she began to feel more comfortable disclosing what she really felt. She said, "To be completely honest, I don't really see any reason why I should stop taking heroin. I have plenty of money to support myself and to pay for my habit. I'm a free agent! I can do what I want, and this is what I want to do." Her argument was cogent and rational, and we told her so. She felt accepted and understood, and said she would be curious to experience hypnosis anyway, since her boyfriend liked it so much. We suspected that although her conscious, rational thinking was airtight, her unconscious thoughts and feelings might have something else to say. We were curious why she had chosen this path for her life, and soon, she was curious too.

She went deeply into hypnosis and was able to do hand levitation, have vivid imagery, and alter her body sensations. After several sessions, she had a significant memory occur to her in trance, something she had not thought about for many years. She recalled being at a large family gathering at the family's summer estate. Everyone was out on the lawn, overlooking a lake. Luscious flowers lined the shoreline and a sweet, light breeze spread through the crowd. Everyone was dressed in beautiful designer clothes. We were reminded of a scene described in *The Great Gatsby*. Melanie was in middle school in her memory and had been snapping pictures to capture the beauty of the moment. Her aunt smiled at her condescendingly, and said, "Well, that's nice dear. Your grandfather was a photo-journalist and won the Pulitzer prize for his work." Then she jolted out of trance, poured out the story, and told us with tears in her eyes how this memory was just one of dozens of similar encounters. She was never taken seriously in her family. No one expected that she would ever achieve anything compared to the legendary achievements of those who went before her. At a certain age, she had made a decision to stop trying.

Now, for the first time in many years, she felt a deep sense of her wish to do something with her life, and she recognized that it did not matter if those other people considered her life insignificant. She was able to see an open future ahead of her and was looking forward to using her unconscious mind as her guide. With this realization, she had a cascade of insights that led her to make a new decision: to check into a drug treatment program. She had listened to her unconscious mind.

Unconscious Change Exercise

Hypnosis can facilitate unconscious learning. Find a restful level of trance, relaxing your muscles and letting yourself have a comfortable bodily experience. As you go deeper into trance, imagine an inspiring scene in nature: it might be a clear sky, clean air, the smell of fresh pine trees, a beautiful garden, the mountains, or the salty ocean air. Breathe deeply and enjoy the feeling of clean air in your lungs. Relax and let your trance deepen. Allow your attention to drift around, toward whatever seems interesting. Your unconscious already knows what is relevant, far better than you can imagine. Associations to important images, experiences, and feelings will take place naturally. You can have an unconscious corrective experience, without consciously knowing it. Or again, perhaps you will know it. If you attempt to anticipate or deliberately program what you will learn, you may limit yourself and thereby miss out on many interesting new spontaneous discoveries. Instead of trying to know, permit yourself to wonder what you will learn. When you are ready, awaken, fully alert.

Overcoming Negative Self-Suggestion

Sometimes people continue a negative habit just because they always have. They think themselves into a corner to justify continuing. Habit leads to inertia, the tendency for a habit already in effect to continue as before, and change seems out of reach. People often have made a valiant effort to change, but each failure confirms the self-diagnosis, "Compulsive . . . incurable." These negative self-suggestions can be altered or bypassed when you work with your unconscious processing. Sometimes habit change involves painful work with memories that lead to significant insights, as with Melanie. But habit change through unconscious learning can be pleasant at times, as Vincent felt, bypassing problems and limitations, leading to new, creative talents that may be far more rewarding than the habit ever was.

Vincent wanted to quit smoking and came for several sessions of hypnosis. We encouraged him to relax and be open to the creative potential of his trance experience. We sensed that he could make new, surprising discoveries before the next session, and suggested that he have some fun with it. He arrived at the next session smiling. He reported that he had a surprisingly wonderful time going out dancing with a girl the night before the session. He had gone to a disco and danced so well that everyone clapped. He told us with much embarrassment that he did not know how to dance nor did he usually go out with girls, since he was comfortably adjusted in a gay lifestyle. Some months later Vincent got in touch to tell us that not only did he continue not smoking, but he had also continued dancing. He entered professional dance contests and was winning them! Furthermore, he discovered that he was an excellent gourmet cook. His hidden natural talent evolved, freed from the restriction of rigid habit. He developed in new, unexpected, and positive directions, due to his creative experiences, which had become available to him through trance.

Exercise in Readying for Change Unconsciously

Go into a very deep trance; take your time. Relax and use any approach to trance that you find effective. Deepen your trance several times; relax more with each suggestion, until you are deeper than you have ever been. Remember, levels vary with individuals and your unconscious will help you find an adequate depth for you.

Can you experimentally produce several different hypnotic effects? Try lightness, warmth, or heaviness of a limb with a nice image, or a slowed experience of time—whatever you enjoy doing in trance. You know that you have begun to set yourself to change your habit. Experiment with altering your awareness, and be open to the unknown.

Each exercise you do in trance can help enlist your unconscious in making a change. Unconscious change can take many forms. You may find something creative and new that you had not considered to replace the old habit. Or perhaps you will have a realization that changes the habit's significance. The realizations could emerge from something distasteful or negative or from something positive and wonderful. Just as your hand can sometimes move seemingly by itself when you write, or you might feel too lazy to do anything at all, so also you can find the craving you usually feel for the substance or satisfaction from the habit can dissipate or be altered. New perceptions can arise from a different image in trance. This can help you change. A new insight may follow, or you may just be able to make a change without insight. Trust your unconscious to individualize.

Unconscious Strength

Explore your reactions to positive suggestions: Can you imagine giving up the problem with little or no discomfort? Your body knows how to not notice many experiences and sensations. Unconscious wisdom can give inner involuntary strength, adding to conscious conviction. You find a new reservoir of confidence to help you. The discovery of your own untapped inner strength becomes the source of change.

You can be calm, using hypnosis when needed, if you are willing to use unconscious processes to help. Your urge need not lead to actually acting upon it. At any point in the chain of action, a link can be broken. Then the habit loses its expression in action.

Associations and Imaginings Exercise

Imagine how you would be without your habit. What a positive sense of accomplishment you will feel! You may wonder why you did not change sooner. What thoughts and images do you have as you project yourself into the future? How did you do it? What are you like? Your thoughts and associations flow from the source of change, but the source is not conscious. Let your unconscious help you in positive ways. Then relax and rest in trance. Wake up refreshed. Repeat this trance often over the next several days. You might want to emphasize suggestion of one aspect over another at each session. Some will find results are immediate, while others may need several sessions. Use trance in the ways that help you.

Conclusion

The relationship between yourself and your unconscious can grow and develop in beneficial ways if you work on it. As the river flows to the ocean and becomes one with it, your sincere intention to resolve your problems can lead you to open up better communication between your conscious and unconscious processes. People have many hidden unrecognized potentials, often unknowingly held in reserve. Use hypnosis to cultivate receptivity to your hidden potential, so you can incorporate your own unrecognized resources into your life. We hope you can apply unconscious learning to accomplish your goals and more. As you change your habits, you may experience a pleasant sense of surprise. Potential can develop in other areas than just the target area. Everything you have experienced and learned can be a resource for positive change. But that is an even greater learning. Learning is infinite.

14

Adjusting and Managing Weight Naturally

The first step on the way to Tao is to be in harmony with, not in rebellion against, the fundamental laws of the universe.

—Zhuangzi, *The Way and Its Power* (in Waley, 1955, p. 55)

YOUR brain has a number of systems that moderate important internal processes. Hypnosis can be very helpful in restoring control when internal equilibrium is lost. There are many ways to rediscover the natural inner balance, and when you do, you will find yourself overcoming problems more easily and naturally than you might have thought possible. The methods also draw upon the principles in Chapter 13 for overcoming addiction and breaking bad habits, so be sure to refer to back to that chapter as well.

How the Brain Regulates Weight

The hypothalamus, located right below the thalamus, is vital for regulating the internal states of the body. It is the seat of the "biological clock," which is central in monitoring the circadian rhythms of sleep and waking, hormonal rhythms, and sexual activity. The hypothalamus helps maintain homeostasis by such means as the constancy of the body's internal temperature.

The hypothalamus is also essential to the regulation of thirst and appetite. An early dual-center hypothesis for the control of eating (Stellar, 1954) proposed that there are two centers for appetite: one which regulates hunger and the other which regulates satiety. For many years, researchers thought that a certain part of the hypothalamus, the ventromedial hypothalamus (VMH), was the satiety center, because lesions to the lateral hypothalamus (LH) seemed to trigger rapid weight loss. But this theory proved to be too simple. Today, the theory that locates appetite control in the hypothalamus integrates a much more complex system of hormones as signals that interact together. One section of the hypothalamus, the arcuate nucleus, is where we find an appetite controller, governed by the circulation of hormones. Five peptides are secreted into the bloodstream, and two types of neurons in the arcuate nucleus are sensitive to these peptides and signal for either a decrease in food intake or an increase. These signals exert effects on second-order neurons in the VMH and LH, which lead to the release of other hormones which stimulate or inhibit appetite.

The hypothalamus also monitors signals to the pituitary gland to direct the release of hormones involved in the HPA stress pathway (See Figure 11.1). The HPA pathway regulates the stress response (described in Chapter 11). Thus, you can see why, from a neurobiological perspective, eating problems are often intertwined with stress (since the hypothalamus also regulates sleep and sex, there are links between stress, sleep disorders, and sexual problems as well).

Getting Started: Your First Week

Anyone considering a weight-loss program should always check with a physician to ensure that there are no medical problems related to your weight. Changes in weight can be due to many factors, so consult with your doctor. If no physical complications are found, then you can do something about your weight.

Willpower is not the determining factor in losing weight. Even with the best of intentions, dieters are subject to the law of reversed effort—that is, the more you try to diet, the more you will tend to think about food! Similar to other habits, using the deliberate, conscious circuits merely serves to place the problem foremost in your mind. Then, conflicts and problems emerge due to negative self-suggestions, thus sabotaging your efforts and discouraging you from succeeding. So, enlist positive unconscious functioning and the ideomotor effect of suggestion to help you accomplish goals. You can use both your conscious and unconscious processes to help regulate your weight. Work with awareness and proper attitudes to set the stage; use suggestion and hypnosis to activate the process; and then allow your natural brain regulation to come back into balance.

First Step: Stop Dieting

Begin your weight loss efforts by not dieting for at least a week. Eat as you normally would when not on a diet. Objectively observe how you normally eat. This is not an invitation to overindulge—simply let your natural tendencies emerge. What happens? Do not try to change your eating habits yet. Notice how you experience eating, and what your eating patterns are. Observe your patterns carefully by initiating the 4-step process of Observe, Question, Imagine, and Allow (introduced in Chapter 12). Keep a journal to help you track your eating patterns if you find that helpful.

Balancing Your Diet

Obtain information on nutrition and proper diet. Become highly informed about food and its effects on the body. Check authoritative sources. Consult expert sources to be accurate. Your doctor may have useful pamphlets, and public libraries are excellent resources. The Internet can be helpful as well, as long as you make sure that the site is not simply an advertisement but is a reputable source of information, such as WebMD. Certain sports or physical activities that you may take part in might require special nutritional requirements as well, so keep that in mind. Compound what you learn from outside sources with your own understandings and wisdom.

After you have gathered this information, set up a well-balanced diet that includes all the food groups. You may wish to follow an established, recognized weight loss program, or consult with a nutritionist. Do not start to diet until you have completed your week of observation and feel ready to commit yourself fully.

Adding Regular Exercise

Getting adequate regular exercise will greatly enhance your weight loss as well as your overall health. Research the benefits of exercise. Learn more about how often is best and what types are best for you. If you are inactive, consider adding a 15-minute walk each day. If you already exercise, try to add a little more time or intensity to your workouts. Be moderate when implementing your changes, but do them.

Erickson once treated an overeating client by requiring that she buy only enough food for one day at a time. Each day she was to walk to the grocery store and purchase her food for that day only. This demanded an absolute commitment to follow his instructions, trust the process, and take extra time, a good test of her resolve. She was forced to evaluate whether she really needed that food for the next day. And to buy the food for the next day, she had to walk every day; a healthy way to use up calories. If you are willing to do this, it can prevent consuming excess food and enlist your personal cooperation with the interesting process you are about to begin.

Working with Self-Suggestion Exercise: Changing Discouragement to Encouragement
Think about any preconceptions you have about the kinds of changes you are hoping to make. Do you feel pessimistic about your weight? If so, where does this negativity come from? Does it derive from your own experience, such as earlier attempts that you made without success? Or are you basing your experience on what other people have told you, such as, "You will never change," "You have large bones," "It runs in the family," or "You have a slow metabolism." Try to trace back to the source of any taken-for-granted attitudes and decisions you might have made in response that might be holding you back, and become aware of them.

These taken-for-granted assumptions may act as negative self-suggestions, interfering with your efforts to change. Notice if you are giving yourself a negative self-suggestion about losing weight. In Chapters 7 and 12 we discussed how people often give negative self-suggestions and we offered some ways to change them. Review the 4-step method for changing negative thoughts consciously: Observe, Question, Imagine, and Allow, as described in Chapter 12. Apply it to some of the subtle, inner discouragement you may be giving yourself without quite realizing it. Notice when and how you do so. Remember not to get annoyed at yourself. Keep an aware, but nonjudgmental attitude as you gradually but definitely change negative self-suggestions into neutral, and then positive, ones.

Truly Tasting

Many dieters will claim they are overweight because they love the taste of food. However, overweight people often consume food so quickly, they taste their food less than they realize, and consequently never feel quite satisfied. Learning to slow down, taste, and experience food can be helpful for overcoming weight problems. It takes time to realize you are full. Developing sensitivity to taste can help get you back on track.

Taste Analyzer

Choose a food to taste. Rate the food in terms of each of the following elements, from least (zero) to most (10).

Sweet	0 1 2 3 4 5 6 7 8 9 10
Sour	0 1 2 3 4 5 6 7 8 9 10
Bitter	0 1 2 3 4 5 6 7 8 9 10
Salty	0 1 2 3 4 5 6 7 8 9 10

Circle the appropriate number for each of the four categories. Do this for your favorite food, a food you like, and a food you dislike. Make up a taste card for each food and try many different foods. Add a brief description at the end of the taste card with the following categories: consistency, color, appearance, temperature, and degree of liking, rating each from 0 to 10 (Bruno, 1972, pp. 96–98). You may like to invite friends or family to try making taste cards too. Tasting foods together can be an enjoyable experience to share.

Eating Mindfully Exercise

Now that you have tasted a number of foods, turn your attention and absorption to eating. Prepare a well-balanced meal that includes some of the foods you put through the taste tester exercise. Set the table carefully, paying close attention to your movements as you put everything on the table. When everything is in place, turn your attention to your body as you slowly sit down. Take a moment to notice how you are sitting on the chair, how your feet meet the floor, and whether your back takes support from the chair. Close your eyes and pay attention to your breathing for a moment. Notice other sensations, such as the aroma of the food. Open your eyes and look carefully at the food in front of you, noticing the colors and arrangement of the food. Then, when you feel calm and centered, begin eating slowly. Chew each bite all the way down and taste the food. Notice its texture, temperature, and flavor. Keep your breathing and body relaxed. Try not to be distracted as you pay close attention throughout the whole meal. If you find your thoughts drifting, stop eating and center yourself again in the moment before you resume eating. When you are finished, clean up carefully, maintaining your mindful awareness.

If you have trouble keeping focused for the whole meal, try again with simply one food, such as a ripe piece of fruit. Eat this one thing mindfully, using the instructions above. As your ability to stay focused improves, extend mindfulness throughout an entire meal.

Mindfulness of Patterns

Just as you mindfully focused on eating a meal, you can use your awareness to observe your eating patterns. You will probably make some connections. For example, people who habitually overeat often indulge at a certain time of day or night. We had a client who claimed that she was a healthy eater. She told us, "I never eat any junk food. I have a very healthy diet." She could not understand why she gained weight from healthy foods like granola, freshly baked, whole-wheat bread, and pasta, and blamed it on her metabolism. But as she became more aware, she realized that she overindulged in healthy foods. The quality of food was high, but the quantity was, too.

Another common pattern is when a particular food triggers overeating. One client would feel compelled to eat an entire gallon of ice cream after she had her first spoonful. One woman overate when she went out with friends, whereas another client only overate when alone. Keep in mind that since patterns are learned, they can be unlearned.

Observing in Trance Exercise

Go into trance. Imagine watching yourself eating, as if in front of a mirror. What do you see? Try imagining yourself eating at different times of the day, including late-night binges and your early morning breakfast. Observe carefully, without drawing a conclusion. Try to just watch.

Exploring Eating Habits Consciously

Now that you have been observing your eating patterns for several days, you can use some cognitive methods to help gather more clarity. Consider whether you eat in reaction to something, such as feeling overtired, stressed, nervous, or worried. Do you have certain foods, times of day, or other events that lead to overeating? Observe and learn about your assumptions and consequent behavior. Remember not to pass judgment on your actions.

After you have made observations of your pattern, consider the following questions: Do you need to change your habit? Do you really want to change? Do you actually believe you can? Answer honestly. Only you really know the true answer. Only you need to know the answer. But the answers to these questions are part of your basis for changing your habit.

Symbolic patterns like overeating are often taken for granted, becoming the constant, inevitable internal state of the sufferer, who becomes trapped in assumptions and beliefs about his or her unchangeable circumstances. Self-hypnosis can be an effective means to overcome this. A new perspective appears, and with it new beliefs can arise. Assumptions can change; conflicts can resolve. Behavior will reflect the change, as self-control becomes your natural response.

How to Not Not-Diet

Maria felt helpless. She had tried to lose weight for years, but seemed to stay stuck at one weight, about 15 pounds over her ideal weight. We asked her what she did to break her diet, and at first she said, "Nothing, I'm always on a diet. I never eat candy, I drink diet soda, and I eat a fairly balanced diet." We encouraged her to not not-diet! She left the session puzzled. When she returned the next week, she was smiling. She said that at first, she could not figure out what we meant, but as she did her daily trances at home, she had an image spontaneously appear of herself cooking. Suddenly she saw herself snacking while she cooked without even realizing that she was doing it! It was a revelation for her, and suddenly she realized that the way to not not-diet was to stop snacking while she cooked. She got a large glass of water ready and drank water instead of snacking while cooking. Over several months, she did lose the 15 pounds.

If you decide you need to eat less, but do not feel you can, think about some of the ways that you prevent yourself from staying on a healthy diet. Then, you can not not-diet by not doing whatever you do do to not lose weight!

Working With Your Unconscious Processes

Conscious insight may help to uncover the source and meaning of self-destructive patterns. But inner change must also take into account your intuitive, unconscious side. Intuition is an essential component of true insight. Insight will include alternative solutions.

The key to resolving one problem, such as overeating, is often linked to another problem, usually something that you might not be aware of. When people have a problem with weight, they may be using overeating as an incomplete attempt to express or solve another problem. All of the related problems are pieces of the puzzle.

An illustration of this point is the case of Alice, who came to see us for hypnotherapy to lose weight. Alice had tried to lose weight for years, but remained 50 pounds overweight. She was outwardly placid and kindly, and upheld a high and admirable moral standard. She often did things for others before thinking of herself. But inwardly, she was uncomfortable. Others could sense her inner tension and frustration even though she was unaware of it. One of the challenges in her family life was that her daughter had temporal lobe epilepsy, with regular bouts of moodiness leading to family tensions. She thought she was handling the daughter well by being kind and good, but her methods were not working.

As her hypnotherapy progressed, Alice felt great waves of anger surge and wash over her in trance. At first, she was surprised by the anger. She had no idea what it was about, But immediately following the wave of anger, she felt like snacking. She began to see that there was a connection, between eating and hostility. With time, she recognized what she felt angry about: her daughter. As she put it, "I'm snacking, instead of smacking!" (Interestingly, "smack" can also mean a unique and interesting taste.) The unconscious often makes connections that the conscious mind might not consider. The urge to "smack" her daughter put her in a bind, since fate had dealt her daughter a neurological problem!

Several sessions following her making the connection between overeating and hostility, Alice had an interesting image when she was in trance. She saw herself climbing a steep path up the side of a mountain. She felt angry that the path was so challenging, but she kept climbing anyway, until she reached the top. A deep feeling of satisfaction washed over her when she looked at the view. At that moment, she woke up with the realization that her family situation presented a challenge to her, and like the steep path, she was getting angry about it. Although she wanted to be a good and pleasant mother, she felt angry about her daughter's uncontrollable behavior. Her anger was unacceptable to her, but her anger was her reaction to the frustration she felt in coping with her daughter's condition. Thus, Alice felt angry with herself as well.

Through trance work, Alice was able to feel and accept her deep anger and understand its source. She became less angry at herself and more tolerant of others. She discovered new ways to cope with her daughter's condition as her reactions found a mature equilibrium. The calmness Alice experienced through trance aided her in developing a true calm within. As she adjusted to the reality of her situation more gracefully, she was able to gently lead her daughter into being calmer and more accepting of herself. The whole family felt better and the situation eased. And most importantly for her personal goals, Alice was finally able to lose weight.

If you have tried to lose weight unsuccessfully, and you know there is no medical reason preventing you from losing weight, consider that something else might be involved. Your unconscious can help you to discover what other problems might be connected, and how to resolve them. These next exercises help you to work unconsciously to uncover what else might be involved and make the changes you need that will allow you to lose weight. If the problem you discover is more than you can handle on your own, seek psychotherapy. A little help from a trained professional could provide the input you need to make positive changes. These exercises can be done along with therapy, and in working at many levels, you will find that your weight issues will resolve.

Exercise in Setting Yourself for Change with Trance

Permit yourself to go very deeply into trance. Let your breathing become steady. As your trance deepens, invite your thoughts to clear. You can let go of unnecessarily tense muscles, perhaps by visualizing a peaceful place where you can be calm and at ease, now or in awhile. Follow your spontaneous response. Do not try to force yourself to be calm—instead, simply wait for it to happen, expecting that it will when you are ready. As you feel calmness develop over time, you can begin to have confidence in your ability to relax and be calm in general. This calm, confident feeling will increase, gradually becoming an expected part of your life. Let this deepen as you relax fully. When you are ready to awaken, suggest that your sensations can gradually return to normal. Wake up refreshed and alert. Repeat this exercise often.

Inviting Unconscious Insight

Now that you are relaxed in trance, suggest to yourself that you would like to have a meaningful image, sensation, thought, memory, or dream. Let it be as vivid as possible. Wait. If nothing occurs now, try again later. Allow your own understandings to emerge either in trance or after you awaken. When you feel ready, come out of trance and notice any thoughts that occur to you.

As with many of the clients described in this chapter, people often have an intuitive sense about connections. Do not judge yourself; simply observe and learn. Give yourself the same compassion and understanding you would give to another. If nothing emerges after several attempts, you may not have a related problem and should continue focusing on issues around eating itself. Beware of filling in the blanks if no other problem is there.

Ideomotor Signaling for Unconscious Response

Ideomotor signaling is one way to communicate using unconscious response. You can learn a great deal unconsciously, if you listen. Listening to your unconscious guides you to better understanding of your difficulty. Review the ideomotor signaling exercises in Chapter 8, then try this one.

Go into a deep trance. Make sure you are sitting or lying so that your hands are free to move. Assign one hand as "yes" and the other as "no." Let your thoughts drift around some of your new learning regarding your eating. As you permit these insights to flow, allow yourself to go more deeply into trance. When you feel ready, ask yourself whether your unconscious understanding agrees with your conscious understanding. Wait for the response in one of your hands. You can check on some of your other understandings of yourself in this way. You may have an intuitive sense. If you have learned and responded well, you have begun to develop inner rapport.

Sometimes you know things but do not consciously understand them. Unconsciously you can access subtle intuitions and other data. By allowing associations and the flow of thoughts, feelings, and memories in trance, positive unconscious processes are freed to make connections, learn, develop and help bring about change.

Loraine requested hypnotherapy from us for a problem with overeating. She was a cashier at a supermarket. She complained of feeling vaguely bored with her life, and she passed her breaks eating. As she checked through the food that customers bought, she was "checking it out for herself," as she told us. She spent much of her working time thinking about what she would eat on her next break.

She enjoyed going into trance and discovered she could relax deeply. Through unconscious analytic exploration of meanings, she realized she was interested in food, but her preferences tended toward the gourmet. Snacking did not satisfy her true hunger. Following this realization, she started to read about gourmet foods and how to prepare them. As time went by she became less and less interested in overeating and eventually went back to school, to become a chef. She evolved from filling herself full to fulfilling herself.

Weight Loss Suggestions

As you understand the issues and begin to make some changes, trance offers opportunities for discoveries that will help you along your path. The following exercises offer some direct and indirect weight loss suggestions. Consider your own individual needs, beliefs, and resources for suggestions that will fit you. You may use what is given in the exercise directly or vary it.

Exercise for Individualizing Weight Loss Suggestions

Go into trance and try some suggestions that can make your weight loss easier. For example, if you overindulge in chocolate, do you wonder when you will want less chocolate? At times, do you forget about chocolate? Aren't you curious what it would be like without this urge? If you tend to eat at night, could you ever feel less hungry at that time? Is it possible to eat less at night? Are you ever too busy to eat, or maybe too tired? If you have discovered that overeating is connected with hostility, can you find a way to forgive and move on? Do you have other creative ideas of your own? Use these suggestions as springboards to coming up with your own positive ways to help you solve any related problems and lose your weight. Vividly imagine the suggestion you use, seeing yourself carrying it out or feeling the sensations that you would feel in doing it. Suggest that the image, thought, or feeling can intensify as you allow your response. You have resources you do not know you have. You must seek them within and allow them to help you now.

Exercise with Indirect Weight Loss Suggestions

Go into a relaxed and comfortable trance. Review your trance learning, which you may or may not need to consciously remember afterwards. Wonder about how your mind, brain, and body integrate as a unit. Contemplate how the nervous system runs all through your body, connecting everything together. Even if you do not know exactly how it all works, your mind–brain system can make connections; it does so all the time. And so, you can make connections and find solutions even when you do not know exactly how to do so. You may have intuitive unconscious surprises, new attitudes, or different perspectives. This becomes possible if you permit your inner light to shine.

Hypnotic Impulse Control

Impulse control may be related to overeating. In order to diet, a certain amount of control over impulses is extremely helpful. Overeaters feel compelled, believing they are helpless to do anything about it when they desire to overeat. Trance gives opportunity for a new experience of potential.

Exercise in Hypnotic Impulse Control

Use your favorite method to enter trance. After you have achieved a comfortable trance, let your attention drift. Suggest to yourself that gradually you will develop an itch. It might be in your arm, leg, or face. As it increases in intensity, try suggesting that you can also have a corresponding counter-impulse to not scratch. The more it itches, the less you will want to scratch. Do not scratch. As you relax the itch weakens. Suggest to yourself that with every breath the itch sensation will diminish until it is completely gone. Imagine a pleasant unrelated memory, or perhaps just forget about the itch altogether. Experiment. Try different methods until you find the technique that works best for you. After a few minutes, if you are on the correct path, the itching sensation will subside, until it totally disappears. Continue to relax. Stay in trance for a few more minutes. Then wake up, fully alert and refreshed.

Trance can be used to help alter a rigidly fixed self-concept. The following exercise will help you accept and feel more comfortable with change.

Altering Your Image Unconsciously Exercise

Invite yourself to go deeply into trance by imagining a profound sense of relaxation in your muscles. Your hands and feet may tingle and begin to feel light. The lightness in your hand begins in your fingertips. Can they become so light they want to rise up? The feeling can move into your hand and up your arm until your whole arm rises upward. As you become increasingly comfortable, imagine your body becoming a few pounds lighter. Enjoy how this feels. Continue to feel yourself getting lighter: one pound lighter, five pounds lighter, then 10, in small increments until you reach your goal. Feel this vividly and enjoy the experience. You can vary this exercise by using pictures and images instead of sensations. See yourself becoming thinner and thinner in a mirror. Notice how natural and comfortable this looks.

Enhancing Progress Exercise

Go into a very deep trance. Invite your unconscious to experience one of the trance phenomena you have done successfully before. Recall the positive experiences you have had in trance, like a calm, comfortable feeling. Enjoy the experience. Encourage your unconscious to be supportive and helpful. You can allow this part of you to strengthen and develop. As you become more comfortable with trance learning, you will find that you can become more comfortable with yourself and all your varied aspects. Let your thoughts drift about this and continue to relax deeply. How long after trance can you feel more comfortable about yourself? Will you be more accepting immediately or perhaps in a few days? Do you feel more positive in the morning or in the evening, at home, when you are tired but at ease, or at work? Are you more comfortable when you are with family, with friends, or by yourself? What positive potentials do you have? Do your friends and family see more potential in you than you see in yourself? You may have undeveloped potential, unrecognized as positive in how you interpret it. When you are ready, awaken refreshed and alert.

Conclusion

Use hypnosis regularly; daily trances are best. Do not chastise yourself for occasional backsliding, simply go on from there. Change of habits will take the time that it needs. Gradual weight loss is best, giving you time to form healthy eating habits permanently. Monitor your progress by noticing whether you find yourself able to stick to realistic goals. Your successes can serve as feedback that you are on a healing course. Be willing to seek harmony and obtain support in this endeavor from family and friends. Come to terms with conflict as you grow in wisdom. A better life awaits you and your family.

15

Activating the Brain's

Pain Reduction System

On the occasion of every accidental event that befalls you, remember to turn to yourself and inquire what power you have for dealing with it.

—Epictetus (in Hadas, 1961, p. 87)

PAIN is something that affects us all. Pain is not just something to avoid; it usually serves a positive purpose. The pain pathways of the nervous system warn you when you are in danger of harming yourself from something that is too hot, cold, or sharp, for example. They can also serve to warn you to take a certain action—such as painful flu symptoms that warn you to stay in bed in order to facilitate your recovery. Or, pain can motivate you to take the time to find out what has caused it. People who do not have the usual pain receptors are negatively affected as a result. Still, despite the many ways that pain can be helpful, there are cases in which the sensation of pain must be relieved, avoided, or diminished so that it can be endured.

Before we proceed, we must caution that if you have pain, you should see your doctor to determine what is causing it. Pain should never be ignored, and so in working with pain you must always do so in conjunction with a doctor. If your doctor tells you that the pain must be endured, you can then use self-hypnosis to help. But please do not be afraid to check into the causes of your pain. In conjunction with medical care, hypnosis can reduce your pain and enhance your quality of life.

The modern-day solution to pain is to take medication, but hypnosis offers an alternative, or a supplement to traditional treatment. Hypnosis has been researched extensively and has been shown repeatedly to be helpful in alleviating pain. Many hypnosis and pain studies offer solid evidence that you can influence the experience of pain far more than you might realize.

Ernest Hilgard, a prominent hypnosis researcher, devoted a great deal of study to understanding how hypnosis alters the sensation of pain. He and his wife Josephine wrote a book on this topic, *Hypnosis in the Relief of Pain* (Hilgard & Hilgard, 1975). They found that, when people were experiencing a painful stimulus or were enduring pain from an illness or condition, the sensation of pain could be significantly decreased or completely relieved using hypnosis. People no longer cried out in pain, grimaced, or held their breath upon receiving hypnosis. On the other hand, their autonomic nervous system–based reactions of increased blood pressure and heart rate were not changed. These findings showed that, despite the fact that the physiological response to the painful stimulus continued, the experience of pain was significantly relieved by hypnosis. We can see that the nervous system serves its protective function when a painful stimulus is present, but people have the capacity to overcome suffering. Some individuals tolerate pain better than others, and this may be largely because the experience of pain can be significantly altered by how it is handled.

The Brain's Pain Pathway

Pain has its own pathway through the central nervous system (Figure 15.1). Pain information is carried rapidly along insulated (myelinated) fibers and slowly along uninsulated (unmyelinated) C-fibers. The axons ascend the spinal chord and the signal is sent to the brain stem, through the medulla and pons, which control pain-related behavior, such as crying out. Then the pain information is distributed to the different thalamic areas and up to the cortex. The cingulate cortex is activated by pain information, especially when you believe the stimulus will be

Figure 15.1. The Brain's Pain Pathway.

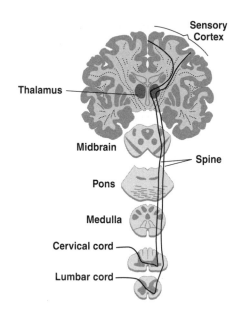

painful. This area influences how the intensely painful is experienced. Thus, psychological approaches that influence expectancy and handling of the emotional element involved in pain will have an effect on how the brain responds, encouraging a lowering of the sensation of pain.

Pain can be controlled through a number of different neurotransmitter pathways. The brain contains natural opiate-like substances called opioids. The brain moderates pain using the opiate neurotransmitter, a type of endorphin, much like how opiate drugs do. The pain signal that comes up through the ascending pain pathways can be controlled and inhibited by the corresponding descending pathway by shifting the balance of neurotransmitters.

Fear of Pain Versus Pain Itself

Your body has natural capacities. When in danger, the HPA pathway activates to help you fight back, run away, or stay still until the danger has passed. Similarly, if you have not eaten for a long time, your body alerts you with hunger pangs, which stimulate you to seek food. And you cannot go without sleep too long before the natural sleep–wake cycle signals to you that you need to sleep. If you just pay attention to your body, you do not have to consciously remember to attend to these basic functions; your body lets you know when these needs must be met, with the inborn, natural abilities of its system.

When you feel pain, you may also feel afraid, because pain often is a signal of danger. Usually when people experience pain from an injury, illness, or childbirth, there is no immediate danger, just the pain. You have probably learned from reading this book that you do not have to be afraid of your natural pain response, because it is simply a built-in pathway in the brain–mind system. The pain pathways do what they do, and what you are left with is the sensation of pain and the fear of that pain sensation. There are many tools you can develop using hypnosis to deal with the fear aspect. Train well and you will learn how to master your fears and thereby control your pain.

You have many sensations in your life: some pleasant, others unpleasant. Zen Buddhism has an interesting interpretation of pain and fear. You might feel a painful sensation, but there is no need to be afraid of sensation itself. Each sensation is merely a sensation. Pain may be very unpleasant and difficult to handle but it is still just what it is, a sensation, and a sensation is nothing to fear. It is just a sensation. By fearing the pain, you add more to it. Instead, simply let the sensation be. Your mind can intensify or lessen the sensation without your realization in awareness. So, if you are under a doctor's care, let yourself feel assured that what can be done is being done. Or if you are waiting for healing, all you can do is withstand the discomfort, and patiently endure it as you wait for the process to run its course. Here, use the 4-step method: *Observe* the pain; *question* its meaning, constancy, and boundaries; *imagine* just as it is moment to moment, but do not add anything to it; and *allow* it to run its course and, in time, diminish.

After you recognize the difference between the sensation of pain and the reaction of fear in response, you can take a new stance toward pain. You may find that your fear eases. Because you do not add to the experience with anticipation and imagination, perhaps you will notice some moments with a little less pain. You will not fear the pain as you develop skills that will help you to endure, lessen, alter, or relieve the pain entirely.

Exercise in Alteration of Pain

Stand, sit, or lie down in a position that produces the least pain possible for you. Focus on the sensation of pain, observe it, and try to contemplate it only as a sensation, and no more. What does it feel like? Is it hot? Pounding? Sharp? Dull? Describe it to yourself, noticing all the details, locating its boundaries. What areas outside the boundaries feel good? Imagine. Try to shift attention to the areas that feel better. Then, allow your awareness to fill out the perception of the body as a greater whole, to put the pain in a new perspective.

Breathe, and allow your body to relax and feel better. People often tighten up against pain, which makes it worse. Allow your mind and body to be as relaxed and calm as possible, and you will feel better. Although very unpleasant and uncomfortable, pain hurts; but still, accept the sensation just for what it is. Do not let it hurt your feelings, so to speak. When you can let go of the hurt, your mind can be at peace, even though you are undeniably extremely uncomfortable. Your sensation is your awareness of the pain, not a punishment. You may have learned from early life experiences that pain is linked to punishment. Your body is not trying to punish you. Your nerves are doing their job—complaining, and with good reason! Accept what is, do not resist, and the pain will be less disturbing. Be one with the pain; suffer with it, not from it. And perhaps then you can find meaning and accomplish what matters to you, as well.

Distraction from Pain Exercise 1

Wouldn't it be nice to have a short vacation from your pain? You can use your memories to offer you a better alternative than pain right now. Go into trance and relax as much as possible. Can you recall a time when you went on a vacation? Perhaps you visited a beautiful place, or maybe it was just a wonderful afternoon off from work when you did exactly what you felt like doing. Using the skills you developed with imagery, visualize this experience now. Picture it vividly, recalling what the weather was like, how the surroundings looked, or perhaps what you were wearing. Recall other people who might have been there, what you did, and the pleasant feelings you had. Enjoy the experience for several minutes. You may be surprised to find that your pain goes away for a moment as you bring yourself fully into this pleasant memory. You may choose another experience that you prefer, with more meaning to you—perhaps time with someone you care deeply for, or perhaps engagement with meaningful work.

Distraction from Pain Exercise 2

Some people may need a different kind of distraction for their pain. Our teacher, Milton Erickson, told us about one of his patients who was suffering from severe pain. She was bedridden and completely discouraged. He asked her this question: Where would your pain go if a hungry tiger were under your bed? The woman vividly imagined that hungry tiger licking his chops under her bed, and suddenly, her pain was gone! Whenever she wanted to get rid of her pain, she just thought of the hungry tiger. You may have your own version of a hungry tiger, and we encourage you to use it.

Relaxation Time Distortion Exercise

Sometimes pain comes in waves. You can work with the timing of pain to give yourself an experience of greater comfort using time distortion. Begin by expanding the time when you do not feel any pain. Notice that you cannot tell the difference been 300 seconds and 320 seconds, or between 320 seconds and 345 seconds. Keep increasing the time in slow increments. Experiment with some of the time distortion exercises in Chapter 8. Let yourself discover creative mental tasks to do in trance.

When a wave of pain comes along, use your time distortion to make the time go by quickly. You cannot tell the difference between 300 seconds and 280 seconds. Let your unconscious shorten the experienced time as much as possible. Or become engrossed in a task that is so compelling that the time just speeds by.

We have discussed the power of expectations to bring about changes in the mind and brain. Pseudo-orientation in time was one technique directly used by Erickson to capitalize on the positive use of expectations, hopes, and wishes. Erickson invented this technique from his creative discovery that, if a person can fantasize that they regress in time, they can also fantasize that they progress in time. People often come up with solutions to their problems by imagining having successfully achieved them. You can apply this technique to help you develop favorable expectancies to assist with pain relief. The boundary of time need not limit you. You can use those common experiences and understandings, "embraced in the general appreciation that practice leads to perfection, that action once initiated tends to continue, and that deeds are the offspring of hope and expectancy" (Erickson & Rossi, 1980, p. 397).

Exercise in Progression Through Time

Imagine now that you are fully recovered from your pain. If you are suffering from an illness, vividly imagine that you have been healthy for quite some time now; if your pain comes from an injury, clearly visualize that all has healed well. If you are feeling emotional pain, picture yourself happy now. What is this pain-free experience like? You can wonder just how it feels, what the sensations are and where you are at that time. Allow your unconscious processes to present you with an image, a feeling, a thought, or whatever comes to mind. Wait now with curiosity about what will occur to you. Then, allow yourself to become immersed in the experience. When you feel ready, come out of trance, but suggest that you could keep some of what you learned about the future with you now, to help you in the present.

Pain Control: Anesthesia and Hyperesthesia

You can alter your experiencing of pain to feel more or less. Anesthesia, or the lessening of pain, is very useful for pain control, whereas hyperesthesia, or increased sensing, can be helpful where greater sensitivity is needed. During pregnancy and childbirth, for example, you probably want to master both of these skills. Sometimes when you have a sprained or broken limb, you need to remain sensitive enough to not put stress on the area, so you may need selective hyperesthesia in order to be sensitive to pressure and textures and promote a safe healing process. Simply dulling your sensitivities might interfere with your ability to handle the situation optimally. On the other hand, the discomforts and pains that occur need not be severe. You can temper the intensity with hypnosis in many different ways that utilize natural abilities you already possess. Both skills have their application. Try to work with both anesthesia and hyperesthesia, and you may find that one enhances the other.

Begin by Lessening the Intensity of Pain

You probably have had the experience of being so busy doing something that you did not notice that you had a sensation. For example, as you are sitting here now, you probably are not thinking about your hand or foot. Then, when you turn your attention there, you might notice that your hand or foot feels cool or warm, light or heavy, or perhaps tingly or even a little numb. This ability to not notice can be expanded for pain control.

Lessening Sensation Trance Exercise

Sit comfortably and allow yourself to go into trance. Let yourself relax very deeply and ask, can your tingling (warm, cool, or whatever sensation you are having in your hand) become very far away? You might experience your hand as being distanced, or just feel the sensations. Wonder, which will it be? Or would your unconscious prefer to feel the sensation lessen until you feel nothing in your hand? Wait for your response and then encourage it to deepen.

Distancing from Sensation: Dissociation Exercise

Go deeply into trance. It's such a nice day, wouldn't you enjoy going to the beach while your body stays here? You are walking on the sand close to the shoreline. Are there any interesting shells? Enjoy the feeling of soft sand between your toes and the sun on your skin. You can hear the waves rolling in on the shore and smell the sweet-salty air. Now you are feeling warm and decide to take a dip. Is the water refreshingly cool or soothingly warm? Let yourself feel completely relaxed and at ease as you swim with the waves.

If the beach is not your spontaneous choice, let yourself go to your own favorite park, woods, mountains, or any other place you might think of.

Transferring Sensations Exercise

Let yourself go deeply into trance. Notice the sensation in one of your hands, which can be comfortable and relaxed. Perhaps you feel warmth or a light tingling, or a refreshing coolness. Let that feeling of comfort spread through your whole hand and out to your fingertips.

When you have developed a comfortable feeling in one hand, try transferring the feeling to the other hand. Place the comfortable hand on top of the other one and imagine the sensations flowing out into the other hand. You might have a picture of a stream, see a color flowing between your hands, or feel a sensation of warmth, coolness, or tingling travel from hand to hand. Experiment with transferring the comfortable feeling to other places, perhaps where you are feeling discomfort, such as in your back, shoulders, chest, or stomach. Wait and allow the experience to develop and increase.

Glove Anesthesia Exercise

Sometimes the best feeling to have is no feeling. You can use your skills in transferring a sensation to give yourself a feeling of numbness. Use the comfortable hand you experienced in the previous exercise to stroke the other hand, to bring about an interesting experience of numbness. Stroke and suggest to yourself that the hand you are stroking will grow numb, heavy, and wooden. This sensation can be similar to the numbness in your jaw brought on by the use of Novocaine by your dentist. It might begin as a tingling or coolness then become very numb. As you continue stroking, the numbness increases. Once you feel that your hand is numb, let the numb hand move slowly to transfer the numbness: to your face or to your abdomen, or to your other arm, wherever you are feeling pain. Press the palm of your hand onto the new area and let the numbness transfer there. As soon as the new area feels numb, let your hand move slowly back down to your lap, with sensations in your hand returning to normal. Now enjoy feeling the numbness in your previously painful area. Experiment with transferring the numb feeling at will.

Exercise in Altering Your Sensations of Pain

Pain sensations do not have to feel quite as painful to you when you broaden the focus of your attention. With each stab or throb of pain you probably can notice some other sensations as well such as pressure, tenseness, heat, or cold. Allow one of these alternative sensations to attract attention, and let your imagination be creative with this compounded perception of the sensations. You do not know exactly what it will be like, but it could be a sensation you can imagine enduring. In fact, allow yourself to be interested in this feeling and its possibilities. You know it helps if you try to cope more comfortably with your pain, so even though it is a strong feeling, do not conceive of it in terms of whether it is just pleasant or unpleasant. Practice with less intense pains you might be having at other times, and give yourself suggestions regularly during trances. Often at first, the effects may not be perceptible. Continue to use your imagination, and you will be able to allow the strong painful sensation you are working on to alter.

The other side of lessening sensation is learning how to heighten the pleasurable experiences that you might be missing. As your enjoyment of life increases, your total sensation of pain will alter, diminish, or be a bit distanced. Reactivate the built-in mechanisms that are already there, the natural reward pathways of the brain, to experience pleasure and happiness again. Then, pain becomes less prominent, or more manageable, so that you can appreciate other important aspects of your life experiences.

Enjoyment of Sensation Exercise

Go into a deep and relaxing trance and then think about some of the things you enjoy. Let them develop fully and think about them. For example, if you are working on the pain felt during pregnancy, can you feel the baby moving? As you turn your attention to your baby, can you sense the heartbeat? Feel attuned to your little one? Or, if you are recovering from an illness, do you have family members or friends who come to visit you? Picture these people now and notice the caring in their eyes, the smell of their perfume, or the colors of their clothes. Perhaps you are lying on a bed. If so, can you pay attention to the softness of the pillow or the comfortable warmth from the blanket? Or you might prefer to recall an enjoyable experience from the past and allow yourself to reexperience it now, recalling as many sensory details as you can. Again, perhaps you can reminisce about meaningful moments of experiences with loved ones, or a great accomplishment of personal significance. Relax as you dwell upon these pleasant sensations.

Exercise in Developing Feelings of Well-Being

Go into trance. Let yourself completely relax, both in body and in mind. You have been working with your pain sensations. There is a certain satisfaction that you can have in making the efforts you are making to bring about a change in your experiencing. Now suggest to yourself that you could enjoy the feeling of satisfaction that you can have for making these efforts. You do not know what that feeling will be, but simply wait until you begin to experience something. Or maybe you will feel a pleasant nothingness—an empty space of quiet and peace. As you rest quietly, you will feel yourself relaxing even more deeply and experiencing a growing sense of emotional well-being. Let that very positive feeling, image, or sensation deepen. Experience this feeling of well-being, enjoying the moment. When you are ready, come out of trance, relaxed and refreshed, but maintaining that positive feeling of well-being.

Conclusion

The first step in pain control is recognizing that you can do something about it. The unconscious provides many tools to diminish suffering, and the close link between mind and body make it possible for the changes to have a powerful effect. Some people will find that practicing these exercises when they are not feeling pain helps them to build their skills. But for others, pain itself might provide a motivation to make a serious effort. Perform the exercises as often as you can for best results. Not only will you feel relief, but you will also gain confidence in your ability to take action even when facing a painful challenge.

16

Altering Anxiety and Fear Reactions in Brain, Body, and Mind

All successful therapies implicitly or explicitly change the patient's image of himself from a person who is overwhelmed by his symptoms and problems to one who can master them.

—J. D. Frank et al., *Effective Ingredients of Successful Psychotherapy*, p. 67

ANXIETY is felt by millions of people. If you have chronic anxiety, you can feel reassured that you are not alone. Herbert Benson, a prominent researcher in meditation and stress reduction, and his research group taught 31 male executives either self-hypnosis or meditation. They found that self-hypnosis elicited a relaxation response which helped the subjects to feel calmer, have lower blood pressure, and experience less stress. They concluded, "The meditational and self-hypnosis techniques employed in this investigation are simple to use and effective in the therapy of anxiety" (Benson et al., 1978, p. 229).

Other studies have found that hypnosis is an effective treatment for anxiety when combined with cognitive behavioral therapy (Schoenberger, 2000). A more recent study tested 89 civilian trauma survivors who suffered from acute anxiety and found that, by adding hypnosis to imagined exposure techniques (similar to those offered later in this chapter), the effects were much stronger than with exposure therapy alone (Bryant, Moulds, Guthrie, & Nixon, 2005). All of these findings are encouraging, because they demonstrate that people can use hypnosis for different types of anxiety, and that it is likely to help reduce anxiety. We combine self-hypnosis with some cognitive behavioral methods in this chapter, to help you enhance the effects of self-hypnosis.

Finding a conscious/unconscious balance that uses hypnosis, while adopting a change in how you think about your anxiety, is most helpful. This chapter will guide you in using hypnosis along with cognitive methods. If you find that you cannot make any change after sincerely trying the exercises in this chapter, you should consult a professional therapist. Just as you would consult a mechanic when your car is malfunctioning and you cannot fix it, your problem with anxiety may be a signal to you that something needs attention and your own unassisted efforts are not enough. Please be willing to seek help from a competent professional psychologist, counselor, hypnotist, or psychiatrist if necessary.

The Neurobiology of Anxiety and Fear

Anxiety involves a number of brain systems that have a strong influence on your mind and body. The autonomic nervous system gets involved through the stress pathway we described in Chapter 11 (See Figure 11.1). But the limbic system, your emotional center, becomes involved as well.

The thalamus, hypothalamus, amygdala and hippocampus play an important role in anxiety. The thalamus acts as the gateway of signals received from the senses, and then sends them on to other parts of the brain for processing (see Figure 4.6). Signals sent to the hypothalamus, the coordinator of internal functions, could set off a stress response, putting your system on high alert. The hippocampus is where memories are stored before being sent on to long-term memory. When the hippocampus is smaller, the individual is less capable of drawing on memory to evaluate the nature of the stressor. But if the correct learning experiences are given, the hippocampus can increase in size.

The amygdala is the emotional center where signals to the hypothalamus that there is something to fear originate, thereby helping to bring about the stress response. It registers the quality and intensity of all our emotions, both pleasant and unpleasant. The basal ganglia surround the limbic system, just below the cortex. They play an important role in coordinating the two areas. Involved in motivation and movement, the basal ganglia act to coordinate emotions and actions, which engage the movement and motivation centers of the basal ganglia. Finally, the cortex itself is activated, accompanied by more thoughts and ruminations about the anxious or fearful situation.

A number of neurotransmitters play a key role in anxiety and fear. Glutamate, the excitatory neurotransmitter, and GABA, the inhibitory one, provide excitation and inhibition throughout the brain. Glutamate and GABA are found in every cell of the body. Serotonin regulates moods, norepinephrine enhances alertness, and dopamine is involved in reward responses. When the system is overactive and tense, there is an imbalance of neurotransmitters, such as not enough GABA. Drug therapies for anxiety often increase the amount of GABA in your system, to inhibit the over-excitation that you feel. But drugs are not the only way to alter the balance of neurotransmitters. Self-hypnosis can also be used to calm the system, thereby creating a more comfortable balance.

Your reaction patterns may feel like they are fixed and unchanging. But if you are willing to make an effort over time, even an entrenched anxiety reaction can be changed. You can learn how to shift your balance back to a calmer center.

Existential Anxiety: Humanistic Categories

Another way to think about anxiety is from a broad humanistic/existential perspective. We all feel anxious to some extent. Anxiety can fall into one of two broad categories: existential or neurotic. Existential anxiety is the healthy recognition of *angst*, meaning that we are thrown into the conditions of our life, with much that is unknown and beyond our control. We must face the tragedy of death, vulnerability, and unpredicted events. In facing our existential anxiety we can live authentically, in tune with life as it truly is. But sometimes, we are just anxious.

Types of Anxiety

The typical ways in which people feel anxiety have been placed into different categories. These labels are tools to help you better understand, and then work to alter, what you may be feeling. But realize that labels can never do justice to your being: You are always more than any label or diagnosis.

Medical / Psychological Categories: Anxiety Disorders

Some anxiety is normal, but when it interferes with living, anxiety is a problem that should be addressed. Intense anxiety afflicts many people, and it can be alleviated with proper treatment. Anxiety takes distinguishable forms, known as disorders, which can be diagnosed and successfully treated. Here are the main types of anxiety disorders:

- *Generalized anxiety disorder (GAD)* involves a broad, general feeling of anxiety that can inhibit people from doing things and going places.
- *Social anxiety disorder (SAD)* is felt in social situations with other people. Sometimes it is specific, such as feeling uncomfortable with public speaking. People with social anxiety feel as if others are judging them negatively.
- *Panic disorder* often manifests as severe physical symptoms, such as rapid, labored breathing or chest pains, when there is no actual physical illness or disease present. Individuals often feel an intense panicky feeling, which usually lasts from one to 10 minutes.
- Specific *phobias* are fears of one thing, such as dogs, heights, spiders, elevators or open spaces. These fears are often, but not always, initiated by a traumatic event involving the thing in question.
- *Post-traumatic stress disorder (PTSD)* may occur after someone has gone through a very traumatic experience such as rape, war, or torture. Not all people who undergo such experiences have an anxiety reaction, but for those who do, it can be very debilitating.
- *Obsessive-compulsive disorder* is also categorized as a type of anxiety.

This is a psychiatric disorder and if you have been diagnosed with it, you should consult with a professional therapist.

Neurotic forms of anxiety develop when people try to avoid the realities of their existential condition, to falsely believe that they can be secure always, that there are no unpredictable tragedies or difficulties that might befall them. Trying to avoid the tragedies of life leads inevitably to disappointment and neurotic anxiety.

Relaxing Into Your Life

When you confront the reality of your existence, with its inevitable tensions, uncertainties, and tragedies, you can begin to accept your condition and accept yourself. Treatments for the different forms of anxiety vary somewhat, but all share one element: the use of learning how to relax and maintain feelings of calm when needed. If you suffer from any kind of difficulty from anxiety, modern medical, psychological, and humanistic wisdom advises you to integrate a program for relaxation into your daily routine. Hypnosis is one of the best methods to help you accept yourself as you are and ease anxiety, by producing feelings of relaxation and calm at will.

The sequence of trance exercises found in Chapter 11 is designed specifically to relax brain, body, and mind. But, many of the other chapters in this book also include trancework for relaxation. Experiment with the different exercises and then use any of the relaxation trances that you find most helpful. What is crucial is that you devote at least a few minutes to relaxation every day (up to 30 minutes daily is ideal). The effects are cumulative: Over time you will notice a generalized lessening of tension, especially as you also work on overcoming the specific type of anxiety that troubles you. The later sections of this chapter will guide you on this path.

When you begin to work on anxiety, commit yourself to the process. Draw confidence from the fact that you can work with your anxiety. You are not being overconfident in expecting that you can be comfortable in your life. If you are willing to make an effort, you can change. And what better place to start than right here, and what better time than right now, by relaxing in trance in the comfort of your own home or chosen environment?

Some people who suffer from anxiety find that when they try to relax, they simply become more anxious. If you have felt this way, you might be more comfortable with an alert trance as your method to relaxation.

Alert Trance for Relaxation Exercise

Find a comfortable position, and allow your eyes to either be open or closed, whichever you prefer. Turn your attention to your breathing and follow the air as it travels in through your nose and down into your lungs, and then out again through your nose. With each breath in and out you become more alert. Your mind becomes clear and your attention focused. You feel a comfortable sensation of tingling developing in your fingertips and/or your toes. Now the tingling can begin spreading through your body, giving you a nice, comfortable feeling of energy: not too much and not too little. As the tingling develops, your mind continues to become more and more alert. You have a pleasant, invigorated feeling. Enjoy the tingling energy, alert and in balance with everything around you.

How Anxiety Develops

Anxiety involves interrelated processes moving from your brain to your mind and body. The mental component, involving certain types of thought patterns, acts much like negative suggestions, and may keep the brain systems reacting as if there is a continued threat of danger. Remember, the brain systems are helping to protect you, and so if you keep telling yourself you are in danger, the brain responds to danger and you feel tense and anxious. Taking a good look at what you might be inadvertently telling yourself may help to deactivate the high-alert response.

Challenging Assumptions with the 4-Step Method:
Observe, Question, Imagine, Allow

- **Observe:** You may have unrealistic expectations about life security. There are contingencies and uncertainties that cannot be controlled—

but there are also situations and certainties that you can affect. Observe what situations you assume to be under your control and those that you feel are beyond your control.

- **Question:** Then, question your assumptions. When you can accept that life includes both dimensions, you will be more realistic about what you can and cannot control. Face what is beyond your control with courage.
- **Imagine:** Vividly imagine taking appropriate action with what is realistically yours to affect and control. For example, if you worry that other people judge you (social anxiety) vividly imagine a situation where you do not care what others think about you. Extend it to people you know only casually, then to those whose opinions you value highly.
- **Allow:** Use trance to invite and allow the image to become clearer. Wait patiently as you relax into the experience and wait for your response.

For this illustration, in a step-wise fashion, you gradually learn to let yourself react to the situation just as it is, without adding the imagined judgments of others to your own response.

As an example of how the 4-step process can work successfully, Jean was a client who suffered with panic attacks. Her worries acted like suggestions that brought about a corresponding physical reaction. She tightened her rib cage, which restricted her breathing and led to a tense feeling in her chest. All these sensations felt like what she imagined to be a heart attack. Then her catastrophic thoughts activated a natural adrenaline response as if there was real danger, even when in reality there was nothing wrong. Jean started by observing what she was telling herself inwardly: "I'm having a heart attack! I'm scared! This is awful!" She questioned these thoughts by checking with her medical doctor, who assured her she had no physical problem. Feeling slightly more confident with the knowledge that she had no heart defect, she began to vividly imagine herself relaxed and healthy. She thought of times when she had felt perfectly healthy in the past. Then she allowed her natural response: a calmer attitude and more relaxed body. She called upon this feeling when she was beginning to panic, and gradually was able to defuse her anxious reaction.

Creative Restructuring Exercise

Once you resolve some of your worries, you begin the process of allowing constructive thoughts to emerge naturally. This exercise can open your perspective even further. Look carefully at this figure:

710

Think of as many possible combinations and permutations of these numerals as you can. Try to open your mind to many possibilities. Spend two or three minutes looking and enumerating what you perceive. Do not read on until you have given yourself a chance to think of as many possibilities as you can.

Now that you have given yourself an opportunity to look, did you consider different combinations of numbers? Does anything else occur to you? What if you look at it from a different perspective? Did you try turning the page upside down to see the word "OIL," for example? We have had some clients look at it sideways to see a sun setting over an ocean wave. Another person combined the shapes to make musical notes.

710 with Your Thinking Exercise

Use the 4-step method to uncover one of your negative or anxious thoughts. Look at one of the thoughts you uncovered. Here is a typical thought when people feel stressed: "Other people are judging me negatively." If this does not apply to you, consider a typically critical thought of your own. Is it possible that you are missing the richness of human interactions? Reframe this perception, by trying a completely new perspective. For example, be the other person looking at you. Now reverse it: "I evaluate others negatively. I am not seeing others as real, emotional human beings. I am just negatively evaluating them." Let new possibilities emerge. You are capable of seeing more than just 710.

Exercise in Briefly Letting Go of Your Fear and Anxiety

Here is another option for creative change. Go into a comfortable trance. Relax all your muscles and let your thoughts settle. You can recall the previous trances and the new learning you have had about your anxiety and fear. Whether or not you consciously know the reasons, ask yourself the following question: Even if you have a very good reason for feeling afraid or anxious, could you be without it for just one minute—or even longer, perhaps one hour, or even a whole day? Vividly imagine this brief period of freedom from your problem. What does it feel like to be without your fear? Think about it. When you are ready, awaken relaxed and refreshed.

Desensitization

Those who have anxieties and fears often amplify them by avoiding them, building them up in their minds, and then becoming more anxious. Although you might seem to feel safer by staying away from something you are afraid of, research has shown that this only makes it worse. A feared object or situation that produces anxiety is overcome by facing it carefully and correctly. A form of therapy called exposure therapy, for example, has the therapist accompany the client to gradually face a feared situation, and then let the reaction dissolve. For example, a fear of elevators is treated by systematically getting closer and closer to an elevator. Eventually the client enters the elevator with the therapist and rides it repeatedly. With nothing negative occurring, she gradually loses her fear.

Sometimes fears are initiated by one real, traumatic event (these are the specific phobias mentioned earlier in the chapter). For example, a fear of dogs can originate with once being bitten by a dog, and then becoming afraid of all dogs. The fear strengthens from avoiding any contact with dogs rather than facing a harmless dog safely. When people repeatedly imagine the traumatic event in their minds, they inadvertently make their anxiety worse.

But just as your imagination keeps the fear alive, so your imagination dispels it. You can use hypnosis to imagine a situation and experience it as if it were really happening. You may have physiological reactions such as sweating, as if you were really in the situation. If you have a fear of something that makes you anxious, try this group of exercises repeatedly, to help alleviate your fear and dissolve your anxiety.

Exercise in Quantifying Your Anxiety and Fear

Begin by enumerating a list of related situations or things, ordering them from 1 (least feared) to 5 (most feared), based on your key fear or anxiety. Write it down. So for example, if you are afraid of heights, begin with a slight hill rated as 1, and end up with a very high ledge rated as 5. If you are working on a social fear, begin with feeling mildly disapproved of or just vaguely noticed as 1 and move on to strongly negative judgments of you by others or being the center of attention as 5. If you feel generalized anxiety, begin with a mild feeling of anxiety felt in the comfort of your home (1) up to a very strong feeling of anxiety out in public (5). If you have suffered a trauma, begin with a very mild situation (1) and then move to a very traumatic situation (5). When you have your list, go on to the next trance exercise.

Progressive Desensitization Trance Exercise

Go deeply into trance. Spend some time developing deep relaxation. Use the relaxation series in this chapter or any other relaxing trances from this book. When you feel very relaxed, think about your fear. Imagine that you are very far away, looking at the feared thing or event from a very safe distance. Relax deeply and begin very slowly to walk toward it. Or if it is a situation, such as a fear of being judged by others, imagine the mildest case, number one on your list (someone making a mild judgment or playful teasing that only slightly bothers you). Keep moving closer or increasing the imagined risk as long as you can maintain your comfortable relaxation. If you start to get anxious, stop, back up a bit, and relax again. Then when you have regained your calm, continue your approach as you imagine yourself completely relaxed.

This process will take some time. Keep returning to the task each day, until you can remain completely relaxed as you get close to the feared object or experience.

When you finally get very close, vividly picture yourself making contact, as you stay completely relaxed. If you feel yourself getting anxious, back away until you can become fully relaxed, wait a moment, and then approach once again.

Do not try not to be afraid, just remain relaxed. Do not push yourself. Only go as far as you can while remaining calm and relaxed. Take the time you need. You may require several sittings to accomplish a complete immersion in the feared object or experience with complete relaxation and inner calm.

Repeat this exercise regularly until you are completely at ease with the feared object or situation.

If you find that you panic at times, with your heart beating fast and your chest feeling tight, you should first have a thorough examination from a medical doctor.

But if the doctor assures you that there is nothing physically wrong, you can experiment with relaxing your breathing. Panicky feelings often build like a spiral: with a feeling of anxiety, people become worried, so they tighten the breathing passages, which makes them feel more anxious and more worried. The cycle builds for several minutes, usually no more than 10 or 15, and then subsides. You can stop the cycle from even getting started by learning how to relax your breathing. Combined with reassuring suggestions that you are OK and that the uncomfortable feeling will pass, you will be able to regain control and eventually stop having this type of experience.

Exercise in Relaxing Breathing for Panic-Related Anxiety

First practice this exercise when you are feeling relatively relaxed. Sit upright so that your breathing passages can be clear. Close your eyes and turn your attention to your breathing. Breathe gently and softly. Feel the air as it moves in through your nose, down into your lungs and then out again through your nose. Place your hands on your rib cage and feel your ribs expand out as you inhale and in as you exhale. Let go of any tensions you feel and relax very deeply with each breath. Do not try to breathe differently than you normally do, except to encourage yourself to breathe gently and relaxed.

Once you feel able to sit quietly and breathe comfortably, try to follow your breathing whenever you are feeling anxious. As you sit quietly and turn your attention to your breathing, suggest to yourself that you can let your breathing rate slow. Place your hands on your rib cage and allow your ribs to expand gently as you inhale and gently move in as you exhale. Tell yourself, "I can relax my breathing now as I have done before. My unconscious knows how to breathe comfortably and now I can allow this to happen." Or find a way to encourage yourself to let go of tense, tight breathing in a way that feels natural to you.

Another view of anxiety is that it is the gap between the now and the later. That is, in anticipating what might be, people imagine dangers, uncomfortable possibilities, or fearful potentials. So, next time you are feeling anxious, try this exercise drawn from the tradition of Eastern meditation to bring yourself fully into the present moment, and you may find your anxious feelings easing.

Staying in the Moment Exercise

People who suffer panic attacks may be able to reduce the intensity of their frightening sensations. This is the beginning of change. Consider the total experience analytically, as a series of sensations, moment by moment, and nothing more. Try to fully experience each sensation as only a sensation. Practice this meditation first at times when you are not anxious and then use the skills you develop to do it when you are feeling uncomfortable.

Sit cross-legged on the floor, with your hands resting comfortably in your lap. If sitting on the floor is uncomfortable for you, sit in an upright chair. Allow your breathing passages to be clear and open by sitting up fairly straight. Close your eyes and turn your attention to your experiencing right now. Start by paying attention to your breathing, following each breath in and out. You might find it helpful to say to yourself, "Now I am aware of breathing in, feeling the air coming into my nose, going down into my lungs and now it is going out through my nose." Follow what you notice at each moment. So you might notice: "Now I am aware of my breathing. Now I notice my chest feels tight. Now I feel a slight letting go of the tightness." Keep following your experience moment by moment. If you notice yourself jumping ahead to something in the future or the past, ground it in the present—for example, you might say, "Now I am imagining the future when I will go to the store" or "Now I am remembering the past when I was afraid of that dog." Keep following your experiencing wherever it goes. If you feel drawn to attend to a sensation, notice that, or if you look at the painting on the wall, notice that you feel like looking. If you leave the present moment, bring yourself gently back to now, as soon as you notice. You will begin to feel centered.

Positive Imagery Exercise

Now that you have worked on your anxieties and fears, let yourself go back into trance. Vividly imagine yourself having a positive experience with your feared object or anxious situation. So, for example, if you fear dogs, imagine yourself playing with a cute little puppy or playing fetch with a handsome German shepherd dog. If you fear heights, imagine yourself enjoying a majestic view from the top of a high mountain. If you suffer from panic attacks, imagine that you are in radiant health, feeling fit and relaxed. If you feel afraid around people, imagine that you are having a wonderful time with people who like you and care about you. If you find yourself feeling generally nervous when you go outside, imagine that you are confident and at ease. Vividly picture your image. Notice every detail: the colors, the aromas, your sensations, feelings, and thoughts. You feel happy and positive. Allow your experience to deepen. Relax and enjoy every minute! When you feel ready to come out of trance, suggest that you can have some of that confidence. You might wonder just how that positive energy will affect your everyday life!

Exercise in Enhancing the Process

Now that you have been working on your difficulty, you can enhance the learning that has begun. Go into trance. When you are fully relaxed, invite your unconscious to review all related thoughts and experiences. You do not need to consciously attend to all this. But you might wonder, what areas seem to need attention? Be open to pursuing these findings, however is best for you. Offer yourself the following suggestions: 1) Discomfort can diminish—it fluctuates and varies naturally, so at times, it must decrease; 2) Your unconscious knows how to outgrow your problem and can communicate this knowledge in the ways that are best; and 3) You may not know for certain when you will have completely outgrown the problem, but you can learn what is necessary to learn in order to benefit. Continuing to relax in trance, review the learning you have had, and allow the growth and development to continue. Then, wake up refreshed and alert, leaving matters to your own unconscious.

Conclusion

When working with yourself in any area, it is important to maintain the nonjudgmental attitude we discussed earlier. Give yourself the time you need to work on your fear or anxiety. Try to be consistent in your trance sessions. When people have fears, there may be more to learn and integrate, beyond the mere symptom. If you have discovered this in your explorations with trance, then hypnosis with a therapist trained in psychotherapy may help to deepen your learning process. Sometimes, fear simply goes away, without demanding attention to deeper change. Be open to the unknown. In the empty space, courage may be found.

17

Achieving Your Personal Best in

Sports and Beyond

Where the mind goes, the body goes; the body follows the mind.

—Miyamoto Musashi

THE quote above, from the famous swordsman, Miyamoto Musashi (1584–1645) could be amended today to include the brain, because where the mind goes, so goes the brain as well. Performance of a skill is moderated through non-declarative, unconscious functioning. Therefore, learning how to let go of the process will help to enhance learning and performance. When the necessary motor skills are first learned during practice of your sport or art, you exercise certain parts of your brain, but once the skills are mastered, other brain areas take over, allowing for that automatic flow you feel at times. Through hypnosis, you can enhance your ability to express your training effortlessly and skillfully. What separates winners from losers among equally skilled participants is the ability to perform in any circumstance, even under pressure, just as you have trained to do. Using hypnosis, you can learn how to step back, to allow your brain–mind–body system to perform optimally.

Exercise to Get Ready

Allow yourself to go into trance. Let your conscious mind think about whatever it wants to, because your unconscious will be more important during this exercise. Invite yourself to feel a sensation in your body, such as a tingling in your fingertips, followed by lightness and movement in your hand, spreading up your arm, or perhaps a comfortable warmth or heaviness. As the sensation increases, you can become curious about the exploration you are going to begin over the next days and weeks. What will it be like to have an intuitive learning which you may or may not understand right away? Imagine this, without guiding your thoughts in any particular direction. Allow your associations to drift in various directions. When you are ready, you can suggest that your sensations will return to normal and you can awaken relaxed and refreshed.

Pressure

Simply trying to suppress your concerns about your performance cannot control the pressure you may be feeling. Almost anything can subtly interfere with how well you do. For example, a snide remark from an opponent at an inopportune moment may activate emotions stemming from your personal insecurities. You can find resources in your unconscious potential to help you alter the meaning of the situation.

A ballet dancer sought hypnotherapy with us for her anxiety during performances and competitions. She worked out very hard when practicing. She usually experienced her performances as uncomfortable, because of the intense audience attention focused on her. Whenever she performed, her anxiety was so great that she would shake with tension all over, which she found extremely embarrassing. She could not imagine herself ever being less nervous. In hypnosis she learned to relax completely and feel calm. She always felt relief from her symptoms during and following trance. She began a learning process. We decided together on an acceptable alternative to shaking all over. She could direct her anxiety into her little finger, which could shake intensely during her performances. Of course, others would probably not notice this, but she would know. The rest of her body was free to perform well, and she could express her secret anxiety subtly hidden, in her little finger. This thought amused her.

After her next dance performance she reported that she found herself dancing well, and smiling to herself about her little secret. She was the only one who had noticed her trembling little finger. From the perspective of the judges, she merely appeared to be enjoying her performance, fully at ease, which added to her high score. This success permitted her to develop further possibilities for herself, both as an artistic performer and later in life, in her career in sales.

Erickson told us about a professional golfer he hypnotized in order to reduce his anxiety during golf tournaments. After treatment, the man learned to totally immerse himself in the experience, approaching each hole as if it were his first without comparison or thought of how he was playing. When he finished the eighteenth hole, he started to tee up again. Everyone asked him what he was doing. He said that he had just started. He believed he was playing the first hole. He was surprised when told that he had won the tournament. He thought he was just beginning!

In both cases, the athletes creatively transformed their performance in the situation. The dancer intensified and redirected her tension, thus mastering the situation. The golfer bypassed performance pressure altogether, by total immersion. The result was a loss of the usual concerns and self-judgments along the way. Pressure can either be intensified or diminished with the help of hypnosis.

Exercise in Altering Your Experience of Pressure

Allow yourself to go into a comfortable trance. Recall the body experience you had in your previous trance, and let it develop again. Once you feel deeply in trance, think about the feeling of pressure you get during competitions or performances. Contemplate the two stories above. The two individuals we described were able to alter the meaning of their situations. Now contemplate your own situation.

If involved in a sport like tennis, marksmanship, or golf—that is, a sport that takes place over a period of time or for points—what would it be like to approach each point, shot, or hole as if it were the first? Or can you imagine your general feeling of anxiety dissolving, if you put your anxiety into your little finger or foot, or even somewhere outside of you? Now, instead, is there a unique, personally creative way you can think about your own situation, so you are free to participate more fully in the moment? If you can accept this as possible, suggest to your unconscious that you can make your own discovery to help you change. Imagine this as a reality for you. Allow thoughts, images, and feelings about this. Wait for your unique response. When you are ready, wake up refreshed and alert.

Training

Nothing can substitute for good training. Getting the most out of your workouts requires more than just physical exercise. The old adage, "You get out of it what you put into it," is a timeless truth. Sometimes athletes have difficulty getting motivated to work hard between competitions. Trance can help you mobilize your resources for better workouts.

Discovering Motivation Exercise

Before your next workout, find a time to go into trance. Relax your body comfortably and let your mind relax as well. Think about a time when you were at your peak. Remember how you felt, how you were ready, how well you moved and performed. Unconscious experience of time is not identical to chronological clock time, consciously experienced. Can you recall a time when you were enthusiastic during a workout as if it were yesterday, today? Or is yesterday too long in the past? Let yourself relax as you turn your attention to remembering. When you are finished, wake up, refreshed.

Motivation is important and individual: What is stimulating for one person may be discouraging to another. For example, after a loss in one game of a series, some people get worried and tense, sending them into a downward spiral. For others, being behind triggers an intense comeback effort for victory. A world-champion badminton player disclosed to us that the secret to her many wins was fear! She was terribly afraid that her opponents were training harder than she was, so she worked out harder and more than she imagined that they did! Her intense, deeply committed effort to master her fear galvanized her to stay on top competitively for many years. Therefore, even fear does not have to be feared. Use negative reactions positively, like this great sportswoman. Act, rather than react.

Exercise in Indirect Suggestion to Mobilize Motivation

Suggest that you have an image occur to you as you orient yourself toward trance. Let your thoughts drift. Then, can you recall the first time you attempted your sport, when you were younger? At first it may have seemed very difficult. Can you recall how you felt about it? Did you find yourself wanting to be involved more and more? Recall your learning process. Reexperience your early enthusiasm and dwell on the details as vividly as possible. When you have considered them for as long as you want, let yourself wake up, refreshed and alert.

Mental practice enhances performance. Research shows that people can acquire nearly as much benefit from actively imagining themselves performing their sport as from an equal amount of time spent actually doing it. In one experiment, 144 high-school basketball players were divided into two groups: one practiced physically, the other only practiced mentally. The physical-practice group spent their sessions actually shooting baskets. The mental practice group spent the same period visualizing aiming and throwing successful shots. The visualizers did nearly as well in a test session as the active practitioners (Clark, 1960). Many other mental-practice studies in varieties of sports uphold these results (Richardson, 1967).

Images for mental rehearsal may be visual or use other senses. For example, for you, imagining the feeling of practicing may be more vivid than the visual image of it. Personal experience can help you find this out. Use the method that works best for you.

Champion Olympic gymnast Mary Lou Retton told us that she always visualized herself doing her routines perfectly before she performed. Many bodybuilders cultivate imagery and metaphors to help them surpass their limits. For example, one bodybuilder we know thinks of his biceps as mountains when he trains; he believes this helps him gain size and strength. You can try mental practice in the next exercise.

Warm-Up Visualization Exercise

Go into trance. When you feel ready, imagine yourself doing your sport very well. For example, if you are a gymnast, imagine that you are doing your routine correctly. If you are a weightlifter, picture yourself easily lifting your limit. Martial artists can experience performing a perfect kick or punch, or an entire form. Runners might imagine running effortlessly with ease. Picture as many details as you can; feel your muscles responding. Focus your attention on this and nothing else. Enjoy the feeling you get from performing your best. If necessary, recall a time when you actually did do well, and remember clearly how this felt. Compare that imaginative experience to how you usually feel when you perform. How is this different? What did you do or feel that was unique to your peak performance? Then, allow yourself to apply this, in your actions.

Exercise in Indirect Visualization of Peak Performance

Find a comfortable level of trance. Invite yourself to go even deeper, through counting your breathing, following a sensation in your body, or another favorite technique. Allow yourself to relax deeply as you respond. Have you ever observed a tiger bounding effortlessly? Have you watched a cat jump smoothly or seen birds fly gracefully in patterns, perfectly coordinated? Let your mind meditate on your own spontaneous images, associations, and thoughts about peak performance. You do not know where your own associations will lead you, in search for useful insights or resources. Allow this process of creative wondering and wandering. Allow your feelings of confidence and your belief in your abilities to build. Continue until you are ready to awaken, refreshed and alert.

Focus

Many people tighten all their muscles at once when making a supreme effort, but this reduces flexibility and responsiveness. Movements become slower, less efficient, and more tiring. All of this is potentially stressful and detrimental to your efforts to do your best. Correct coordinated tensing and relaxing can enhance your efficiency and smoothness, improving sports performance.

Focus in the martial arts involves relaxation followed by tensing of contributory muscles at the moment of impact. This leads to optimum speed and strength combined. You can incorporate this concept into any sport by deliberately relaxing unnecessary tensions and tensing only when necessary. Be careful not to tense unrelated muscles—for example, in a tennis stroke, do not tighten your shoulders as you swing. In running, keep your upper body relatively relaxed, but gracefully coordinated.

You can use simple, isolated movement patterns to learn how to control muscle groups. It is possible to learn how to tighten and focus on one muscle group while you keep the rest of your body relaxed. This skill will give you more control over your body and lead to a deeper level of relaxation all over.

Differential Focus on Muscle Groups Exercise

Lie down in a place where you can be undisturbed. Scan your body with your awareness from top to bottom, noticing any particularly tight areas. You need not do anything about them yet. Start with your toes and feet. Tighten them as you pay attention to the sensation. Hold your feet tight while you keep the rest of your body relaxed for a minute. Then fully relax your feet along with the rest of your body. Pay close attention to the sensation of relaxation and compare it to how the contraction felt. Remain relaxed for a minute. Tighten your feet a second time, then after a minute relax fully. Remember how your feet felt when tensed and when completely relaxed. Notice the differences. Next, tighten your legs, including calf, thigh, knee, in both the front and back, but remember not to tighten anything else, and then relax. Repeat twice for each body part. Move up your body: stomach, chest, back, neck and shoulders, arms, hands, head. When you have scanned through your whole body, tighten everything at once, and then relax. You should feel a much greater relaxation when you let go. Tensions can be relaxed more fully with repeated practice.

Exercise in Applying Differential Focus for Your Sport

Repeat this exercise several times over the next few days. Go back over important areas. For example, if you are a runner, try tightening your quadriceps while relaxing the backs of your legs, and keeping the upper body relatively relaxed. Then shift the tension pattern, by tightening the backs of your legs slightly, while relaxing in the front. Shift several times.

For weightlifters, think of a particular lift—for example, the bench press—and deliberately reduce tension in unrelated areas. For example, breathe well and do not clench the jaw, while focusing on the visualized lift with the important muscles. Pay attention to the overall sensation of your body with the particular muscle set that you can feel is ideal for you during the bench press. Tighten your chest and ready your body to do a bench press. Usually readiness for the lift includes having the lower back slightly arched, rib cage expanded, shoulders back or forward. This kind of work can add to your muscular control, with subtle but certain effects which will produce a smooth performance and enhanced endurance. When actually performing the lift, add feedback from a training partner to fine-tune the action.

Improving Performance with Suggestion

For some people, specific direct suggestions can have a significant effect. Before you go into trance, think about your sport and pinpoint something you would like to improve. If you are a runner, you might like to increase your pace; a weight lifter may strive to lift more weight; a soccer player might work on ball control and kicking accuracy; a tennis player might wish to improve his backhand or serve; while a martial artist may want to increase accuracy or focus. Decide upon your target to improve, and then begin.

Direct Suggestion Exercise

Go into a comfortable trance. Think about your target area. Next, invite your unconscious to produce an image or a sensation to help you improve. Be willing to be open to a creative image. For example, tennis players or golfers could imagine that a friendly breeze helps smooth their swing, while runners might imagine a huge hand pushing or guiding them along, or a lightness in their legs that makes running seem effortless. A weight lifter may suggest the weight feels lighter than expected. Let your unconscious play with this idea and develop your own technique which fits with what you want to improve. Enjoy an overall relaxation in trance and then awaken refreshed and alert. Expect positive changes in performance, but give them time to take effect.

Induced Suggestion Exercise

Some induced suggestions, such as heaviness or lightness during trance, may help you gain inner control. Experiment with calming your heart and breathing. Suggest to yourself that this will happen and then wait for the response. For feedback, you can measure how well you control these involuntary functions by checking your pulse or timing your breaths. During competition, the ability to optimize these functions can be very useful.

The athlete who would truly excel must surpass the limitations of method, and even transcend technique itself (Simpkins & Simpkins, 2007). Technique becomes "no technique." For mastery, you must lose yourself. Instead of expressing yourself through the sport, let the sport express itself through you. Champion bodybuilders' efforts to develop their physiques may begin from personal motivations, but ultimately, they become sculptors, shaping their muscles like clay. The techniques of martial arts practitioners may stem from a love of tournament sport or a need for self-defense, but committed practitioners become peaceful and imperturbable. Artistry transcends the individual motivations as the process evolves. At a certain point the external technique is replaced by Oneness. Then "it" happens. As Herrigel wrote:

> This state, in which nothing definite is thought, planned, striven for, desired or expected, which aims in no particular direction and yet knows itself capable alike of the possible and the impossible, so unanswering is its power. (1971, p. 41)

Surprisingly, higher levels of play take place when you do not consciously think of play. Instead, you permit the process of playing the sport to be spontaneous and unintentional, without concepts, words, or labels.

A Zen master named Shoju was visited by a number of swordsmen who wanted to improve their swordsmanship. He invited them to have some tea and they had an enjoyable conversation. The Zen master's talk over tea inspired them, but they remained skeptical that the teachings could help them in swordmanship. They believed that when it came to practical combat, their rigorous martial arts training was all they needed to be skilled.

The master challenged them to try to strike him with their swords. He said that he would only use his fan to protect himself. They scoffed at the idea, but the master insisted. Amazingly, the swordsmen could not find an opening to attack and eventually had to admit defeat. Another monk who had watched the entire encounter asked how this was possible, since the master had never practiced with a sword. Shoju answered:

> When the right insight is gained and knows no obstruction, it applies to anything, including swordplay. The ordinary people are concerned with names. As soon as they hear one name, a discrimination takes place in

their minds. The owner of the right eye sees each object in its own light. When he sees the sword, he knows at once the way it operates. He confronts the multiplicity of things and is not confounded. (Suzuki, 1973, p. 204)

This can be applied in a practical sense to winning and losing. The moment you start to worry about whether you are going to win or lose, or think about how well you are doing or how skilled your opponent is, you distract yourself from your practice.

The exercise that follows is drawn from Zen meditation. Practice it daily over a period of time and you will begin to experience for yourself what Zen masters have known for centuries: Practice is enlightenment (Simpkins & Simpkins, 1999b; 2009).

Discovering Clear Mind Exercise

This exercise is best performed sitting cross-legged and upright. Close your eyes and relax. Begin by following your breathing as it goes in and out. Watch each breath, and eventually you will feel calmer. Next imagine a blue sky, a clear still body of water, or a blank screen. As thoughts try to interfere, let them flow past without attaching yourself to them. Do not let yourself follow the train of thought; simply notice it, let it pass, and return to the image. Finally, let your image pass. Stay with the emptiness. Do this with any distraction that comes up: outer sounds, inner feelings, or thoughts. Always return to clear mind. Repeat this exercise often, and you eventually will find that it becomes easier to clear your mind of thoughts. After you are comfortable with the exercise, try it while performing your sport. Let your body move without deliberate thought, simply allowing your personal excellence to express itself fully.

Conclusion

Using self-hypnosis, higher levels of skill become possible. You draw effortlessly from the performance pathways of your brain, which take care of movement and skill-learning automatically. The months spent in deliberate, thoughtful training to prepare for a competition use lower brain pathways in the cerebellum. But at the actual point of performance, transcend technique and allow the habit pathways that operate unconsciously to let your actions flow naturally. Thoughts or feelings do not hinder the free performance of what has been mastered. With mind, brain, and body functioning as one, you cannot help but do your best!

Final Thoughts

Begin your journey from where you are
To the horizon of your destiny's star

—C. Alexander Simpkins

YOU have experienced self-hypnosis, and have felt the positive effects it can bring.

You are not living in isolation, locked into your personal unchanging sensations and experiences, but actually living in a unity, between inner and outer, conscious and unconscious, mind and brain. And this unity can be your source for transformation at any moment.

Any sensation, thought, feeling, or behavior can be a place to start, by accepting the responsiveness that is already being expressed, and working with it sensitively in trance. Through the ideomotor link, you can imagine something different, and in so doing, initiate an automatic process toward change. All of these abilities are built-in and natural: Your sincere, open absorption sets it in motion.

Self-hypnosis offers you options: to change things around, to experience anew, to grow, and to learn. You might choose to draw upon the wider context of your perception to include other people, your environment, or anything else that is already there around you. At other times you may find it helpful to narrow your focus inward, to gain a closer perspective, thereby learning something new about your inner world. All of these novel experiences change your brain, loosening the bonds of old, redundant patterns and forming new neuronal connections, thus fostering potential.

Your potential is unwritten—you are the creator of your destiny. We hope that self-hypnosis inspires you to continue reaching out beyond the horizon.

References

Barabasz, A. E. (2000). EEG markers of alert hypnosis: The induction makes a difference. *Sleep and Hypnosis, 2*, 264–269.

Barabasz, A. E., & Barabasz, M. (2008). Hypnosis and the brain. In M. R. Nash & A. J. Barnier (Eds.), *The Oxford handbook of hypnosis: Theory, research, & practice* (pp. 337–363). Oxford, England: Oxford University Press.

Baudouin, C. (1921). *Suggestion and autosuggestion.* New York, NY: Bodd, Mead, and Co.

Benson, H. (1975). *The relaxation response.* New York, NY: William Morrow & Co.

Benson, H., Frankel, F. H., Apfel, R., Daniels, M. D., Schniewind, N. E., Nemiah, J. C., & Rosner, B. (1978). Treatment of anxiety: A comparison of the usefulness of self-hypnosis and meditational relaxation technique. An overview. *Psychotherapy & Psychosomatics, 30*, 3–4, 229–242.

Bernheim, H. (1973). *Hypnosis and suggestion in psychotherapy.* New York, NY: Jason Aronson.

Bertrand, A. (1823). *Traité du somnambulisme et des differentes modifications qu'il presente.* Paris, France.

Binet, A., & Féré, C. (1888). *Animal magnetism.* New York, NY: D. Appleton and Co.

Braid, J. (1960). *Braid on hypnotism: The beginnings of modern hypnosis.* New York, NY: The Julian Press.

Bramwell, J. M. (1903). *Hypnotism, its history, practice, and theory.* London, England: Grant Richards.

Breuer, J., & Freud, S. (1957). *Studies on hysteria.* J. Strachey (Trans.). New York, NY: Basic Books. (Original work published 1895)

Bruno, F. (1972). *Think yourself thin.* New York, NY: Barnes and Noble Books.

Bryant, R. A., Moulds, M. L., Guthrie, R. M., & Nixon, R. V. (2005). The additive benefit of hypnosis and cognitive behavior therapy in treating acute stress disorder. *Journal of Consulting and Clinical Psychology, 73*, 334–340.

Cannon, W. (1942). Voodoo death. *American Journal of Public Health*. 2002, 92, 1593–1596.

Carrer, L. (2002). *Ambroise-Auguste Liebeault: The hypnological legacy of a secular saint*. College Station, TX: Virtualbookwork.com Publishing.

Chaves, J. F. (1993). Hypnosis in pain management. In J. W. Rhue & S. J. Lynn (Eds.), *Handbook of clinical hypnosis* (pp. 511–532). Washington, DC: American Psychological Association.

Clark, R. (1960). Effect of mental practice on the development of a certain motor skill. *The Research Quarterly, 31*, 4, 25–29.

Cooper, L. T., & Erickson, M. H. (1982). *Time distortion in hypnosis: An experimental and clinical investigation*. New York, NY: Irvington Publishers.

Coué, E. (1923). *How to practice suggestion and autosuggestion*. New York, NY: American Library Service.

Crawford, H. (2001). Neuropsychophysiology of hypnosis: Attentional and disattentional processes. *International Journal of Clinical and Experimental Hypnosis, 42*, 4204–4232.

Davidson, R., Goleman, D., & Schwartz, G. (1976). Attentional and affective concomitants of meditation: A cross-sectional study. *Journal of Abnormal Psychology, 85*, 235–308.

Descartes, R. (1968). *Discourse on the method and the meditations*. New York, NY: Penguin Books (Original work published 1641)

De Bono, E. (1976). *Teaching thinking*. London, England: Temple Smith.

De Pascalis, V. (1998, December). Brain mechanisms and attentional processes in hypnosis. INA-BIS '98. Fifth Internet World Congress on Biomedical Sciences. McMaster University, Hamilton, Ontario, Canada. Retrieved Jan. 30, 2010, from http://www.mcmaster.ca/inabis98/woody/de_pascalis0311//index.html

De Pascalis, V., Magurano, M. R., Bellusci, A., & Chen, A. C. (2001). Somatosensory event-related potential and autonomic activity to varying pain reduction cognitive strategies in hypnosis. *Clinical Neurophysiology, 112*, 1475–1485.

De Pascalis, V. (2007). Phase-ordered gamma oscillations and the modulation of hypnotic experience. In G. A. Jamieson (Ed.), *Hypnosis and conscious states: The cognitive neuroscience perspective* (pp. 67–89). Oxford, England: Oxford University Press.

Domjan, M. (1998). *The principles of learning and behavior* (4th ed.). Pacific Grove, CA: Brooks/Cole.

Duyvendak, J. J. L. (1992). *Tao Te Ching: The book of the way and its virtue*. Boston, MA: Charles E. Tuttle Co., Inc.

Egner, T., Jamieson, G. A., & Gruzelier J. (2005). Hypnosis decouples cognitive control from conflict monitoring processes of the frontal lobes. *Neuroimage, 27*, 143–49.

Erickson, M. H. (1943). Hypnotic investigation of psychosomatic phenomena: Psychosomatic interrelationships studied by experimental hypnosis. *Psychosomatic Medicine*, January 5, 51–58.

Erickson, M. H. (1958). Naturalistic techniques of hypnosis. *The American Journal of Clinical Hypnosis, 7*, (1), 3–8.

Erickson, M. H. (1965). A special inquiry with Aldous Huxley into the nature and character of various states of consciousness. *American Journal of Clinical Hypnosis, 8*, (14), 14–33.

Erickson, M. H., & Rossi, E. L. (1979). *Hypnotherapy*. New York: Irvington Publishers.

Erickson, M. H. & Rossi, E. L. (1980a). *Hypnotic alteration of sensory, perceptual and psychophysiological processes by Milton H. Erickson*. New York, NY: Irvington.

Erickson, M. H., & Rossi, E. L. (1980b). *The nature of hypnosis and suggestion by Milton H. Erickson.* New York, NY: Irvington.

Erickson, M. H., Rossi, E. L., & Rossi, S. (1976). *Hypnotic realities.* New York, NY: Irvington Publishers.

Frank, J. D., Hoehn-Saric, R., Imber, S. D., Liberman, B. L., & Stone, A. (1978). *Effective ingredients of successful psychotherapy.* New York: Brunner/Mazel.

Frank, J. D., & Frank, J. B. (1991). *Persuasion and healing.* Baltimore, MD: The Johns Hopkins University Press.

Frankl, V. (1988). *The will to meaning: Foundations and applications of logotherapy.* New York, NY: New American Library.

Ganzel, B. L., Morris, P. A., & Wethington, E. (2010). Allostasis and the human brain: Integrating models of stress from the social and life sciences. *Psychological Review, 117,* (1), 134–174.

Gazzaniga, M. S. (2000). Cerebral specialization and interhemispheric communication: Does the corpus callosum enable the human condition? *Brain, 123,* 1293–1326.

Goetz, C. G. (1987). *Charcot, the clinician: The Tuesday lessons.* New York, NY: Raven Press.

Goetz, C. G. (2000). Battle of the titans: Charcot and Brown-Séquard on cerebral localization. *Neurology, 54,* 1840–1847.

Gordon, B. (1949). The physiology of hypnosis. *Psychiatric Quarterly, 23,* 317–342.

Gravitz, M. A. (1991). Early theories of hypnosis: A clinical perspective. In S. J. Lynn & J. W. Rhue (Eds.), *Theories of hypnosis: Current models and perspectives* (pp. 19–42). New York, NY: The Guilford Press.

Gravitz, M. A. (1993). Etienne Felix d'Henin de Cuvillers: A founder of hypnosis. *American Journal of Clinical Hypnosis, 36,* (1), 7–11.

Gravitz, M. A. (1994). The first use of self-hypnosis: Mesmer mesmerizes Mesmer. *American Journal of Clinical Hypnosis, 37,* (1), 49–52.

Green, J. P., Barabasz, A. F., Barrett, D., & Montgomery, G. H. (2005). Forging ahead: The 2003 APA Division 30 definition of hypnosis. *International Journal of Clinical and Experimental Hypnosis, 53,* 259–264.

Gruzelier, J. H. (1998). A working model of the neurophysiology of hypnosis: A review of the evidence. *Contemporary Hypnosis, 15,* 3–21.

Hadas, M. (1961). *Essential works of stoicism.* New York, NY: Bantam Books.

Harmon, T. M., Hynan, M. T., & Tyre, T. E. (1990). Improved obstetric outcomes using hypnotic analgesia and skill mastery combined with childbirth education. *Journal of Consulting and Clinical Psychology, 58,* (5), 525–530.

Herrigel, E. (1971). *Zen in the art of archery.* New York, NY: Vintage.

Hilgard, E. R. (1965). *Hypnotic susceptibility.* New York, NY: Harcourt, Brace & World, Inc.

Hilgard, E. R. (1977). *Divided consciousness: Multiple controls in human thought and action.* New York, NY: John Wiley & Sons.

Hilgard, E. R., & Hilgard, J. (1975). *Hypnosis in the relief of pain.* Los Altos, CA: William Kaufman.

Howard, R. J., Fytche, D. H., Barnes, J., McKeefry, D., Ha, Y., Woodruff, P. W., Bullmore, E.T., Simmons, A., Williams, S. C., David, A. S., & Brammer, M. (1998). The functional anatomy of imagining and perceiving color. *Neuroreport, 9,* 1019–1023.

Hull, C. L. (1933). *Hypnosis and suggestibility: An experimental approach*. New York, NY: Apple-ton-Century-Crofts, Inc.

Huxley, A. (1962). *Island*. New York, NY: Harper & Row.

Hyams, J. (1982). *Zen in the martial arts*. New York, NY: Bantam.

James, W. (1896). *The principles of psychology* (Vols. 1–2). New York, NY: Henry Holt & Co.

James, W. (1918). *Selected papers on philosophy*. London, England: J. M. Dent & Sons Ltd.

Janet, P. (1925). *Psychological healing: A historical and clinical study. In two volumes*. London, England: George Allen & Unwin Ltd.

Johnson, S. (2008). *Hold me tight*. New York, NY: Little, Brown and Company.

Kalat, J. (2007). *Biological psychology*. Belmont, CA: Thompson-Wadsworth.

Kirsch, I., Montgomery, G., & Sapirstein, G. (1995). Hypnosis as an adjunct to cognitive-behavioral psychotherapy: A meta-analysis. *Journal of Consulting & Clinical Psychology, 63*, 214–220.

Klein, C. H. V. (1905). The medical features of the papyris ebers. *JAMA, 45*, 1928–1935.

Kosslyn, S. M., Thompson, W. L., Costantini-Ferrando, M.F., Alpert, N. M., & Spiegel, D. (2000). Hypnotic visual illusion alters color processing in the brain. *American Journal of Psychiatry, 157*, 1279–1284.

Kroger, W. S. (1977). *Clinical and experimental hypnosis*. Philadelphia, PA: J. B. Lippincott.

Legge, J. (1971). *Confucius*. New York, NY: Dover Publications, Inc.

Marcel, G. (1966). *The philosophy of existentialism*. New York: The Citadel Press.

McKeon, R. (1941). *The basic works of Aristotle*. New York, NY: Random House.

Mead, G. H. (1934). *Mind, self, & society from the standpoint of a social behaviorist* (Vol. 1). Chicago, IL: University of Chicago Press.

Melis, P. M., Rooimans, W., Spierings, E. L., & Hoogduin, C. A. (1991). Treatment of chronic tension-type headache with hypnotherapy: a single-blind time controlled study. *Headache, 3*, (10), 686–689.

Miller, M. E., & Bowers, K. S. (1986). Hypnotic analgesia and stress inoculation in the reduction of pain. *Journal of Abnormal Psychology, 95*, 6–14.

Miltner, W. H. R., & Weiss, T. (2007). Cortical mechanisms of hypnotic pain control. In G. A. Jamieson (Ed.), *Hypnosis and conscious states: The cognitive neuroscience perspective* (pp. 51–66). Oxford, England: Oxford University Press.

Mitchell, D. B. (2006). Research report: Nonconscious priming after 17 years. *Psychological Science, 17*, (11), 925–929.

Mitchell, D. B., & Brown, A. S. (1988). Persistent repetition priming in picture naming and its dissociation from recognition memory. *Journal of Experimental Psychlogy: Learning, Memory, and Cognition, 14*, 213–222.

Munro, H. S. (1911). *Handbook of suggestive therapeutics, applied hypnotism, psychic science*. St. Louis, MO: C. V. Mosby Company.

Musashi, M. (2005). *The book of five rings*. T. Cleary (Trans.). Boston, MA: Shambhala Pocket Classics. (Original work published c. 1645)

Oakley, D. A. (2008). Hypnosis, trance and suggestion: Evidence from neuroimaging. In M.R. Nash & A. Barnier (Eds.), *Oxford handbook of hypnosis* (pp. 365–392). Oxford, England: Oxford University Press.

Park, L. C., & Covi, L. (1965). Non-blind placebo trial: An exploration of neurotic patients' responses to placebo when its inert content is disclosed. *Arch. Gen. Psychiat, 12*, 336–345.

Pattakos, A. (2008). *Prisoners of our thoughts: Victor Frankl's principles for discovering meaning in life and work.* San Francisco, CA: Berrett-Koehler Publishers.

Pavlov, I. (1927). *Conditioned reflexes: An investigation of the physiological activity of the cerebral cortex.* New York, NY: Dover Publications, Inc.

Platonov, K. (1959). *The word as a physiological and therapeutic factor.* Moscow, Russia: Foreign Languages Publishing House.

Posner, M. L. (1978). *Chronometric explorations of mind.* Hillsdale, N. J.: Erlbaum.

Posner, M. L., & Peterson, S. E. (1990). The attention system of the human brain. *Annual Review of Neuroscience, 13*, 25–42.

Rainville, P., Hofbauer, R. K., Paus, T., Duncan, G. H., Bushnell, C. &. Price, D. D. (1999). Cerebral mechanisms of hypnotic induction and suggestion. *Journal of Cognitive Neuroscience, 11*, 110–125.

Ray, W., Blai, A., Aikins, D., Coyle, J., & Bjick, E. (1998). Understanding hypnosis and hypnotic susceptibility from a psychophysiological perspective. INABIS, December 7–16, 1998. Fifth Internet World Congress on Biomedical Sciences. McMaster University, Hamilton, Ontario, Canada.

Raz, A., & Shapiro, T. (2002). Hypnosis & neuroscience: A cross talk between clinical and cognitive research. *Archive of General Psychiatry, 59*, 85–90.

Raz, A., Shapiro, T., Fan, J., & Posner, M. I. (2002). Hypnotic suggestion and the modulation of Stroop interference. *Arch. Gen. Psychiatry, 59*, 1155–1161.

Richardson, A. (1967). Mental practice: A review and discussion, part I. *The Research Quarterly, 38*, (1), 32–36.

Rossi, E. & Jensen, M. (2010). How we light and brighten the lamps of human consciousness: The ideo-plastic paradigm of therapeutic hypnosis in an era of functional genomics and bioinformatics. Prepublication interview. *American Journal of Clinical Hypnosis.*

Rossi, E. (2007). *The breakout heuristic: The new neuroscience of mirror neurons, consciousness, and creativity in human relationships.* Phoenix, AZ: Milton H. Erickson Press.

Rossi, E., Iannotti, S., Cozzolino, M., Castiglione, S., Cicatelli, A., & Rossi, K. (2008). A pilot study of positive expectations and focused attention via a new protocol for therapeutic hypnosis assessed with DNA microarrays: The creative psychosocial genomic healing experience. *Sleep and Hypnosis: An International Journal of Sleep, Dream, and Hypnosis, 10*, (2), 39–44.

Rossi, E. L. (2002). *The psychobiology of gene expression.* New York, NY: Norton.

Rossi, E. L., & Lloyd, D. (2009). *Ultradian rhythms from molecules to mind: A new vision of life.* New York, NY: Springer-Verlag.

Schoenberger, N. (2000). Research on hypnosis as an adjunct to cognitive-behavioral psychotherapy. *International Journal of Clinical and Experimental Hypnosis, 48*, 150–165.

Scoville, W. B., & Milner, B. (1957). Loss of recent memory after bilateral hippocampal lesions. *J. Neurol. Neurosurg. Psychiat., 20*, 11–22.

Selye, H. (1974). *Stress without distress.* New York, NY: Signet Books.

Shaffer, G. W., & Lazarus, R. S. (1952). *Fundamental concepts in clinical psychology.* New York, NY: McGraw-Hill Book Company, Inc.

Sidis, B. (1898). *The psychology of suggestion.* New York, NY: D. Appleton.

Simpkins, C. A., & Simpkins, A. M. (1999a). *Simple Taoism: A guide to living in balance.* Boston, MA: Tuttle Publishing.

Simpkins, C. A., & Simpkins, A. M. (1999b). *Simple Zen: A guide to living moment to moment.* Boston, MA: Tuttle Publishing.

Simpkins, C. A., & Simpkins, A. M. (2001). *Timeless teachings from the therapy masters.* San Diego, CA: Radiant Dolphin Press.

Simpkins, C. A., & Simpkins, A. M. (2004). *Self-hypnosis for women.* San Diego, CA: Radiant Dolphin Press.

Simpkins, C. A., & Simpkins, A. M. (2007). *Meditation from thought to action with audio CD.* San Diego, CA: Radiant Dolphin Press.

Simpkins, C. A., & Simpkins, A. M. (2008). An exploratory outcome comparison between an Ericksonian approach to therapy and brief dynamic therapy. *American Journal of Clinical Hypnosis, 50,* (3), 217–232.

Simpkins, C. A., & Simpkins, A. M. (2009). *Meditation for therapists and their clients.* New York, NY: Norton.

Simpkins, C. A., & Simpkins, A. M. (2010). *The dao of neuroscience: Combining Eastern and Western principles for optimal therapeutic change.* New York, NY: Norton.

Solomon, R. L. (1980). The opponent-process theory of acquired motivation: The costs of pleasure and the benefits of pain. *American Psychologist, 35,* (8), 691–712.

Spiegel, D. (2008). Intelligent design or designed intelligence? Hypnotizability as neurobiological adaptation. In M. R. Nash & A. J. Barnier (Eds.), *The Oxford handbook of hypnosis: Theory, research and practice.* (pp. 179–200). Oxford, England: Oxford University Press.

Spanos, N. P., & Chaves, J. F. (1991). History and historiography of hypnosis. In S. J. Lynn & J. W. Rhue (Eds.), *Theories of hypnosis: Current models and perspectives* (pp. 43–78). New York, NY: The Guilford Press.

Sperry, R. W. (1974). Lateral specialization in the surgically separated hemispheres. In F. O. Schmitt & F. G. Worden (Eds.), *Neurosciences: Third study program* (pp. 5–19). Cambridge, MA: MIT Press.

Springer, S. P. & Deutsch, G. (1981). *Left brain, right brain.* San Francisco: W. H. Freeman.

Squire, L. R., & Kandel, E. R. (2000). *Memory: From mind to molecules.* New York, NY: Henry Holt & Company.

Stellar, E. (1954). The physiology of motivation. *Psychology Reviews, 61,* 5–22.

Stroop, J. R. (1935). Studies of interference in serial verbal reactions. *Journal of Experimental Psychology, 18,* 643–662.

Suzuki, D. T. (1973). *Zen and Japanese culture.* Princeton, NJ: Princeton University Press.

Suzuki, S. (1979). *Zen mind, beginner mind.* New York, NY: Weatherhill.

Taylor, E. (1982). *William James on exceptional mental states.* New York, NY: Charles Scribners Sons.

Tellegen, A., & Atkinson, G. (1974). Openness to absorbing and self-altering experiences ("absorption"), a trait related to hypnotic susceptibility. *Journal of Abnormal Psychology, 83,* 268–277.

Triplet, R. G. (2006). The relationship of Clark L. Hull's hypnosis research to his learning theory: The continuity of his life's work. *Journal of the History of the Behavioral Sciences, 18,* (1), 22–31.

Vaitl, D., Gruzelier, J., Jamieson, G. A., Lehmann, D., Ott, U., Sammer, G., . . . Weiss, T. (2005). Psychobiology of altered states of consciousness. *Psychological Bulletin, 131,* (1), 98–127.

Vogt, B. A., Finch, D. M., & Olson, C. R. (1992). Functional heterogeneity in cingulate cortex: The anterior executive and posterior evaluative regions. *Cerebral Cortex, 2,* 435–443.

Waley, A. (1958). *The way and its power.* New York, NY: Grove Weidenfeld.

Waite, A. E. (2002). *The hermetic and alchemical writings of Paracelsus.* Whitefish, MT: Kessinger Publishing.

Watson, B. (1993). *The Zen teachings of master Lin-Chi.* Boston, MA: Shambhala.

Watzlawick, J., Weakland, J. H., & Fisch, R. (1974). *Change.* New York, NY: Norton.

Whitehorn, J. C. (1956). Stress and emotional health. *The American Journal of Psychiatry, 112,* (10), 773–781.

Williams, R. and Williams, V. (1994). *Anger kills: Seventeen strategies for controlling the hostility that can harm your health.* New York, NY: HarperCollins.

Williams, M. A., Morris, A. P., McGlone, F., Abbott, D. F., & Mattingley, J. B. (2004). Amygdala responses to fearful and happy facial expressions under conditions of binocular suppression. *Journal of Neuroscience, 24,* (12), 2898–2904.

Wolberg, L. (1948). *Medical hypnosis* (Vols. 1–2). New York, NY: Grune & Stratton.

Yapko, M. (1995). *Essentials of hypnosis.* New York, NY: Brunner/Mazel.

Yapko, M. (2001). *Treating depression with hypnosis: Integrating cognitive-behavioral and strategic approaches.* New York, NY: Brunner/Routledge.

Yapko, M. (2006). *Hypnosis and treating depression: Applications in clinical practice* (3rd ed.). New York, NY: Routledge.

Yapko, M. (2009). *Depression is contagious.* New York, NY: Free Press.

Index

Note: Figures and photos are noted with an *f.*